How to Use

Microsoft® Office 97
Small Business Edition

Visually in Full Color

Julia Kelly

Contents at a Glance

GN00801830

SAMS

A Division of Macmillan Computer Publishing, USA
201 W. 103rd Street
Indianapolis, Indiana 46290

How to Use Microsoft® Office 97
Small Business Edition

International Standard Book Number: 0-7897-1646-1

Library of Congress Catalog Card Number: 98-84270

Printed in the United States of America

First Printing: July 1998

00   99   98   4   3   2   1

This book was produced digitally by Macmillan Computer Publishing and manufactured using computer-to-plate technology (a film-less process) by GAC/Shepard Poorman, Indianapolis, Indiana.

Trademarks

Executive Editor
Jim Minatel

Aquisitions Editor
Jamie Milazzo

Development Editor
Noelle Gasco

Technical Editor
Kurt Hampe

Managing Editor
Thomas F. Hayes

Project Editor
Karen A. Walsh

Copy Editor
Krista Hansing

Indexer
Chris Barrick

Production
John Etchison
Heather Stephenson

Cover Designers
Aren Howell
Gary Adair
Nathan Clement

Book Designers
Nathan Clement
Ruth Harvey

About the Author

Julia Kelly, cybergirl in cowspace, ex-jet jockey, and former mad scientist, has also done time as a stable cleaner, hardware store cashier/barrista, theme park candy girl, veterinary cat holder, Caribbean pilot, and teacher of diverse topics.

She currently lives on her farm in north Idaho, where she writes books, teaches classes, builds databases, chops wood, and shovels snow.

Acknowledgements

As with all computer books, this one was a team effort, and I want to thank all the team members who made the process bearable and successful: my terrific agent, Margot Maley, at Waterside Productions; delightful acquisitions editor, Jamie Milazzo; excellent (and funny) technical editor, Kurt Hampe; and wonderfully patient development editor, Noelle Gasco.

Dedication

To God, for making my bizarre livelihood as a writer possible.

And to my grandmother, who finally believes (I think) that I can make a living doing this.

Contents

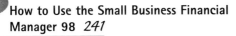

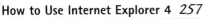

How To Use This Book

The Complete Visual Reference

Each chapter of this book is made up of a series of short, instructional tasks, designed to help you understand all the information that you need to get the most out of your computer hardware and software.

Click: Click the left mouse button once.

Double-click: Click the left mouse button twice in rapid succession.

Right-click: Click the right mouse button once.

Pointer Arrow: Highlights an item on the screen you need to point to or focus on in the step or task.

Selection: Highlights the area onscreen discussed in the step or task.

Click & Type: Click once where indicated and begin typing to enter your text or data.

Click & Drag

Release

How to Drag: Point to the starting place or object. Hold down the mouse button (right or left per instructions), move the mouse to the new location, and then release the button.

Key icons: Clearly indicate which key combinations to use.

Each task includes a series of easy-to-understand steps designed to guide you through the procedure.

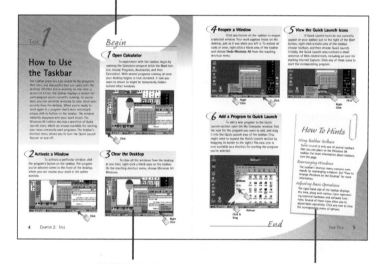

Each step is fully illustrated to show you how it looks onscreen.

Extra hints that tell you how to accomplish a goal are provided in most tasks.

Menus and items you click are shown in **bold**. Words in *italic* are defined in more detail in the glossary. Information you type is in a `special font`.

Continues

If you see this symbol, it means the task you're in continues on the next page.

Introduction

One of the many differences between small businesses and big businesses is that in a small business, you get to be a master-of-all-trades. One person (or maybe just a few people) is responsible for not only the actual work of the business but also for correspondence, marketing and public relations, bookkeeping and accounting, and time management.

With Microsoft Office 97 Small Business Edition, you can blend features of different programs together because all the programs are integrated with each other. For example, because Excel is the best program for creating charts but Word is the best program for writing reports, you can write a business analysis in Word and paste a chart you created in Excel; then you can send the completed document as an attached file in an Outlook email message.

This book provides a visual, easy-to-learn introduction to each of the programs included in the updated version of Microsoft Office 97 Small Business Edition. Each task is designed to teach you what you need to know quickly so you can accomplish the task at hand and get back to your real job. In this book you'll learn how to use the following applications:

- ✓ *Word 97*. As one of the most popular Windows-based word processing programs available, Word 97 offers many options. With it, you can create everything from a short memo to a long report and format everything for a customized professional look.
- ✓ *Excel 97*. Excel 97 is a number-crunching program in which you can calculate and analyze numerical data, and easily find specific information in a large table by sorting and filtering data.
- ✓ *Publisher 98*. Publisher 98 is an easy-to-use desktop publishing program that guides you through the process of creating newsletters, brochures, business cards, and Web pages.
- ✓ *Outlook 98*. Outlook 98 is communication central. It includes a calendar, a to-do list (Tasks), a business diary (Journal), an address book (Contacts), and a post office.
- ✓ *Small Business Financial Manager 98*. The Small Business Financial Manager 98 is a report generator that works in Excel. If you have a lot of business data, perhaps in another accounting program such as Quicken or Peachtree, you can use the Financial Manager to copy, calculate, and arrange that data into standard business reports such as balance sheets, cash flows, and income statements.
- ✓ *Internet Explorer 4*. Microsoft's new Web browser is a lot more than a browser. When you install Internet Explorer 4, you can install the new Active Desktop, which makes your desktop look and act like a Web page and gives you access to the Internet from just about anywhere.
- ✓ *Expedia Streets 98*. Expedia Streets 98 is a map generator that looks up street addresses and gives you as detailed a view as you want. You can also plan cross-country trips by looking up the mileage and printing out all the maps you need for the trip.

You can learn how to use a program by starting with Task 1 and working through the tasks in order, or you can learn how to accomplish a specific task such as Word's Mail Merge by reading just that task. Either way, the procedures are distilled into quick bites of information and hints so that you can finish a project efficiently.

We think you'll enjoy learning from this book, and we know you'll gain enough information to approach your Microsoft Office 97 Small Business Edition software with confidence.

Task

2

1

Getting Started with Office 97 Small Business Edition

*I*f you're new to Microsoft programs, there are a few procedures that are common to all of them and that work the same way in each program, such as opening and closing the program, as well as getting help while you work. You'll also need to open, save, print, and close documents (or files) in each program. All these procedures come into play whether you're writing a letter in Word 97, compiling an expenses list in Excel 97, or creating business cards in Publisher 98. These procedures are just a bit different in Microsoft Expedia Streets 98, and I'll save those how-to explanations for Chapter 9, "How to Use Expedia Streets 98."

This chapter also covers the new Web-style window, which appears when you install the Standard or Full installation of Internet Explorer 4 and then choose the Active Desktop. This section takes the mystery out of the new windows and shows you how to customize them right upfront, which is particularly helpful for those of you who install software first and then read the book. If you haven't installed Internet Explorer 4 yet, you can read Task 4 in this chapter after you install it. If you need help installing each of the programs, see Chapter 10, "How to Install the Microsoft Office 97 Small Business Edition Programs." ●

How to Open and Close Programs

Every computer task begins with opening the program you want to use and ends with closing the program you've been using. Everything else you learn in this book comes in between.

If you're already familiar with Windows 95 programs, you still might find something new in this task. If you're new to Windows 95 or to computers in general, this task shows you how to find and open the program you need, and how to close the program before you turn off your computer.

Begin

1 Click Start

On the left end of your taskbar (the gray bar at the very bottom of your screen), click the **Start** button. If you don't see the taskbar, someone may have set it to AutoHide to create more screen space; point your mouse pointer at the very bottom of the screen, and the taskbar should pop into view after a moment.

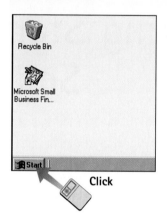

Click

2 Open the Programs Menu

On the Start menu, point to **Programs**.

3 Click a Program

A list of all the programs in your computer appears; click the one you want to open. Some programs have a right-pointing triangle on their right; when you point at them, another menu of programs appears. Keep pointing at programs until you get to the final submenu, and then click the program you want to open.

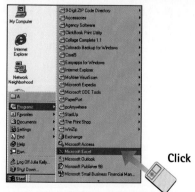

Click

4 Before You Close the Program

Save and close any open documents before you close the program. To close the displayed document, choose **File**, **Close**. If the document contains any unsaved changes, you'll be asked whether you want to save them; click **Yes**.

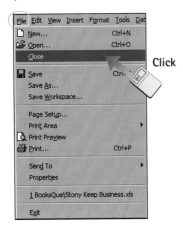

Click

5 Close with One Click

When all open documents are closed, click the **X** button in the upper-right corner of the program window to exit the application.

Click

6 Close with Two Clicks

You can also close the application with menu commands. When all open documents are closed, choose **File**, **Exit**.

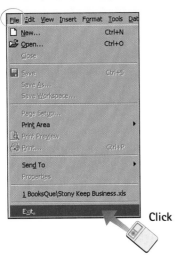

Click

End

How to Get Help

Every computer user, from novice to pro, needs help now and then. All the programs in Microsoft Office 97 SBE provide help in a variety of guises, including the Office Assistant (an animated figure), the Contents and Index (a table of contents, index, and search engine for the program's help files), and the What's This? mouse pointer.

The Contents and Index and the What's This? mouse pointer are available whenever you want them; the Office Assistant often shows up whether you want it or not, but you can hide it or uninstall it if this helper becomes annoying.

Begin

1 Use the Office Assistant

For friendly help that attempts to guess what you want to know, click the Office Assistant button (the question-mark icon) on the Standard toolbar. An animated assistant appears with help topics, tips, and a search feature. To get help, click a topic option, or type a question and click the **Search** button. To hide the Office Assistant, click the **X** box on its title bar.

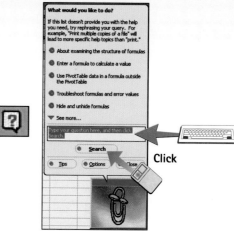

Click

2 Change the Office Assistant

Click the Office Assistant's **Options** button. On the **Options** tab, click check boxes to turn on or off specific behaviors. On the **Gallery** tab, scroll through different characters by clicking the **Next** and **Back** buttons; then choose **OK**.

3 Look Up Help Book-Style

To look up help topics yourself, choose **Help, Contents and Index**.

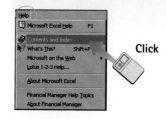

Click

4 Use the Table of Contents

The Help Topics dialog box has three tabs. The **Contents** tab is a table of contents for the help files and works like a book's table of contents. Double-click topics and subtopics to find help files for your question.

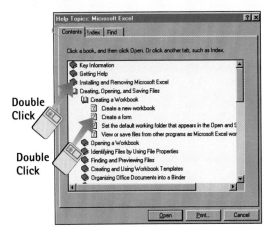

Double Click

Double Click

5 Use the Index

The **Index** tab is an alphabetical index of all the help file topics and works like a book's index. Type the first few letters of your topic to scroll to that alphabetical location in the index list, and then double-click a topic in the list to open the help file. If the index lists several related help files, double-click a likely title.

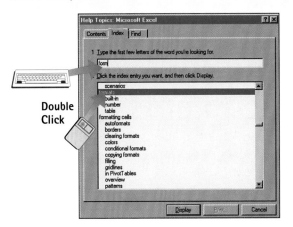

Double Click

6 Search the Help Files

The **Find** tab is a search engine that searches the full text of all the help files for specific words and phrases. When you first open the **Find** tab, the program needs to create a list of words to search (it's quickest to leave the default **Minimum database size** option selected and click **Next**).

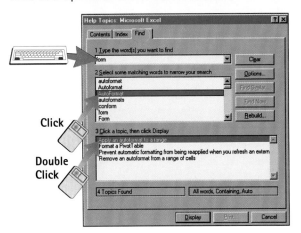

Click

Double Click

End

How-To Hints

Get Quick, Brief Explanations

For help on a menu command, toolbar button, or window item, choose **Help, What's This?**. Click the item you're curious about, and a ScreenTip appears with an explanation. Click anywhere to remove the ScreenTip.

Dialog Box Help

To get What's This? help in dialog boxes, right-click the words you don't understand, and click the **What's This?** button that appears. Most dialog boxes have a small question-mark button in the upper-right corner that performs the same function.

Want More Office Assistant Characters?

You can download more assistants from Microsoft's Web site. Choose **Help, Microsoft on the Web, Free Stuff**. On Microsoft's home page, read the instructions and click **Download Now** under the assistant you want. Use the default selected options in the dialog boxes that prompt you to save the assistant file.

How to Open, Save, Print, and Close Documents

Before you learn the more complex procedures in each program, you must master the most basic procedures. Fortunately, the basic procedures—opening, saving, printing, and closing documents—are the same in each of the Microsoft Office 97 SBE programs, so you need to learn them only once.

In every program, a single document is a file, with a unique filename, stored in a folder somewhere on the hard drive.

Begin

1 Start a New Document

To start a new document in any program, click the **New** button on the Standard toolbar. A new, blank document (such as a Word document or an Excel workbook) appears and awaits your input.

Click

2 Open an Existing Document

To open an existing document (a file) in any program, click the **Open** button on the Standard toolbar. In the Open dialog box, navigate to the folder in which your file was saved. Double-click the filename to open the document.

Double Click

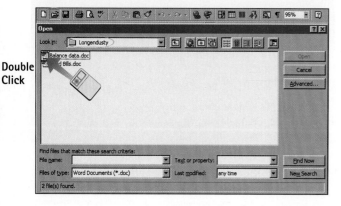

3 Save a Document

Click the **Save** button on the Standard toolbar. If the document was previously saved, the changes you made are automatically saved in the existing file. If the document is new, the Save As dialog box appears. Type a name in the **File name** box, and then choose **Save**.

Cli

4 Print the Document

To print the displayed document, choose **File**, **Print**. In the Print dialog box, you can either set printing options (such as number of copies or specific pages to print) or leave all the default option settings. Choose **OK** to begin printing. If you click the **Print** button on the toolbar, the document is printed with default settings.

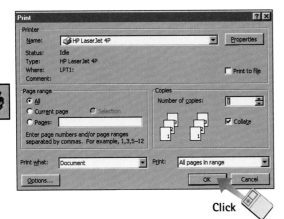

Click

5 Close the Document

To close the displayed document, choose **File**, **Close**. If the document has any unsaved changes, you'll be prompted to save it—click **Yes** to save and close, choose **No** to close without saving, and choose **Cancel** to keep the document open.

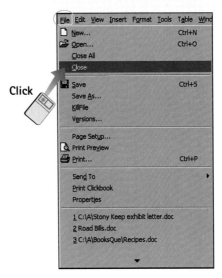

Click

End

How-To Hints

Close with One Click

To close a document quickly, click the small **X** button in the upper-right corner of the document window.

Close the Program and Documents Together

To close the program and all open documents in one step, click the small **X** button in the upper-right corner of the program window; you'll be prompted to save any unsaved documents before they're closed.

Save a Copy of a Document Under a Different Name

To save a copy of a file with a different name, click **File**, **Save As**. In the Save As dialog box, type a new name in the File name dialog box, and choose **Save**.

Print a Document with One Click

To print a document quickly, click the **Print** button on the Standard toolbar.

How to Use Web-style Windows and the Web Toolbar

The new Web-style folder windows differ somewhat from the familiar Windows 95 folder windows. You can return the windows to the familiar "classic" Windows 95 style, or you can use the new Web style, which is larger and displays more information. You can also pick and choose which new Web-style features you want.

Begin

1 The New Web-style Window

The new windows are much bigger and have a Web-page look to them. To read the properties for a file or folder, point to its name, but don't click; the properties appear in the window's left panel. To open a file or folder, click its name once.

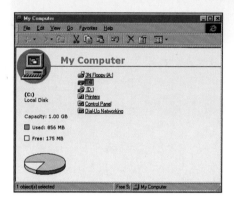

2 Web-style Navigation

To navigate back toward your hard drive, click the Up button. To go forward through several levels of folders, click each folder. To go backward and forward to folders or Web sites you have already opened, click the **Back** and **Forward** buttons. To turn button labels on or off, right-click the toolbar and click **Text labels**.

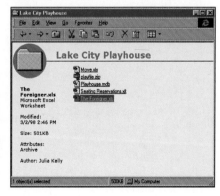

3 Use the Address Toolbar

To launch your browser and surf the Web, right-click the menu bar and click **Address Bar**. Click in the Address bar and type the Web site's address, or *URL*, starting with either **http** or **www**. Press Enter to launch your browser.

4 Go Where You've Been Before

Click the down arrow on the Address bar to select a folder or Web site you've previously visited.

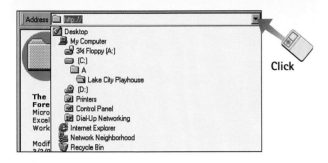

Click

5 Go to a Favorite Site

To go to a Web site you've saved in your Favorites folder, click **Favorites**, and then click the site you want. Your browser launches and goes to the Web site. See Chapter 7, "How to Use Internet Explorer 4," to learn how to save Web sites to your Favorites list when you're searching the Web.

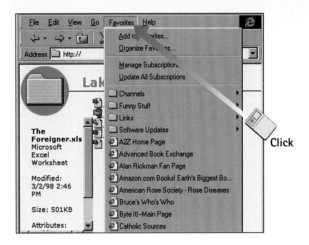

Click

6 Hide the Left Panel

To hide the left panel of the new window (because it takes up a lot of room), choose **View, as Web Page**. You can make the panel reappear by choosing **View, as Web Page** again.

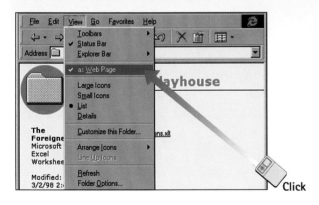

Click

7 Change Window Features

Choose **View, Folder Options**. For the new Web-style window and the entire Active Desktop, click the **Web style** option and choose **OK**. For the classic Windows 95–style window, click the **Classic style** option, and choose **OK**. To pick and choose, click the **Custom, based on settings you choose** option, and choose **Settings**. In the Custom Settings dialog box, click the options you want, and choose **OK**.

End

Task

2

How to Use Word 97

If you use nothing else in Microsoft Office 97 Small Business Edition, chances are you'll at least use the Microsoft Word application. Word processing is quite likely the most common pastime in the computer world, and Word 97 can do pretty much whatever you need a word processor to do—and then some. Microsoft Word has a lot more features than any one user will ever need, but every user will find all the features his specific tasks require.

Even though a lot of features are available, you don't need to use or understand them all. You can start off with very simple tasks, such as writing letters and making lists, and get to know the rest of Word's features one by one as you need them. Take your time and learn Word at your own pace; in no time, you'll be comfortable with it.

Word does a lot of repetitive work for you, such as automatically generating numbered or bulleted lists and creating form letters or mailing labels from a contact database. You can change font and paragraph characteristics so that a document is automatically double-spaced and paragraphs have automatic first-line indents, and you can set tabs that align text to the left, right, or center. You can create headers and footers that automatically appear on every page in a document, and you can create reusable templates of your own. You can even customize built-in templates in which lots of formatting is already done for you. Whatever you want, there's a way to do it in Word.

A Tour of the Word Window

When you start Word, the program window (named Microsoft Word) appears, and one blank document window (named Document1) appears. Usually, both windows are *maximized*—the program window fills the whole screen, and the document window fills the whole program window. When both windows are maximized, two restore buttons (one for each window) are displayed in the set of buttons located in the upper-right corner of the window's screen. If you see a maximize button for either window, click it. (The maximize button appears in place of the restore button; its icon looks like a single large square.) You can also maximize any window by double-clicking its title bar. Usually, you'll want to keep both windows maximized because it gives you more room to work.

Begin

1 The Title Bar

The title bar tells you what's in the window. When the document window is maximized, it must share the title bar with the program window, so the title bar contains the names of both the program (Microsoft Word) and the file. Document1 is a temporary name for your document. When you save the document for the first time, you'll replace that name with a recognizable name you choose.

W Microsoft Word - Document1

2 The Typing Area

The typing area in a new document is blank except for three symbols. The insertion point (a vertical, blinking bar also known as the cursor) shows you where the next character you type will appear. The end-of-file mark (a horizontal bar) shows you where the document ends. You use the mouse pointer to select text and to move the insertion point. When the mouse pointer is in the typing area, it resembles an I-beam.

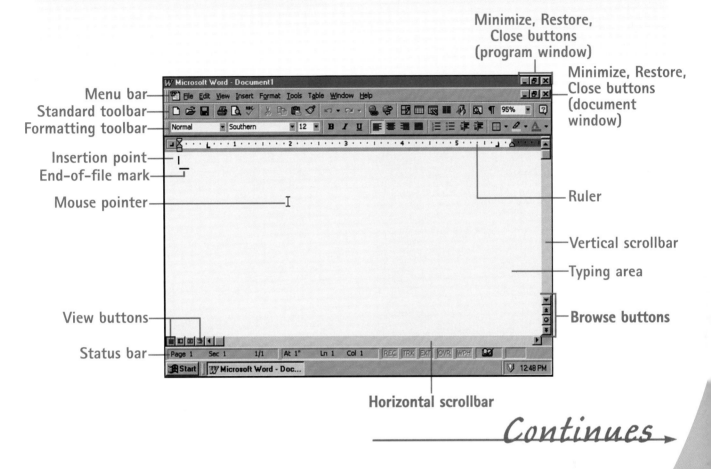

Minimize, Restore, Close buttons (program window)

Minimize, Restore, Close buttons (document window)

Menu bar

Standard toolbar

Formatting toolbar

Insertion point

End-of-file mark

Mouse pointer

Ruler

Vertical scrollbar

Typing area

View buttons

Browse buttons

Status bar

Horizontal scrollbar

Continues

3 Select Menu Commands

The Word menu bar contains menus, which in turn contain all the available Word commands. All the tasks you need to perform are available through menu commands. To use the menu commands, click the menu name to display the menu, and then click the command you want.

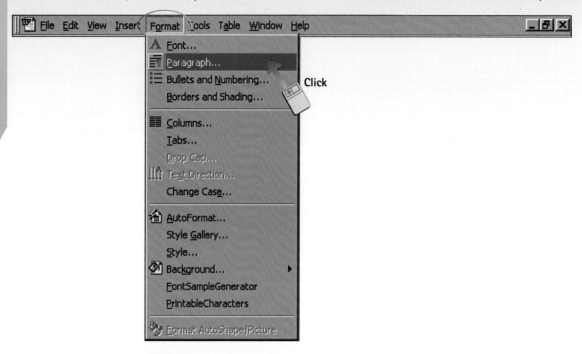

4 Use Toolbars

The Standard toolbar contains shortcuts for frequently used commands such as those to open, save, and print documents and those to undo mistakes. The Formatting toolbar (below the Standard toolbar) contains shortcuts for commands that change the appearance of the document. The ruler (below the two toolbars) shows where your margins are, and it enables you to set tabs and indents. If you don't see the ruler, you can display it by choosing **View**, **Ruler**.

5 View and Navigate

The View buttons (in the lower-left corner of the document window) enable you to change the way your document is displayed onscreen. By default, Word uses Normal view, which is fast-scrolling and looks like one endless page. The Browse buttons (in the lower-right corner of the document window) enable you to quickly jump from one part of your document to the next. The status bar indicates the current page, the total number of pages, and the location of your insertion point on the page.

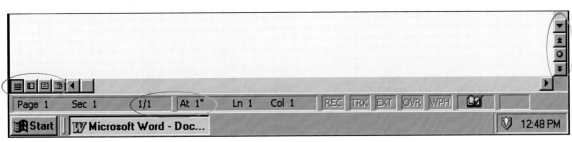

End

How-To Hints

Toolbars Hidden?

If you don't see the Standard or Formatting toolbars, or if you see other toolbars you want to hide, choose **View, Toolbars**. On the menu that appears, click the name of the toolbar you want to show or hide.

Scrollbars Hidden?

If your screen doesn't show either of your scrollbars or your status bar, choose **Tools, Options**. Near the top of the Options dialog box, click the **View** tab if it isn't already showing. Then, under Window, click any check box that isn't already marked—**Status bar**, **Horizontal scrollbar**, and/or **Vertical scrollbar**—and then choose **OK**.

See Button Names

To see a button name, place the mouse pointer over the button for a moment; a _ScreenTip_ appears with the button name.

Use Shortcut Menus

To open a shortcut menu that contains often-used commands, click an object with the right mouse button (called a right-click); then use the left mouse button to click the command you want. Almost everything in the Word window has its own shortcut menu.

Choose Menu Commands from the Keyboard

To choose menu commands with the keyboard, press the Alt key, press the underlined letter in the desired menu, and press the underlined letter in the desired command. For example, to display the Format menu, press Alt+O; when the Format menu is displayed, press P to choose the Paragraph command. To close a menu without choosing a command, press Esc.

How to Enter and Edit Text

Every great literary masterpiece began with a blank page. In keeping with that time-honored tradition, Microsoft Word opens with a blank document window, ready for you to begin typing a bestselling novel, a personal letter, or an interoffice memo.

The flashing insertion point indicates where the next character you type will appear. So, if you're ready to begin your journey on the road to literary fame and fortune, simply start typing.

Begin

1 Start a New Paragraph

Each time you press Enter, you start a new paragraph. Press Enter to end short lines of text, to create blank lines, and to end paragraphs. Don't press Enter to start new lines within a paragraph; Word wraps the lines for you. If you later add or remove text or change page margins, Word adjusts the line breaks to fit.

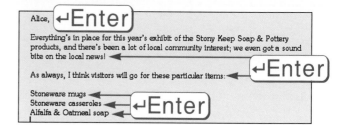

2 Indent Lines of Text

Press the Tab key to indent the first line of a paragraph. If you keep pressing Tab, you increase the indent one-half inch at a time. To indent all the lines in the paragraph instead of just the first one, right-click in the paragraph and click **Paragraph** on the shortcut menu that appears. Click the **Indents and Spacing** tab at the top of the dialog box, and set indentation settings under **Indentation** in the **Left** box (a setting of 0.3 is usually good).

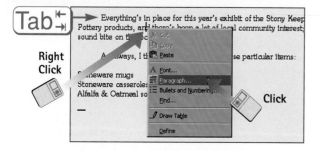

3 Create Lines

To type the same character repeatedly, hold the key down. Word automatically converts some repeated characters into different types of lines, as shown here. For example, if you type three or more asterisks (*) and press Enter, Word replaces them with a dotted line. Do the same with the equal sign (=) for a double line, the tilde (~) for a wavy line, the pound (#) symbol for a thick decorative line, the hyphen (-) for a single line, or the underscore (_) for a thick single line.

4 Type Uppercase Letters

To produce all uppercase letters without having to hold down the Shift key, press the Caps Lock key once before you begin typing. Press the Caps Lock key again when you're ready to switch off this feature. Caps Lock affects only the letter keys, not the number and punctuation keys, so you always have to press Shift to type a character on the upper half of a number or a punctuation key, such as @ or %.

STONY KEEP SOAP & POTTERY ANNUAL EXHIBIT

Alice,

5 View Nonprinting Characters

Click the **Show/Hide** button in the Standard toolbar to see where you pressed the spacebar, Tab, and Enter keys. A dot represents a space, an arrow represents a tab, and a paragraph mark indicates where you pressed Enter. You can use the Show/Hide button to check whether you accidentally typed an extra space between two words (you see two dots instead of one) or to see how many blank lines you have between paragraphs. To turn off Show/Hide, click it again.

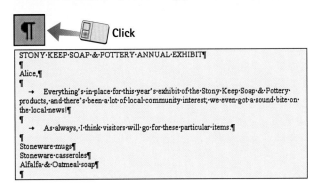
Click

STONY·KEEP·SOAP·&·POTTERY·ANNUAL·EXHIBIT¶
¶
Alice,¶
¶
→ Everything's·in·place·for·this·year's·exhibit·of·the·Stony·Keep·Soap·&·Pottery·products,·and·there's·been·a·lot·of·local·community·interest;·we·even·got·a·sound·bite·on·the·local·news!¶
¶
→ As·always,·I·think·visitors·will·go·for·these·particular·items.¶
¶
Stoneware·mugs¶
Stoneware·casseroles¶
Alfalfa·&·Oatmeal·soap¶
¶

6 Select and Delete Characters

To delete text, select the text and press Delete. To select text, place your cursor at the beginning of the text you want to select; then hold down the left mouse button, drag the cursor to the end of the text, and release the mouse button. You can delete extra spaces, tabs, and paragraph marks the same way you delete regular characters, with the Backspace and Delete keys.

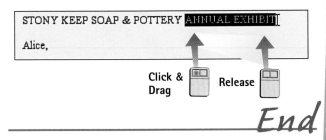

STONY KEEP SOAP & POTTERY ANNUAL EXHIBIT

Alice,

Click & Drag   Release

End

How-To Hints

Move Around with Keys

Within a block of text you can use the arrow keys to move backward and forward, or up and down between lines.

Add or Delete Blank Lines and Page Breaks

If you want to create a blank area on the page, press the Enter key repeatedly to insert new blank lines. If you want to start a new page, press Ctrl+Enter to insert a manual page break; to remove a manual page break, click the page break line and press Delete.

Quick Selection Techniques

To delete a word, double-click the word to select it, and press Delete. To delete an entire sentence, press Ctrl while you click in the sentence to select it, and press Delete. To delete an entire paragraph, triple-click (three rapid clicks) in the paragraph to select it, and press Delete.

How to Move and Copy Text

After you've tried electronic cutting, copying, and pasting, you'll never go back to using any other method for your editing. If you've ever created a document using a typewriter and inadvertently left out an important step or paragraph, you know what I mean. You have to retype the whole thing! That's not so with electronic word processing. Word makes it easy to pick up characters, words, sentences, paragraphs, and more, and move them to a new location.

You can use menu commands, shortcut menu commands, toolbar buttons, keyboard shortcuts, and drag-and-drop techniques to move and copy text; everyone finds his own favorite method. To move text, cut it from its position and paste it somewhere else; to copy text, make a copy of the text and paste it elsewhere.

Begin

1 Select Text to Cut or Copy

Select the text you want to cut or copy. To select text, place your cursor at the beginning of the text you want to select; then hold down the left mouse button and drag the cursor from the beginning to the end of the text, and release the mouse button. The selected text is highlighted, as shown here.

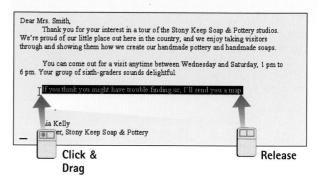

Click & Drag   **Release**

2 Move and Copy Text

To move the text with toolbar buttons, click the **Cut** button in the Standard toolbar. The text is deleted from your document, but it remains in a special Windows storage area called the Clipboard.

To copy the text with toolbar buttons, click the **Copy** button in the Standard toolbar. When you copy text, nothing appears to happen because the text remains in its original location, and a copy of the selected text is sent to the Clipboard.

3 Paste Text

Click to place the cursor where you want to paste the text. If necessary, you can open another document or switch to another already open document to paste text there. Click the **Paste** button in the Standard toolbar to paste the text. The text is pasted into the document beginning at the position of the insertion point.

4 Move Text Using Drag and Drop

To move text by dragging and dropping it, select the text you want to move. Click in the selected text and hold down the mouse button; then drag the mouse to place the dotted vertical line (the drag-and-drop cursor) where you want to paste the text. Release the mouse button to drop, or paste, the cut text.

> Dear Mrs. Smith,
>   Thank you for your interest in a tour of the Stony Keep Soap & Pottery studios. We're proud of our little place out here in the country, and we enjoy taking visitors through and showing them how we create our handmade pottery and handmade soaps.
>
>   Yo can come out for a visit anytime between Wednesday and Saturday, 1 pm to 6 pm. Y   ˜ of sixth-graders sounds delightful.
>
>   t have trouble finding us, I'll send you a map.
>   e you soon,

Release   **Click & Drag**

5 Copy Text Using Drag and Drop

To copy text with the same drag-and-drop method, select the text you want to copy. Click in the selected text and hold down the mouse button, then drag the mouse to place the dotted vertical line (the drag-and-drop cursor) where you want to paste the text. Press and hold the Ctrl key while you release the mouse button to drop, or paste, the copied text.

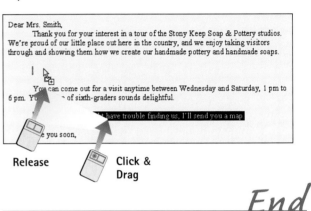

> Dear Mrs. Smith,
>   Thank you for your interest in a tour of the Stony Keep Soap & Pottery studios. We're proud of our little place out here in the country, and we enjoy taking visitors through and showing them how we create our handmade pottery and handmade soaps.
>
>   You can come out for a visit anytime between Wednesday and Saturday, 1 pm to 6 pm. Yo   ˜ of sixth-graders sounds delightful.
>
>   have trouble finding us, I'll send you a map
>   e you soon,

Release   **Click & Drag**

End

How-To Hints

Move, Copy, and Paste from the Keyboard

The keyboard shortcuts for the Cut, Copy, and Paste commands are Ctrl+X for Cut, Ctrl+C for Copy, and Ctrl+V for Paste. These keyboard shortcuts are standard for all Windows-based programs.

Move or Copy Text to Other Programs

You can also cut or copy text to a document in another program that supports object linking and embedding (OLE). Cut or copy the desired text, and then switch to the other program and open the document in which you want to paste the text; position the insertion point, and use the Paste command provided in that program.

If You Have Two Documents Open

To switch to another open Word document, click the Window menu, and then click the document name from the menu. To switch to a different open program, click its button on the taskbar to bring it in front of Word.

Paste Again and Again

After you cut or copy text, a copy of it remains in the Clipboard, so you can repeatedly paste more copies of the text without cutting or copying it again. The Clipboard contents are replaced only when you use the Cut or Copy command again. The Clipboard empties when you exit Windows.

TASK 4

How to Use the Spelling and Grammar Checker

The Spelling and Grammar Checker enables you to check the spelling and grammar of an entire document as you type, or all at once. Because most of us tend to forget about running the Spelling Checker when we finish typing, the Automatic Spelling Checker can save errors by pointing them out and making them difficult to ignore.

To see if the Automatic Spelling Checker is turned on, type a misspelled word such as **werd**. When you type a space or punctuation mark following the word, a red wavy line appears under the word; that red wavy line is the Automatic Spelling Checker at work.

Begin

1 How Word Flags Errors

When you type, a red wavy line appears under any word that Word can't find in its dictionary to tell you that word may be misspelled; a green wavy line indicates a possible grammatical error. To turn the Automatic Spelling Checker on or off, choose **Tools**, **Options**. On the **Spelling & Grammar** tab, click the **Check Spelling as you type** check box.

> Check the spelling checker by typing a werd word;
>
> Sometimes you're grammar checker helps, but it's not a substitute for a High school English class.

2 Right-click the Error and Correct It

Right-click the word that's marked with a red wavy line. A shortcut menu appears with possible alternative spellings. To choose an alternative spelling from the shortcut menu, click on that suggestion. If your spelling is correct (for example, someone's last name), click **Add**; the word is added to Word's dictionary. If you don't want to add the word to the dictionary, click **Ignore All**.

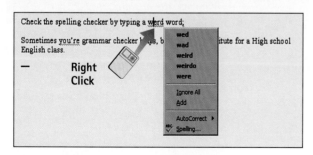

3 Fix a Grammatical Error

If the wavy underline is green, Word detects a possible grammatical error. Right-click the error and click a command to fix or ignore it. (You can speed up the spelling checker by turning off the grammar checker. Choose **Tools**, **Options**. On the **Spelling & Grammar** tab, clear the **Check grammar as you type** check box.)

> Check the spelling checker by typing a weird word;
>
> Sometimes you're grammar checker helps, but it's not a substitute for a High school English class. For example, in this case the grammar checker is totally clueless.
>
> **you are**
> Ignore Sentence
> Grammar...

Right
Click

4 Check the Whole Document

If you decide to ignore the wavy lines while you type and check the whole document when you finish (instead of while you type), choose **Tools, Spelling and Grammar** to run the spelling and grammar checker. The Spelling and Grammar dialog box appears when it encounters a word that does not conform to the program's grammatical rules. As you can see, the grammar checker isn't always reliable.

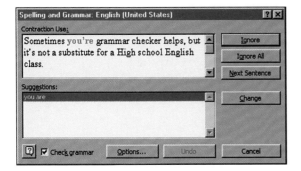

5 Correct a Misspelling

The Spelling and Grammar checker stops at a word that's not listed in its dictionary. Suggestions for spelling are listed in the **Suggestions** box (same as on the shortcut menu). Click the spelling you want, and click **Change** to correct the single instance; click **Change All** to correct every instance of the misspelling in the document. To run the spelling check faster, clear the **Check grammar** check box so that grammar is not checked along with spelling.

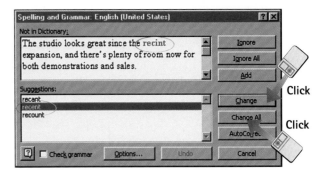

6 If It's Not a Misspelling

If the word is correctly spelled and you plan to use it again, click **Add** to add the word to Word's dictionary so it won't go unrecognized in the future.

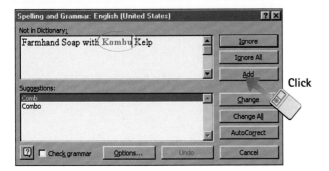

7 Please Ignore the Word

Sometimes a document uses a word that's abbreviated or otherwise oddly spelled. Although you want the word spelled that way in this document, you don't want to add it to Word's dictionary. Click **Ignore** to ignore this particular instance or **Ignore All** to ignore every instance of the spelling in this document.

End

5

How to Use AutoCorrect

Word's AutoCorrect feature can save you time by automatically correcting misspelled words as you type. AutoCorrect comes with a list of common misspellings, you can add your own common misspellings to the list to personalize it to your work habits. All the words and phrases in AutoCorrect are available to every document you open in Word.

What makes AutoCorrect even more useful is that you can use it to do your typing for you. If you often type a particular word or long phrase, you can create an AutoCorrect entry that types the word for you when you type a short acronym. For example, I got tired of typing the word "AutoCorrect," so I created an AutoCorrect entry. Now I type "ac" and a space, and Word types the whole word for me, capitals and all.

Begin

1 Try AutoCorrect

Test AutoCorrect to see how it performs—type **teh**, and press the Spacebar or type a punctuation mark such as a comma or a period. Because "teh" is a common misspelling, AutoCorrect corrects it to "the" before you realize you mistyped it.

> The quick brown fox and teh

2 Undo AutoCorrect's Changes

If you type something you don't want corrected (for example, "Mr. Edmund Teh"), press Ctrl+Z to undo the correction before you type any other characters. The AutoCorrection is undone, and you can continue typing.

> Mr. Edmund Teh

3 Remove Words from AutoCorrect

To remove a word from the AutoCorrect list, choose **Tools**, **AutoCorrect**, and then click the **AutoCorrect** tab. In the **Replace** text box, type the first few letters of the word you want to delete from AutoCorrect; the list of words and replacements scrolls to the point in the list where you can find your word. Click your word in the list, and click **Delete**.

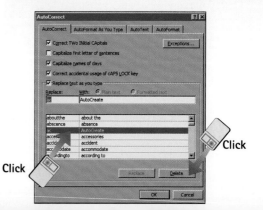

4 Add Words to AutoCorrect

To add a word or phrase to the AutoCorrect list, open a document and type it. Select it, choose **Tools**, **AutoCorrect**, and click the **AutoCorrect** tab. Your word(s) appear in the With box. In the **Replace** box, type the word or acronym you want to type in your document, and choose **OK**. If you want to add more words, click **Add** after each word. Choose **OK** to finish.

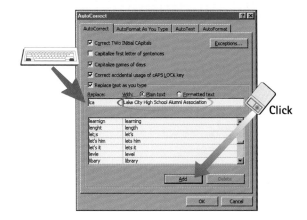

Click

5 Add Formatted Words

To add formatted word(s), open a document and type the text, including any formatting such as italics, bold, or color. Select the word(s), choose **Tools**, **AutoCorrect**, and click the **AutoCorrect** tab. Your word or phrase appears in the With box, fully formatted. In the **Replace** box, type the word or acronym you want to type in your document, and choose **OK**.

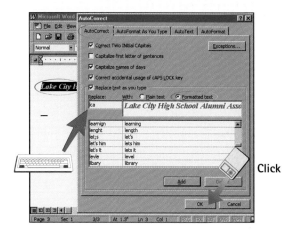

Click

End

How-To Hints

Choose Plain or Formatted Text

You can elect to replace an AutoCorrect acronym with a fully formatted word or phrase, or with unformatted text, by clicking the **Plain text** or **Formatted text** option above the With box.

Turn AutoCorrect On or Off

To turn AutoCorrect off or on, choose **Tools**, **AutoCorrect** and clear or mark the **Replace text as you type** check box on the **AutoCorrect** tab.

AutoCorrect Does More

Set or turn off other convenient automated options, such as capitalization of weekday names and the first word in sentences, by marking or clearing those check boxes on the **AutoCorrect** tab in the AutoCorrect dialog box.

How to Use AutoText

AutoText can save you time by inserting a long block of formatted text, such as a paragraph or a table, each time you click a short AutoText entry. For example, you can create a standard introduction for weekly reports or an empty table that you can use repeatedly in a document (each inserted table will have identical dimensions). AutoText entries can be of any length, from a short sentence to an entire letter, and they're easy to save and use.

Begin

1 Type an AutoText Entry

If the AutoText toolbar isn't already displayed, choose **View**, **Toolbars**, **AutoText** to display it. In any document, type the text you want to include in your AutoText entry and apply any formatting you want.

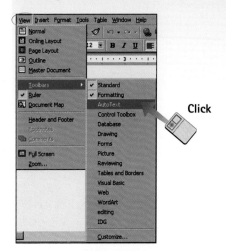

Click

2 Open the AutoText Dialog Box

Select the text—if you want to include any paragraph formatting you've applied (such as line spacing, indents, or alignment), be sure to include the hidden paragraph mark at the end of the text. Then click the **New** button in the AutoText toolbar.

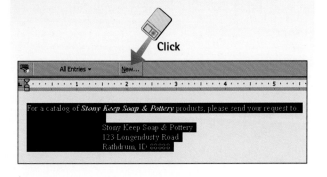

Click

3 Name Your Entry

In the Create AutoText dialog box, type a name for the entry in the entry box, and choose **OK**. Although you can have AutoText names that are more than one word long, it's best to use a name that's short and memorable.

4 Insert the Entry in a Document

To use the entry, click in your document where you want to paste the entry, and then click the **All Entries** button on the AutoText toolbar. On the list of AutoText categories, point to the category where your entry is stored, and click the name of the entry. The entry is pasted into your document.

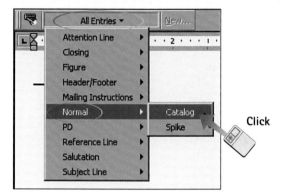

Click

5 If You Can't Remember the Entry

If you can't remember the name of the AutoText entry you want, click the **AutoText** button on the AutoText toolbar. In the **AutoText** tab of the AutoCorrect dialog box, click possible names in the list of entries, and look at the partial entry in the Preview box. When you've selected the name you want, click **Insert**.

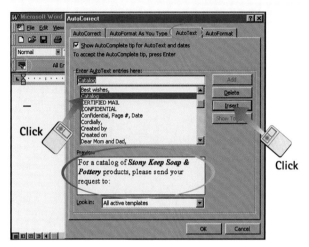

Click

Click

6 Delete an AutoText Entry

To delete an AutoText entry, click the **AutoText** button on the AutoText toolbar to display the **AutoText** tab of the AutoCorrect dialog box. Click the entry, click the **Delete** button, and click **OK**.

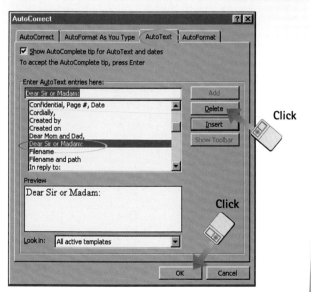

Click

Click

How-To Hints

Print an AutoText List

You can print a list of AutoText entries for a quick reference to what text each entry contains. Choose **File**, **Print**; in the Print dialog box, click the down arrow in the **Print what** list box. Click **AutoText entries**, and then choose **OK**.

Edit an AutoText Entry

First insert the entry into your document, and then make your changes. Select the text again, and be sure to include all the text you want in the entry. Click the **New** button in the AutoText toolbar, type the name of the existing entry, and choose **OK**.

Automatic AutoText

After you type the first few letters of an AutoText entry's name, a ScreenTip containing the name may appear next to the characters you typed. If you press **Enter**, the AutoText entry is inserted there. If you continue typing, the ScreenTip goes away.

End

How to Format Text

Formatting refers to all the techniques that enhance the appearance of your document. In Word, you can roughly divide formatting techniques into three categories: character, paragraph, and page.

Character formatting includes all the features that can affect individual text characters. The primary character formatting features are boldface, italic, underline, font, and font size. Paragraph formatting includes line spacing, indents, alignment, tabs, paragraph spacing, and so on. Page formatting includes page orientation, margins, and page breaks.

The most commonly used formatting features are applying boldface, italic, and underline to text. As a matter of fact, these features are so frequently used that they have their own buttons on the default Formatting toolbar.

Begin

1 Character Formatting

To boldface text, select the text and then click the **Bold** button on the Formatting toolbar.

To italicize text, select the text and then click the **Italic** button on the Formatting toolbar.

To underline text, select the text and then click the **Underline** button on the Formatting toolbar. The Underline button produces a single underline. If you want a different type of underlining, use the Font dialog box instead.

2 Open the Font Dialog Box

If you want to see what a font style will look like before you apply it, select the text and then choose **Format, Font** to display the Font dialog box.

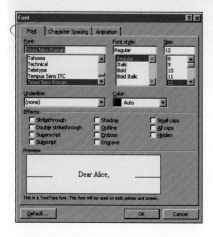

3 Choose a Style

At the top of the dialog box, click the **Font** tab if it isn't already in front. In the Font Style list, choose **Bold**, **Italic**, or **Bold Italic** to boldface and/or italicize your text.

Click

4 Underline Text

To underline text, click the down arrow on the Underline list box to display the list of choices, and click the desired underline style.

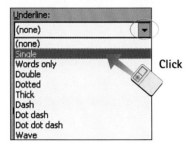

Click

5 Choose a Color

To color text, click the down arrow on the Color list box to display the list of choices, and click the desired color.

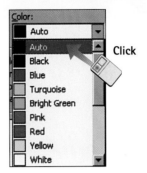

Click

6 Preview and Apply Styles

You can preview your choices in the Preview area at the bottom of the dialog box.

When you've made your selections, choose **OK** to close the dialog box and apply the changes to the selected text.

Click

End

How-To Hints

More Font Effects

Check out the special effects available in the Font dialog box. Click an effects check box (such as **Outline** or **Shadow**), and look at the preview.

Undo Basic Formatting

To remove boldface, italics, or underline, select the text and then click the appropriate toolbar button again.

Format from the Keyboard

To format by using the keyboard, select the text and use these keyboard shortcuts: Ctrl+B for boldface; Ctrl+I for italics; Ctrl+U for underline; or Ctrl+Shift+D for double underline. Type asterisks before and after a word to boldface it (as in "*poodle*"), or type underscore characters before and after a word to italicize it (as in "_poodle_"). As soon as you type the next word, Word deletes the asterisks or underscores and applies the formatting.

More Formatting Techniques

If you want to boldface, italicize, or underline a single word, you don't have to select the word first. Just click anywhere in the word and then apply the formatting using any of the methods described on this page. If you want to format individual characters, select those characters and then apply formatting.

How to Copy Character Formatting

If you apply several different character formats—such as a font, a font size, and a format (bold, italic, underline)—to a block of text in your document, and then later decide you'd like to apply the same formatting to another block of text, you don't have to apply those formats one by one to the new location. Instead, you can use the Format Painter button to take all the formats from the original block of text and "paint" them across the new text.

Begin

1 Select Text

Select the text that has the formatting you want to copy (characters, words, whole paragraphs, headings, and so on). To select text, place your cursor at the beginning of the text you want to select, hold down the left mouse button and drag the cursor to the end of the text, and release the mouse button.

Click & Drag   **Release**

Stony Keep Soap & Pottery

1998 Annual Exhibit

It's time once again for the annual Stony Keep Soap & Pottery exhibit, studio tour, and sale. Lots of great new works, as well as consistent favorites, will be on sale at special Annual Exhibit prices!

2 Click Format Painter Button

Click the Format Painter button in the Standard toolbar.

3 Mouse Pointer Changes

Your mouse pointer changes to a paint-brush pointer.

Stony Keep Soap & Pottery

1998 Annual Exhibit

It's time once again for the annual Stony Keep Soap & Pottery exhibit, studio tour, and sale. Lots of great new works, as well as consistent favorites, will be on sale at special Annual Exhibit prices!

Studio Tour

Take the studio tour: watch pots being thrown on the potter's wheel, and all-vegetable soaps being created.

Recent Works

Check out the recent works in clay, both functional and purely artistic, by Stony Keep's resident artists.

4 Select the Text to Format

Drag the paintbrush pointer across the text where you want to paint the format.

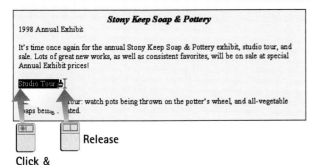

Release

Click & Drag

5 Release the Mouse

Release the mouse. The formatting is applied to the block of text (click anywhere to de-select the text).

6 Format Several Blocks of Text

To paint the same formatting to several different blocks of text more quickly, double-click the **Format Painter** button. Format Painter remains turned on, so you can paint the formatting repeatedly. For example, you can paint across all the headings in the document shown here. When you're finished painting the formatting, click the **Format Painter** button again to turn it off.

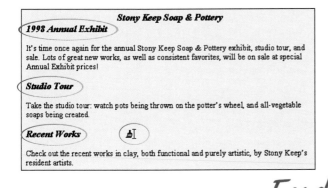

End

How-To Hints

Other Ways to Copy Formatting

Another way to copy formatting is to first apply formatting to a selection with the Font dialog box (by using the Font dialog box, you can apply several formatting characteristics at once); then select a block of text where you want to copy the formatting, and choose **Edit**, **Repeat Font Formatting**. You can also press F4 or Ctrl+Y to repeat an action.

How to Change Fonts and Font Sizes

For many people, playing with fonts is one of the more entertaining aspects of word processing—but it's easy to go overboard and format the document to the point that it becomes excessively busy and difficult to read. Resist this temptation if you want your document to have a professional appearance. Two—or at most three—fonts per document is usually enough.

Begin

1 Select the Text

Select the text whose font you want to change. To select text, place your cursor at the beginning of the text you want to select; then hold down the left mouse button and drag the cursor to the end of the text, and release the mouse button.

2 Select a Font

On the Formatting toolbar, click the down arrow on the Font list box to display a list of your installed fonts. Scroll through the list, and click the font you want to apply to the selected text. Fonts you've used recently appear above a double line at the top of the list; below the double line is an alphabetical list of all the fonts.

3 Select the Text

After you've chosen a font, you can make it larger or smaller by changing the font size. To change the font size, select the text you want to resize (this can be whole words, paragraphs, or individual characters).

Stony Keep Soap & Pottery

1998 Annual Exhibit

It's time once again for the annual Stony Keep Soap & Pottery exhibit, studio tour, and sale. Lots of great new works, as well as consistent favorites, will be on sale at special Annual Exhibit prices!

4 Locate a Font Size

On the Formatting toolbar, click the down arrow on the Font Size list box to display the list of font sizes.

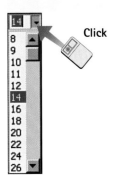

Click

5 Select a Font Size

Scroll, if necessary, to find the size you want, and then click on the number to apply it to the selected text. (You can also click in the Font Size box and type a point size that's not included on the list.)

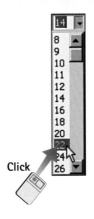

Click

6 Using the Font Dialog Box

The quickest way to experiment with fonts, sizes, and other characteristics is to use the Font dialog box. Select the text you want to format, and then choose **Format**, **Font**. Play with different format characteristics, and check the results in the Preview box.

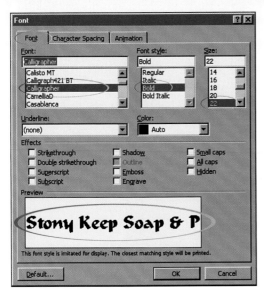

End

How-To Hints

Types of Fonts

The number and type of available fonts depend on what's been installed on your computer, but most computers have a wide selection of TrueType fonts. These are displayed in font lists with a TT symbol next to their names. The advantage of TrueType fonts is that they look the same onscreen as they do when printed, so what you see is what you get (WYSIWYG).

Special Effects

If you want to spice up the appearance of a heading, try some of the special effects in the Effects area of the Font dialog box. Shadow, Outline, Emboss, and Engrave can all add a nice decorative touch to small blocks of text.

Which Font Is Applied?

The buttons and list boxes on the Formatting toolbar—for font, font size, font style, and so on—display the formatting at the location of the insertion point. This comes in handy when you aren't sure which font is applied to a particular block of text. All you have to do is click in the text and then look at the Formatting toolbar to see what characteristics are in effect.

How to Change Line and Paragraph Spacing

Line spacing is the amount of space between lines within a paragraph. Word assumes single spacing, which provides just enough space between lines so that letters don't overlap. Double spacing is good for rough drafts of documents because it gives you extra room to write in edits by hand. One-and-a-half spacing makes text easier to read by separating lines with an extra half-line of blank space.

Paragraph spacing is the amount of space between paragraphs. Documents with an extra half-line of space between paragraphs are easier to read, and you don't need to type an extra blank line between paragraphs.

Begin

1 Select the Paragraphs

To change the line spacing of several adjacent paragraphs, select the paragraphs first. To change the line spacing of only one paragraph, click in that paragraph. To change the line spacing for the entire document, press Ctrl+A to select the entire document. In the example shown here, all the body text paragraphs are selected.

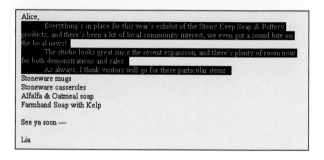

2 Open the Paragraph Dialog Box

Choose **Format**, **Paragraph** to display the Paragraph dialog box.

Click

3 Select Line Spacing

At the top of the Paragraph dialog box, click the **Indents and Spacing** tab if it's not already in front. Then click the down arrow on the Line spacing list box. Click a line spacing, either **Single**, **1.5 Lines**, or **Double**.

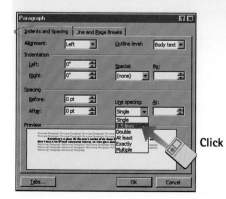

Click

4 Select Paragraph Spacing

To change paragraph spacing for the selected text, click the small arrows to set numbers in the Before and After boxes under Spacing. Experiment with different spacing to find one that sets the paragraphs apart for easy reading but that doesn't take up too much space on the page. The Before box sets spacing at the top of the paragraph(s); the After box sets spacing at the bottom of the paragraph(s). Choose **OK** to close the dialog box.

5 View the Results

The line spacing for this paragraph was changed to one-and-a-half, and the paragraph spacing is 0 Before, 6 After.

> Alice,
>
> Everything's in place for this year's exhibit of the Stony Keep Soap & Pottery products, and there's been a lot of local community interest; we even got a sound bite on the local news!
>
> The studio looks great since the recent expansion, and there's plenty of room now for both demonstrations and sales.
>
> As always, I think visitors will go for these particular items:
>
> Stoneware mugs
> Stoneware casseroles
> Alfalfa & Oatmeal soap
> Farmhand Soap with Kelp

End

How-To Hints

More Line Space

For a line spacing other than those offered, click in the At box (next to the Line spacing list box) and type a line-spacing value. For example, type **3** for triple spacing.

Paragraph Formatting Is Carried Forward

A new paragraph takes on the formatting of the preceding one. So, if you're typing a double-spaced paragraph and you press Enter to start a new paragraph, the new paragraph will also be double-spaced. You can change the line spacing of the new paragraph—or of any paragraph—by following the steps on these pages.

How to Use Tabs

Default tabs in Word are positioned at every half-inch across the ruler. Each time you press the Tab key, your insertion point moves to the next tab stop, pushing over any text to the right of the insertion point. In regular body text, these default tabs work just fine. When you want to create a list with two or more columns of text, however, it's easier if you replace the default tabs with custom tabs at the exact locations where you want to line up your text.

Begin

1 Decide the Type of Tab Stop

You can create four kinds of custom tabs: left, center, right, and decimal. At the left end of the ruler, Word uses the symbols shown here to represent the different types. Use left tabs to align text on the left, right tabs to align text on the right, center tabs to center text across the tab, and decimal tabs to align numbers on the decimal point.

2 Select the Type of Tab

Use the **Tab Alignment** button to select which type of tab to create. Click the button repeatedly to cycle through the four tab symbols. The left tab symbol shows by default, so you must click the **Tab Alignment** button only if you want to create a center, right, or decimal tab. Shown is a column of names created with a left tab.

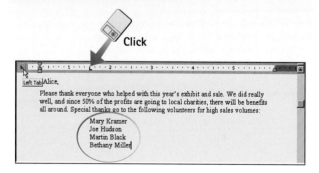

3 Create a Custom Tab

Select the text (the paragraph, line, or entire document) where you want a custom tab, and then create the custom tab by clicking at the desired position on the ruler. The symbol for the tab appears on the ruler. Your custom tabs appear in the text where you created them (and the paragraphs that follow).

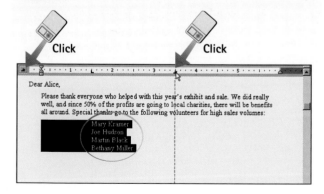

4 Create More Custom Tabs

Repeat steps 2 and 3 to add additional custom tabs. In this example, a left tab is used to line up names in the list, a decimal tab lines up the dollar amounts on their decimals, and a right tab lines up the date at the right.

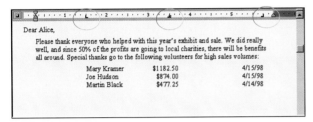

5 Use Custom Tabs

To use the custom tabs, press the Tab key to move out to the first custom tab stop, and type your text. If you've created another custom tab in the same line, press Tab again to move to that tab stop, and type the text. Press Enter to start each new line of text.

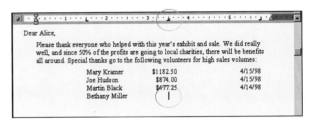

6 Move a Custom Tab

To shift the position of a custom tab, select all the lines in the text where you want to reposition the tab. Then point to the tab, and drag it along the ruler to a new position.

Release   Click & Drag

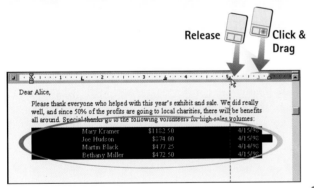

End

How-To Hints

Remove Custom Tabs

To remove a custom tab, use the left mouse button to drag it from the ruler straight down into the text area of the document window, and then release the mouse.

See Where the Tabs Are

To see what custom tabs are in effect for a certain paragraph, click anywhere in the paragraph, and then look at the ruler.

Restore Default Tabs

To restore the default tabs below a paragraph that contains custom tabs, click in the paragraph where you want the default tabs to begin, and simply drag the custom tabs off the ruler (see the first hint). When no custom tabs exist, default tabs work instead.

Delete Tab Spaces

If you accidentally press the Tab key too many times, delete the extra tabs by pressing Backspace or Delete, just as with deleting typed characters.

Formatting Custom Tabs

You can also set custom tabs in the Tabs dialog box (choose **Format, Tabs**). With this method, you can create bar tabs, which you can use to add vertical lines and tabs with dot leaders to your document.

How to Create Numbered and Bulleted Lists

Word's Numbered and Bulleted List features automatically add numbers or bullets when you're typing a list, and they indent the text so that it doesn't wrap underneath the numbers or bullets (see the sample document). What's more, when you type the first item in a list and press Enter, Word automatically turns on the feature for you. (If it doesn't, see the second item in the How-To Hints on the facing page.)

Begin

1 Turn on the Numbered List Feature

To create a numbered list: type **1.** followed by a space, then type the text for the first item, and press Enter. Word turns on the Numbered List feature (the Numbering button on the Formatting toolbar now looks like it's pushed in), inserts a "2." to begin the next line, and creates a hanging indent so that the text in items that take up more than one line won't wrap under the number.

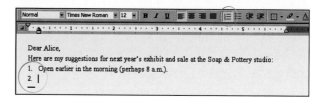

2 Turn on the Bulleted List Feature

To create a bulleted list, type an asterisk (*) followed by a space, type the text for the first item, and press **Enter**. Word turns on the Bulleted List feature (the Bullets button on the Formatting toolbar looks pushed in). The program changes the asterisk to a bullet, inserts another bullet to begin the next line, and creates a hanging indent.

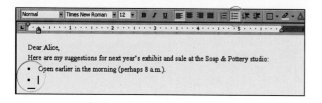

3 Type Your List

Continue typing items, pressing Enter at the end of each item to start a new numbered or bulleted line.

Dear Alice,
Here are my suggestions for next year's exhibit and sale at the Soap & Pottery studio:
1. Open earlier in the morning (perhaps 8 a.m.).
2. Have a half-price table for seconds and lumpware — folks will buy lots of this stuff if it priced well below normal.
3. Have a Kids' Hour, when kids can have studio time to make something.
4. Get an espresso cart and barrista in for the duration of the exhibit.
5. |

4 Turn Off the Numbers or Bullets

After you type the last item, press Enter twice to turn the numbered or bulleted list off, or click the Numbering or Bullets button on the toolbar to turn it off. The first Enter starts a new numbered or bulleted line, and the second Enter clears that line and turns off the feature.

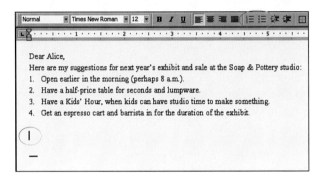

5 Change Numbers to Bullets

If you want to change the numbers to bullets (or vice versa), select the entire list and then click the Bullets or Numbering button on the Formatting toolbar.

6 Change Bullet Symbols

In this example, the numbered list has been changed to a bulleted list, and each individual bullet has been modified to be a different symbol. To change the bullet symbol, select the list items you want to change, and then choose **Format**, **Bullets and Numbering**. Select a new symbol on the **Bulleted** tab, and then choose **OK**.

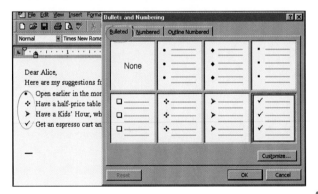

End

How-To Hints

Renumbering Is Automatic

When you cut and paste to change the order of items in a numbered list, Word keeps the numbering sequential.

Turn Off Automated Lists

To turn Automatic Bulleted Lists or Automatic Numbered Lists on or off, choose **Tools**, **AutoCorrect**, and click the **AutoFormat As You Type** tab. Mark or clear the Automatic bulleted lists and Automatic numbered lists check boxes, and choose **OK**. If you disable these features, you can still turn numbered or bulleted lists on and off manually by clicking the Numbering or Bullets toolbar buttons.

Change the Number Format

You can change the format of the numbers in your list. Select the list, choose **Format**, **Bullets and Numbering**, and experiment with the options on the **Numbered** tab of the Bullets and Numbering dialog box.

How to Create a Table

If you want to create a complex list or chart, the best option is to use a Word table. A *table* is a grid of rows and columns, and each box in a table is called a *cell*. Tables are flexible; you can use them to create anything from simple charts to invoices, employee lists, or résumés.

Word enables you to create tables in two ways: You can use the **Insert Table** button on the Standard toolbar (or the **Table**, **Insert Table** menu command) to specify how many rows and columns you want. (Word then creates an empty table for you.) Or, you can use the **Draw Table** button on the Tables and Borders toolbar to draw the table with your mouse. Regardless of how you create the table, you can easily adjust the number of rows and columns at any time.

Begin

1 Create a Table the Fast Way

To create a table the quick way, click where you want to place the table, and then click the **Insert Table** button on the Standard toolbar. In the grid that appears, you can tell Word how many columns and rows you want in the initial table; drag to select squares that represent cells in the table (two rows and three columns are selected for the table shown here).

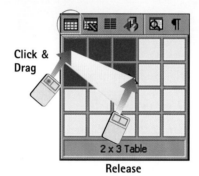

2 Adjust Column Width

A table with the number of rows and columns you selected appears on the page. The table stretches across the width of the page. To make a column narrower, point to a vertical border and drag it to a new position; drag the right table border to narrow the entire table.

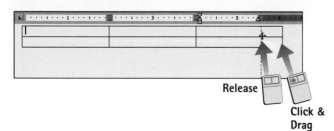

3 Enter Text in the Table

Click in a cell and begin typing; the text in each cell behaves like a paragraph. If you press Enter, a new paragraph begins in the same cell. You can format the text in each cell the same way you format text in a normal paragraph.

Item	Price	About the Item
Rice bowls	$6 each $22/set of four	A *rice bowl* is at least as deep as it is wide, and has a pleasing, ergonomic shape. Rice bowls are ideal for serving rice when you serve Japanese cuisine.
Hand mugs	$4 each	A *hand mug* has no handles — instead, the curvature of the mug form fits your hand. Filled with a hot beverage, it's a wonderful hand warmer on a cold day!

4 Create a Table Another Way

To draw an asymmetrical table cell by cell, click the **Tables and Borders** button on the Standard toolbar. The Tables and Borders toolbar appears, and the mouse pointer becomes a pencil (the document switches to Page Layout View).

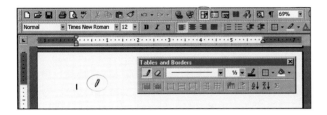

5 Draw the Outside Border

Click the **Draw Table** button if it isn't already selected, and then use the **Line Style**, **Line Weight**, and **Border Color** buttons to choose the type and color of the line you want for the outside border of your table. Drag the mouse to draw a rectangle for the outside border of the table.

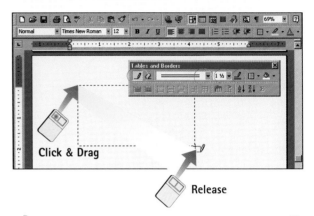

Click & Drag

Release

6 Draw the Inside Borders

Select a different line type or color for the inside borders, if you want; then draw internal lines to delineate rows and columns. As you drag, a dashed line shows you where the line will be inserted. Release the mouse as the line extends across the entire width or height of the table. You can draw a table as complex as you want with this method.

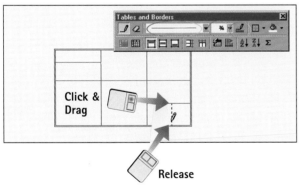

Click & Drag

Release

End

How-To Hints

Enter Text in a Table

To enter text in a table, click in a cell with your mouse and then type. Press Tab to move cell-by-cell to the right, and press Shift+Tab to move cell-by-cell to the left. (To insert a tab character in a cell, press Ctrl+Tab.) To add a new row at the bottom of a table, click in the far-right cell in the last row, and then press Tab.

Insert and Delete Rows

To insert a new row within a table, click in the row below where you want the new row inserted, and click the **Insert Rows** button on the Standard toolbar; or choose **Table, Insert Rows**. To delete a row, click in the row and then choose **Table, Select Row**; then choose **Table, Delete Rows**.

Enter Text Above the Table

If you created a table at the top of a document and later decide you want to type text above the table, click at the beginning of the upper-left cell in the table and press **Enter**; Word inserts a blank line above the table.

How to Add Borders and Shading

You don't have to know anything about graphics to add attractive borders and shading to headings and paragraphs of body text. You can even create a decorative border around the entire page. This task shows you how to work with the Borders and Shading dialog box, but you can also issue most of the commands with the Tables and Borders toolbar (click the **Tables and Borders** button on the Standard toolbar).

The borders and shading formats apply to tables and table cells as well as to paragraphs that aren't in tables; all use the same techniques.

Begin

1 Open the Dialog Box

Click anywhere within the paragraph (or table cell) to which you want to add borders and shading, or select adjacent paragraphs (or table cells) if you want to add borders and shading around the group. Choose **Format**, **Borders and Shading** to display the Borders and Shading dialog box.

Click

2 Select a Setting

Click the **Borders** tab if it isn't already in front. If you see an option under Setting that closely matches the type of border you want to add, click it.

Click

3 Customize Your Border Style

Customize your border lines by scrolling through the Style list and clicking the desired style. Use the Color and Width drop-down lists to change the color and width of the lines. To design a border from scratch, choose **Custom** under Setting, select a style, color, and width for one of the lines, and then click the line in the sample box under Preview.

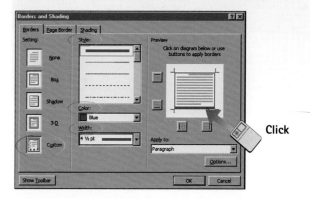

Click

4 Add Shading

To add shading, click the **Shading** tab at the top of the dialog box, and then click the color you want under Fill. When you've made all your selections in the Borders and Shading dialog box, choose **OK**.

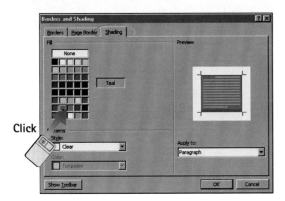

Click

5 Make the Box Bigger

To change the distance between the top and bottom borders and the paragraph text, simply point to the border you want to adjust, drag it up or down, and then release the mouse.

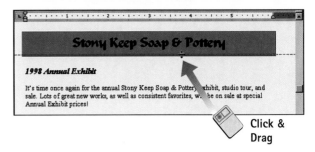

Click & Drag

6 Create a Page Border

To create a border around your page, click the **Page Border** tab in the Borders and Shading dialog box, specify the type of border you want, and choose **OK**. Word creates the border around every page in your document.

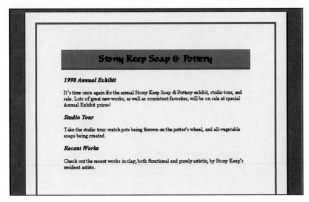

End

How-To Hints

Separate Borders Around

To put separate borders around two adjacent paragraphs, insert a blank line between the two paragraphs; then apply borders around the two paragraphs separately.

Narrow Borders

If you don't want the right and left borders on a paragraph to extend all the way to the margins, indent the paragraph an equal amount from the left and right (choose **Format, Paragraph**, and change the indentation on the **Indents and Spacing** tab).

Automatic Borders

To quickly add a single-line horizontal border, click the line where you want the border to go, type **- - -** (three hyphens; no spaces), and press Enter. To create a double-line border, type **===** (three equal signs), and press Enter. To enable/disable this feature (it's turned on by default), choose **Tools, AutoCorrect**, click the **AutoFormat As You Type** tab, mark or clear the Borders check box, and choose **OK**.

How to Change Page Margins

The default margins in Word are 1 inch on the top and bottom of the page and 1.25 inches on the left and right. These margins are fine for most documents, but like all features in Word, they can be changed. Wider margins can give the page a more spacious feel, and narrower margins come in handy when you're trying to fit lots of text onto one page (especially when you find you have just a line or two more than will fit).

Begin

1 Open the Page Setup Dialog Box

Choose **File**, **Page Setup**. (It doesn't matter where the insertion point rests, and you shouldn't have any text selected.)

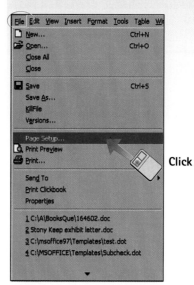

Click

2 Click the Margins Tab

In the Page Setup dialog box, click the **Margins** tab if it's not already active.

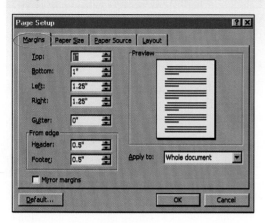

3 Enter New Margin Settings

Type new margin settings in the Top, Bottom, Left, and Right boxes (the settings are measured in inches). Choose **OK** to apply the new margins.

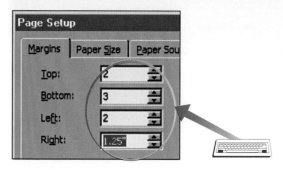

4 Preview Your Settings

On the Standard toolbar, click the **Print Preview** button to switch the document to Print Preview. Print Preview gives you a whole-page view of your document, and it's easier to check margin settings for a good visual appearance.

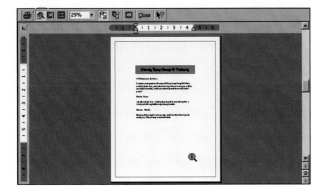

5 Drag Margins to Change

You can also change margins visually, rather than by setting inch measurements, in either Print Preview or Page Layout view. The margins are displayed as gray bars at each end of the horizontal and vertical rulers; you can drag a margin to reset it.

End

How-To Hints

Watch Your Printable Area

Be careful about setting margins too narrow—most printers have a minimum margin that's not printable (commonly, a margin of less than .25 inches falls outside the printable area).

Change the Default Margins

If your company wants margin settings on all its documents that differ from Word's default margins, you can set the default margins to match those used in your company. This way you won't have to change the margins each time you start a new document. To set new default margins, follow steps 1 through 3, but before you choose **OK** in step 3, click the **Default** button. When Word asks whether you want to change the default settings for page setup, click **Yes** and then choose **OK**. You can change the default margins as often as you like.

How to Use Headers and Footers

A *header* is text that appears at the top of every page, and a *footer* is text that appears at the bottom of every page. You might want to use headers and footers to display the document title, your name, the name of your organization, and so on. You can also insert fields in headers and footers—a *field* is a holding place for information that Word updates automatically, such as the current date. Built-in AutoText entries also are set up for headers and footers.

Begin

1 Choose the Header/Footer Command

To add a header and/or a footer to a document, choose **View, Header and Footer**.

Click

2 Create a Header

Word switches to Page Layout view, places the insertion point in the header area, and displays the Header and Footer toolbar. You type and format text in a header or footer just as with normal body text; the only difference is that text entries in the header and footer show up on every page in the document. Word automatically creates two custom tabs in the header and footer areas. You can use, create, delete, and move these custom tabs just like custom tabs in the body of the document.

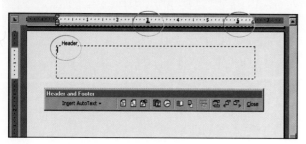

3 Create a Footer

To create a footer, click the **Switch Between Header and Footer** button to place the insertion point in the footer area. You can switch between the header and footer by clicking this button. You can select built-in header and footer entries from the AutoText button on the Header and Footer toolbar.

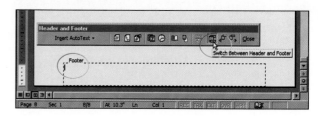

4 Add Automatic Fields

Click the **Date** button to insert a field for the current date.

Click the **Time** button to insert a field for the current time.

Click the **Page Number** button to insert the current page number.

Click the **Number of Pages** button to insert the total number of pages in the document.

Click the **Format Page Number** button to change the appearance of the page number.

Click the **Close** button in the Header and Footer toolbar to return to the body of the document.

5 An Example of a Header

In this example, the header includes formatted text in the center, and a current date field on the right.

End

How-To Hints

Work Faster in Page Layout View

Headers and footers aren't visible in Normal view, but you can see them in both Page Layout view and in Print Preview. After you've created a header or footer, you can switch to the header or footer area from within Page Layout view by double-clicking the pale gray header or footer text. You can then switch back to the body text by double-clicking the pale gray body text.

Different Odd and Even Pages

If you want different headers or footers on odd and even pages of your document (which is common for documents that are bound), choose **File, Page Setup**, and click the **Layout** tab; mark the **Different odd and even** check box, and choose **OK**. You can use the **Show Next** and **Show Previous** buttons in the Header and Footer toolbar to switch between the headers and footers for odd and even pages.

How to Use the Document Map

The *Document Map* gives you a bird's-eye view of your headings as you're working. As its name suggests, this map shows you where you are in a long document, and you can use it to quickly jump from section to section. The Document Map works best if you format your headings with heading styles, as shown in the examples on this page, or outline levels. If Word doesn't find heading styles or outline levels, it searches for paragraphs that look like headings within the larger body text (for example, short lines formatted in a larger font size), applies outline levels to them, and then displays them in the Document Map.

Begin

1 Switch to Document Map

Click the **Document Map** button in the Standard toolbar.

2 Document Map Opens

Word opens the Document Map on the left side of the document window and uses indentation to show the levels of the various headings in the outline. In this example, the heading SUMMER RECIPES (formatted as Heading 1) contains three subheadings—Salsa, Pesto, and Vegetable Salad (formatted as Heading 2)—which, in turn, contain subheadings for the individual recipes (formatted as Heading 3).

3 Move to a Heading

To move to a particular heading in your document, click the heading in the Document Map. If the heading is wider than the Document Map pane, Word displays a ScreenTip containing the entire heading when you point to it.

4 The Section Appears

In this example, clicking on the Roasted Corn and Tomato Salsa heading in the previous step instantly brings that section of the document into view.

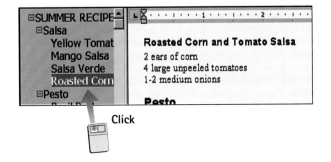

Click

5 Expand/Collapse the Section

You can expand or collapse the view of headings that contain subheadings in the Document Map. Clicking on a minus sign hides all the subheadings beneath the heading, and clicking on a plus sign displays them.

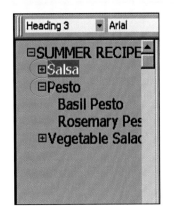

6 Expand/Collapse the Whole Map

If you want to expand or collapse the view of the entire Document Map, right-click anywhere in the Document Map to display the shortcut menu shown here, and click the deepest heading level you want to view. To close the Document Map, either double-click the Document Map's right border, or click the **Document Map** button on the Standard toolbar.

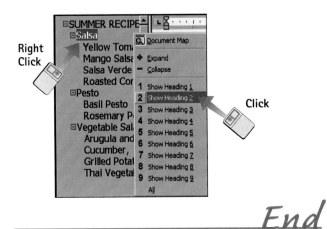

Right Click

Click

End

How-To Hints

Adjust Map Pane Width

To adjust the width of the Document Map pane, point to the boundary between the Document Map and the document. When you see the two-headed arrow and Resize ScreenTip, drag to change the width.

A Blank Document Map

If the Document Map is blank, it means that Word couldn't find any paragraphs formatted with heading styles or outline levels, or any paragraphs that looked like headings. If this happens, follow the directions in Task 18, "How to Use Outline View," to apply heading styles or outline levels to your headings; then redisplay the Document Map.

Rearrange Headings in Outline View

If you need to change the levels of some of your headings or move headings in your document, use Outline view instead of the Document Map (see Task 18).

How to Use Outline View

Outline view is similar to the Document Map, but it's intended to help you modify the structure of your outline instead of simply helping you navigate. In Outline view, you can move headings—and any body text or subheadings they contain—by dragging-and-dropping them, and you can hide and display heading levels by clicking on toolbar buttons. You can also apply heading styles or outline levels to your headings while you're using Outline view.

Begin

1 Choose Outline View

Choose **View**, **Outline** (or click the **Outline View** button in the lower-left corner of the document window).

Click

2 The View Switches

Word switches to Outline view and displays the Outlining toolbar. The numbered buttons on the toolbar refer to heading levels in the outline. Click a number button to display that level of headings; click the **All** button to display the entire document, both headings and body text.

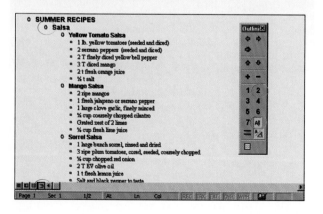

3 Collapse the Outline

In this example, clicking on the 2 button in the previous step collapsed the outline to show only headings formatted with the Heading 2 style and higher.

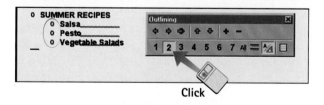

Click

4 Select a Heading to Move

To move a heading (along with its sub-headings and body text) to a new location in the document, first select the heading by clicking on the plus sign next to it (all the heading's subtext is selected along with the heading). When you point to the plus symbol, the mouse pointer changes shape to become a four-headed arrow.

```
○  Yellow Tomato Salsa
      □  1 lb. yellow tomatoes (seeded and diced)
      □  2 serrano peppers  (seeded and diced)
      □  2 T finely diced yellow bell pepper
      □  3 T diced mango
      □  2 t fresh orange juice
      □  ¼ t salt
  ⊕ Mango Salsa
      □  2 ripe mangos
      □  1 fresh jalapeno or serrano pepper
      □  1 large clove garlic, finely minced
      □  ¼ cup coarsely chopped cilantro
      □  Grated zest of 2 limes
      □  ¼ cup fresh lime juice
○  Sorrel Salsa
```

5 Move the Heading

Drag the plus symbol up or down in the outline. As you drag, the mouse pointer becomes a two-headed arrow, and a faint horizontal line with a small black arrow indicates where the heading will move. When the line is in the right location, release the mouse. Word moves the heading and all its contents to the new location.

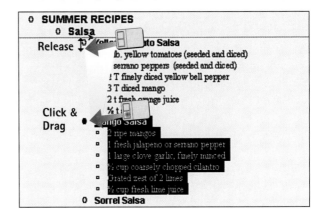

6 Promote or Demote Heading Levels

To change a heading's outline level, drag the plus symbol to the right or left—left to promote the heading to a higher level, and right to demote the heading to a lower level. As you drag, the mouse pointer becomes a two-headed arrow, and a faint vertical line with a small black arrow indicates where the heading will move. When the level is in the right location, release the mouse. All the heading's subtext is promoted or demoted along with the heading.

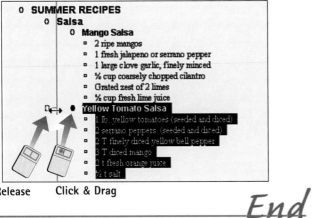

Release   Click & Drag

End

How-To Hints

Expand or Collapse Sections

To expand or collapse the subheadings and text under an individual heading, double-click the heading's plus symbol.

Switch Views

When you're done using Outline view, use the View menu or the View buttons in the lower-left corner of the document window to switch to Normal or Page Layout view.

View Outline Without Formatting

To view your headings in Outline view as plain, unformatted text, click the **Show Formatting** button on the Outlining toolbar to hide the formatting.

How to Use a Template

Word templates are well-designed and easy to use. A paint-by-numbers approach to document creation, templates show you exactly what type of text to enter where.

The advantage of using a template instead of an ordinary document to store text and formatting you want to reuse is that you can't accidentally overwrite a template. Here's a common problem: If you open a document you're using as a blueprint, revise it, and then accidentally choose **File**, **Save** instead of **File**, **Save As** to save the filled-in version, you overwrite the original document and lose your blueprint. But when you start a new document based on a template, fill in the blanks, and save it, Word saves the new document separately from the template, leaving the template in its original form.

Begin

1 Open the New Dialog Box

Choose **File**, **New** to display the New dialog box. In this situation, you can't use the **New** button on the Standard toolbar as a shortcut. (When you click the **New** button, Word assumes you want to start a new document based on the Normal template; it doesn't give you the chance to choose a different template.)

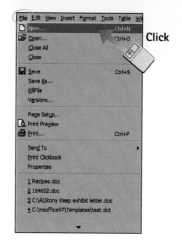

Click

2 See Where Templates Are Stored

The Normal template (which is used by the New toolbar button to start a new document) is stored in the **General** tab.

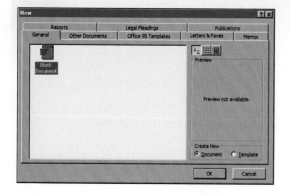

3 Preview Templates

Try clicking on a few template names. When a template is selected, Word displays a preview of it on the right side of the dialog box (if a preview is available).

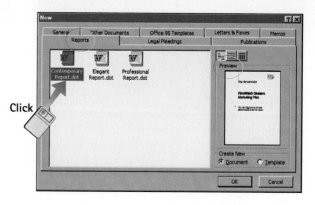

Click

4 Select a Wizard

Some templates are called wizards. *Wizards* are specialized templates that enable you to customize the document you create (see Task 20, "How to Revise a Template"). The **Letters & Faxes** tab shown here contains wizards for creating envelopes, faxes, letters, and mailing labels. Be sure the **Document** option, in the lower-right corner of the dialog box, is selected, and then double-click the icon for the template you want to use (Elegant Letter in this example); or click the icon and then choose **OK**.

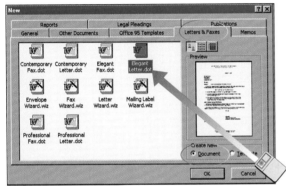

Double Click

5 Enter Text into the Template

Word creates a new document based on the template you chose. Many templates, such as the one shown here, provide instructions to "Click here and type" to help you fill in your text. You may also see some cross-hatched boxes; Word uses these for formatting purposes only—they won't print. Click the first "click here" instruction to select it, and type your text.

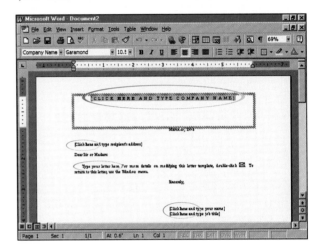

6 Finish the Document

The text you typed replaces the "click here" text. Continue replacing all the "click here" instructions with the text you want in the document. When you have completed the document, use the regular methods to save, print, and close it.

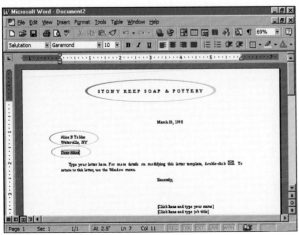

How-To Hints

Use Template Instructions

Some templates, such as the one shown in this task, include a sentence or two of instructions in the body of the document. After you've read the instructions, select the text and type over it.

Check Headers and Footers

Be sure to check the header and footer areas of the template. Many templates have dummy text in these areas that must be replaced. (See Task 16, "How to Use Headers and Footers.")

End

How to Revise a Template

After using a template for a while, you may notice some text or formatting that you consistently want to change. You can make the change in each individual document you base on that template, but it's much more efficient to modify the document once by changing the template. Remember that editing a document based on the template does not affect the underlying template; you must open the template itself to revise it.

Begin

1 Open a File

Click the **Open** button in the Standard toolbar, or choose **File**, **Open**.

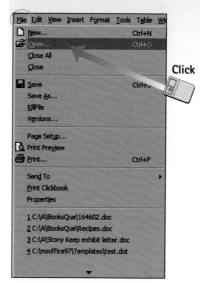

Click

2 Choose a Template File Type

In the lower-left corner of the Open dialog box, click the down arrow on the Files of type list box, and click **Document Templates**.

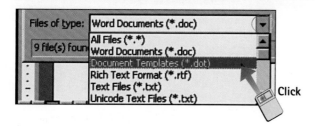

Click

3 Navigate to the Templates Folder

Navigate to the folder where the template is stored—either the Templates folder itself or a subfolder of Templates. The Templates folder is usually a subfolder of the Microsoft Office folder, which is generally located on your hard drive. The usual path is c:\Microsoft Office\Templates. Double-click the subfolder where your template is stored.

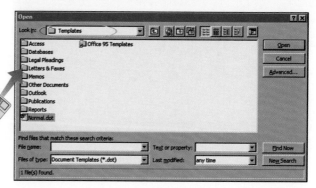

Double Click

4 Select a Template

Double-click the template icon (in this example, the "SSS&P Letterhead" in the Letters & Faxes subfolder), or click the template icon and then choose **Open**.

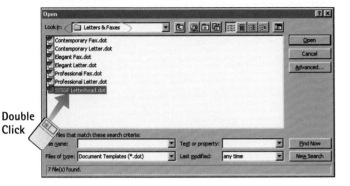

Double Click

5 Make Your Changes

Make your changes to the text or formatting of the template. In this example, a box border is added to the letterhead, and the address is reformatted to fit on one line.

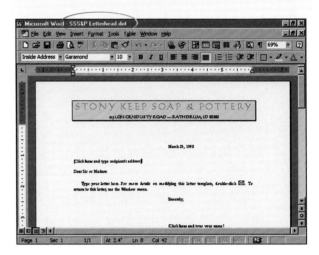

6 Save the Template

Save and close the template. The next time you use the template, you'll open the modified version of the document.

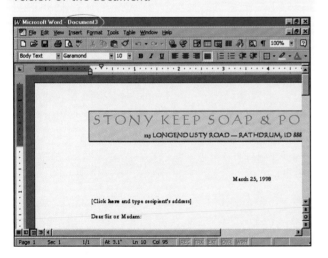

End

How-To Hints

Create Different Versions of Template

To create different versions of the same template, perhaps with different color schemes or different audiences, choose **File, New**. In the New dialog box, click the **Template** option in the lower-right corner before you open the template on which you want to base a new version. This opens a copy of the template that you can save as a different version, with a different name. After you save this new version of the template, its icon appears on the **General** tab next time you choose **File, New**.

Delete a Custom Template

To delete a custom template, open the New dialog box; right-click the icon for the template you want to delete, and click **Delete**. Choose **OK** to close the dialog box.

How to Use a Wizard

Wizards differ from standard templates in two ways: They offer a great deal of hand-holding, and they help you tailor the template to suit your preferences. Other than that, the result is the same. Wizards typically ask you a series of questions about what text and formatting you want included in the document. When a wizard has gathered all the information it needs, it creates a document that contains all your preferences. Wizard-generated documents are the same as documents based on standard templates, complete with click-here instructions to help you fill in the text.

Begin

1 Open the New Dialog Box

Choose **File**, **New** to display the New dialog box. (You cannot use the **New** button on the Standard toolbar if you want to create a new document from a template or a wizard).

Click

2 Select a Wizard

Click the tab that contains the wizard you want to use, click the wizard name, and choose **OK** to start the wizard. (This example uses the Memo Wizard in the **Memos** tab.)

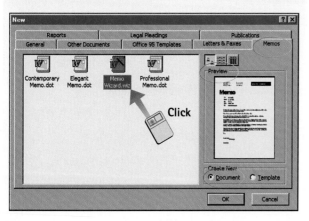

Click

3 Start the Wizard

Word displays the first step of the Wizard dialog box, called Start. As you progress through the wizard, Word highlights the current step on the left side of the dialog box. Click **Next** to move to the next step.

Click

4 Step Through the Wizard

Each wizard step presents questions and alternative choices. In this step, the Memo Wizard needs to know which style you prefer for your memo. Make your selection, and click **Next** again. Continue working your way through the steps. If you want to go back to a previous step, click the **Back** button until you reach the step you want.

Click

5 Finish the Wizard

When you reach the Finish step, click **Finish** to tell the wizard to create the new document.

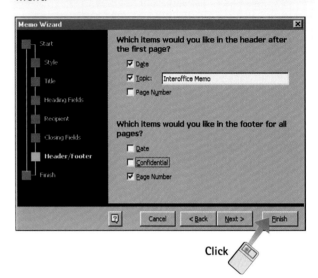

Click

6 Finish Your Document

After a moment or two, Word displays a document in Page Layout view with the text and formatting you requested. This document works like a document based on a template; wherever you see click-here instructions, replace them with actual text. Then save, print, and close the document.

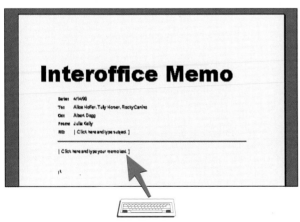

How-To Hints

A Faster Wizard

If you've used a wizard before and know that you want to keep all the default answers to the questions, you can save time by clicking the **Finish** button on the Start page (see step 3) to complete the questionnaire without changing the default choices.

Zoom to a Different View

Some wizards display the document at a reduced zoom setting so that you can see more of it on your screen. If you want to enlarge the document to make it easier to read, display the Zoom Control list in the Standard toolbar, and click 100%. You may then need to use the horizontal scrollbar to scroll the right and left margins into view.

End

How to Create Form Letters with Mail Merge

Mail Merge enables you to create form letters or mailing labels. You create a single document and then let Word create many identical copies of the document and merge a different name, address, and so forth into each copy of the document. Mail Merge uses a *data source* (for example, a table of records of names, addresses, and associated information) that's separate from the document. A data source might be an Excel worksheet, an Access or FoxPro table, or a table in another Word document; if the data source doesn't already exist, you can create a Word data source using Mail Merge.

Begin

1 Open a Saved Document

Start by opening the document into which you want to merge data. If you're creating a form letter, type and save the letter, and open it in Word. If you're creating mailing labels, open a blank document. This task uses a form letter to demonstrate Mail Merge; creating mailing labels is very similar.

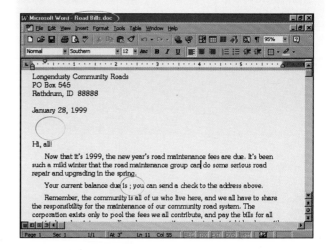

2 Open the Mail Merge Helper

Choose **Tools**, **Mail Merge** to open the Mail Merge Helper, which is a combination dialog box and wizard that walks you through the process.

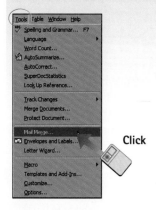

Click

3 Select a Document Type

In step 1 of the Mail Merge Helper, click the **Create** button to display a list of document types. For a form letter, click **Form Letters**.

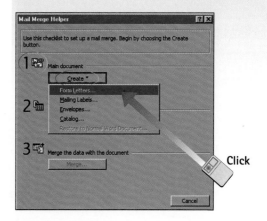

Click

4 Click the Active Window Option

In the next dialog box, click the **Active Window** button (because your form letter is already displayed in the active window).

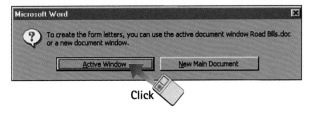

Click

5 Choose the Get Data Button

Read the text at the top of the Helper—it tells you to choose the **Get Data** button. At this point, you can either use an existing data source, or create a new data source and type all the names and addresses you want to merge into the letter. See Task 23, "How to Use an Existing Data Source," to learn how to continue using an existing data source. See Task 24, "How to Create a New Data Source," to learn how to create a new data source at this point.

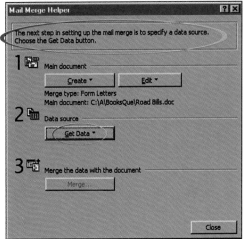

End

How-To Hints

Use Merge Fields

If you want to use an existing letter as your main document, open it, save it under a new name so you don't lose the original, and remove all the information you'll replace with *merge fields* (data to be merged, such as name or address) from the data source. Then continue with step 2 in this task.

How to Use an Existing Data Source

A data source is actually a simple database, so to prevent confusion you should understand two database-related terms: record and field. A *record* is all the information about one person in your data source; this is a row in the database table. A *field* is one category of information within each record; it is a column in the database table. Typical fields include first name, last name, address, and so on.

It's easiest to use a data source that already exists in your computer. Follow the steps in this task to use an existing data source. If your merge data is not stored in an electronic file, skip this task and use Task 24 to create a new data source.

Begin

1 Choose Open Data Source

If you haven't done so yet, open your main merge document (your form letter). In the Mail Merge Helper dialog box, click the **Get Data** button, and then click **Open Data Source**.

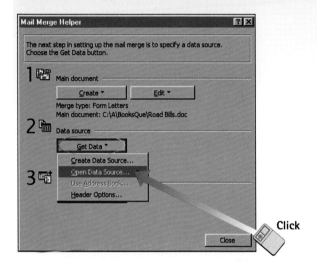

Click

2 Look for the Data Source File Type

In the Open Data Source dialog box, navigate to the folder where your data source file is stored. Click the down arrow next to the Files of type box, and click the file type for your data source.

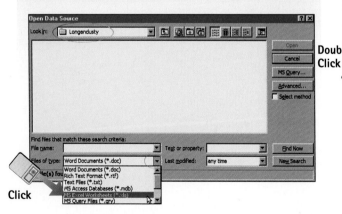

Click

3 Select the Data Source File Type

The files of the type you selected are listed in the dialog box; double-click your data source file.

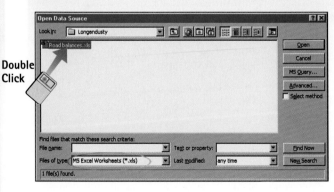

Double Click

4 Open the Data Source File

The file's program starts and the file opens in the background. You'll see a dialog box asking you further questions to define the data source, depending on the file type you opened. In this example, an Excel file is the data source, and the table containing the names and addresses is a range named Balance. Follow any steps and questions to tell Word where your data source is (in this example, I'll double-click the named range **Balance**).

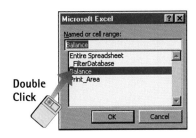

Double Click

5 Open the Mail Merge Toolbar

If this is the first time you've merged this document, there won't be any *merge fields* (fields that insert information from the data source) in the document yet. Click **Edit Main Document** to set up merge fields. The Mail Merge toolbar appears above your document.

Click

6 Insert Merge Fields

Click in your document text where you want to insert a merge field (for example, First Name in the address block of a letter). On the Mail Merge toolbar, click **Insert Merge Field** to drop a list of all the field names into your data source. Click the field name you want to insert, and type any punctuation you need (space, comma, and so on). Continue inserting field names one by one in the document text until all the field names this document needs are in place. Then go to Task 25, "How to Run the Mail Merge," to run the merge.

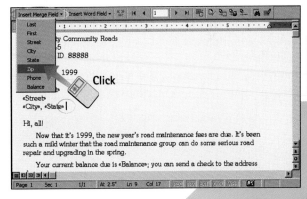

Click

End

How-To Hints

Keep the Data Source Simple

If you use an Excel worksheet as a data source, make it easier to use by doing one of two things: Either keep your contacts list in a workbook that contains no other worksheets, or keep the list on its own worksheet and name the data range on the worksheet. This helps Word locate and define your data source range.

Use Field Names

If you use an Excel data source, be sure your source range has a row of column labels (these are the **field names**) at the top of the table, and no blank rows within the table. If you use an Access or other database data source, the database handles these items.

Use Your Address Book

To use your Exchange or Outlook address book as a data source, click **Use Address Book** in step 1 (instead of Open Data Source). Follow the steps and questions in the dialog boxes to help Word locate the address book.

How to Create a New Data Source

If you haven't created a data source for your Mail Merge yet, you can create it now while you set up your merged document. The new data source will be a table in a separate Word document, and the Mail Merge Helper will create both the data source and a data entry form that makes it easy to enter your data. You'll be able to save and edit the records you enter in the new data source, so you can create the data source once and reuse it endlessly.

Begin

1 Create a New Data Source

If you haven't done so yet, open your main merge document (your form letter). Then click the **Get Data** button in the Mail Merge Helper dialog box, and click **Create Data Source**.

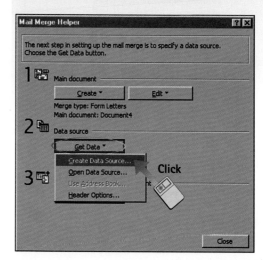

2 Set Up Field Names

The Create Data Source dialog box contains a list of default data fields. To make your data source easier to handle, remove any field names you don't need by clicking the field name in the list, and then clicking **Remove Field Name**. To add a new field that's not in the default list, type it in the Field name box and click **Add Field Name**. When the list of field names is complete, choose **OK**.

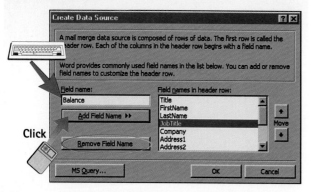

3 Save Your Data Source

In the Save As dialog box that appears, navigate to the folder where you want to save your data source. Give your data source an identifiable name, and choose **Save**. The new data source will be a Word document.

4 Open a Data Entry Form

In the next dialog box, click **Edit Data Source** to add data to your new, empty data source.

Click

5 Enter Data

Word creates a Data Form dialog box to help you enter data. Type appropriate data in each field, and press Enter to move the insertion point to the next field. When you finish typing an entry in the last field for a record, press Enter to start a new record. When you finish entering all your records, choose **OK**. The Mail Merge toolbar is displayed above your document, and you're ready to insert merge fields into the document text.

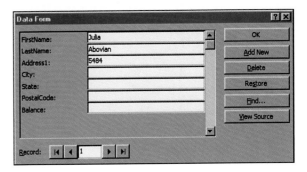

How-To Hints

Edit and Delete Records

At the bottom of the Data Form, the **Record** box indicates the record in use. To edit a previous record, you can click the red arrows next to the **Record** box to click through the records one by one until you find the record you want. To delete a record, display it and click **Delete**.

Data Is Always Available and Current

The new data source is attached to the main document; every time you open the main document, Word knows where to find the data source and displays the Mail Merge toolbar automatically. Any future merges you perform in the main document always use current data in the data source.

Open the Data Source

The easiest way to edit the data source is to open it through the main document. First open the main document; then click the **Edit Data Source** button at the right end of the Mail Merge toolbar. Make your revisions in the Data Form, and then choose **OK**. Save and close the main document, and click **Yes** to save the data source attached to the main document.

6 Insert Merge Fields

Click in your document text where you want to insert a merge field (for example, First Name in the address block of a letter). On the Mail Merge toolbar, click **Insert Merge Field** to drop a list of all the field names into your data source. Click the field name you want to insert, and type any punctuation you need (space, comma, and so on). Continue inserting field names one by one into the document text until all the field names this document needs are in place. Then go to Task 25 to run the merge.

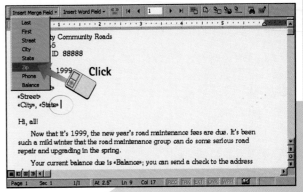

Click

End

How to Run the Mail Merge

In this final step of the merge process, Word merges the main document with the data source. The product of the merge is a document called Form Letters1 that contains all the merged letters.

Begin

1 Start with the Main Document

Open your completed (and saved) main document onscreen. To check that the merge codes are in the proper places and that the information in the data source is entered correctly, click the **View Merged Data** button on the Mail Merge toolbar.

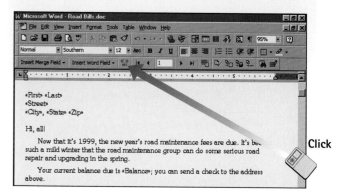

Click

2 Check That Data Merges Correctly

Word displays the data from the first record of your data source in place of the merge fields. Use the red arrows next to the **View Merged Data** button to check the data from a few more records; each time you click one of the buttons, the merge fields show data from a different record. If you spot a problem, you can edit either the main document or the data source.

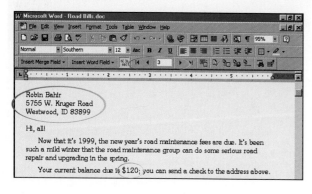

3 Show the Mail Merge Helper

When everything is set up properly, click the **View Merged Data** button again to turn it off. Click the **Mail Merge Helper** button on the Mail Merge toolbar to show the Helper; if you get lost in this process, the Helper will tell you what you need to do next.

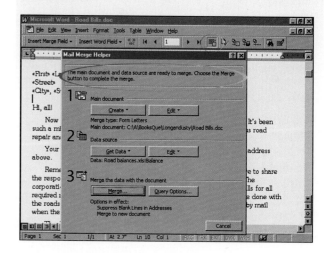

4 Start the Merge

The Helper tells you that you're ready to merge; click the **Merge** button at step 3 in the Helper.

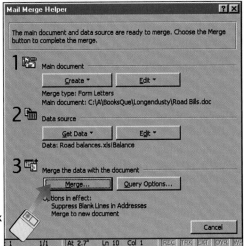

Click

6 Print the Merged Documents

Word separates the new documents with page breaks, so each new document begins on a new page (even though all the pages form one long document file). When you're ready, print the final merged document. Then close the final merged document without saving it (you don't normally need to save the many identical merged letters) and save and close the main document. If asked, click **Yes** to save the data source.

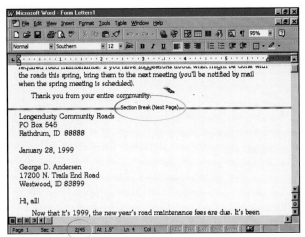

5 Run the Merge

In the Merge dialog box that appears, click **Merge** to merge all your records into the document. Depending on how many records are in your data source, Word could take anywhere from a few seconds to several minutes to merge the data; a new page in the document is created for each record in the data source. When the merge is finished, Word displays the merged documents on your screen in a document named Form Letters1.

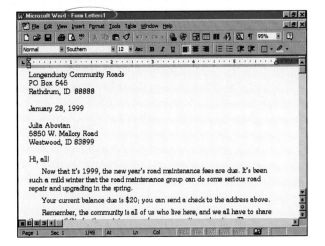

How-To Hints

Save Space

To conserve hard disk space, you don't need to save the merged letters. (The final merged document could be hundreds of pages long if you have a lot of records in your data source.) Next time you need the final merged document, just open the main document and run the merge again.

Merge Faster

The **Merge to Printer** button on the Mail Merge toolbar runs a merge by sending the merged documents directly to the printer (you don't get a chance to check for mistakes onscreen first).

End

How to Insert a Graphic

The difference between a document that elicits yawns and one that sparkles and demands attention is often the addition of graphics. It takes only a mouse click or two to insert a spiffy graphic. This task walks you through the process of inserting clip art images from the Microsoft Office 97 Small Business Edition CD#2.

Begin

1 Click to Place the Graphic

Click in the text to place the insertion point where you want to insert the graphic.

Click

2 Display the Clip Gallery

Choose **Insert**, **Picture**, **Clip Art**. Word switches to Page Layout view. If you see a message that says more clip art is available on Microsoft Office Small Business Edition Disk #1, choose **OK** to close it; the Microsoft Clip Gallery 4.0 dialog box appears.

Click

3 Browse the Images

The Clip Gallery contains tabs for clip art, images (photographic images), sounds, and videos. The examples in this chapter use clip art, but you can use similar methods to work with other types of clips. On the **Clip Art** tab, click the various categories to browse the available images.

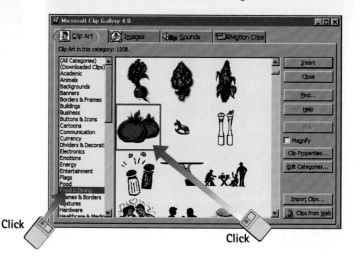

Click

Click

Click

4 Magnify and Insert an Image

To see a selected image more clearly, click the **Magnify** check box. When you click an image, it enlarges a bit and its filename appears under the clip. If you find an image you want to use, select it and click **Insert**.

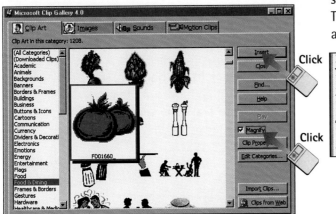

Click

Click

5 Work with the Image

Word inserts the image in your document. It also displays the Picture toolbar, which contains buttons for helping you work with images. The white squares surrounding the image (called sizing handles) indicate that it's currently selected; you can select a graphic image at any time by clicking on it. To delete an image from your document, select it and press the Delete key.

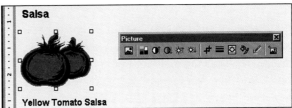

6 Resizing an Image

To resize an image, drag a sizing handle with the mouse. To resize an image without altering its proportions, drag a corner handle instead of a side handle. To resize an image from the center out (instead of out to one side), press and hold down Ctrl while you drag a handle.

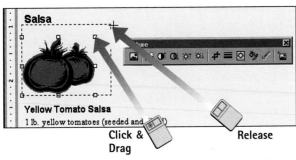

Click & Drag

Release

End

How-To Hints

Add More Images

You can add images to the Microsoft Clip Gallery. Click the **Import Clips** button in the Microsoft Clip Gallery 4.0 dialog box; in the Add Clip Art to Clip Gallery dialog box, locate and select the graphics file you want to add, and choose **Open**. When Word displays the Clip Properties dialog box, click to mark the categories where you want this image displayed, and enter any keywords, separated by spaces, that you want to associate with this image to use in searches later. Then choose **OK**.

Use Your Own Art

To insert an image of your own that you haven't imported into the Clip Gallery, choose **Insert**, **Picture**, **From File**. In the Insert Picture dialog box, locate and click the image file on your hard drive, and choose **OK**.

How to Format a Graphic

Word enables you to format graphics images in many different ways, whether to insert an image, display the Drawing and Picture toolbars, or experiment. You can change the way the text wraps around the image. You can also lighten an image's coloring to turn it into a watermark; finally, you can even place a graphic image behind your text.

Begin

1 Wrap Text Around an Image

By default, Word doesn't allow text to wrap around graphics images. In many cases (such as when you're placing a picture in a news article), you need to change this setting so that the text wraps around one or both sides of the image. In this example, the recipe text block should wrap around the right side of the image instead of shifting below it.

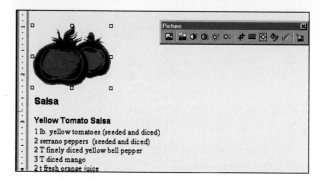

2 Change Image Properties

To change the way your text wraps around an image, select the image; then right-click the image and click **Format Picture** on the shortcut menu to display the Format Picture dialog box.

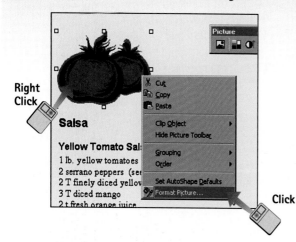

Right Click

Click

3 Change How Text Wraps

Click the **Wrapping** tab. Under **Wrapping style**, click the type of wrapping you want. Under **Wrap to**, click an option to specify how the text should wrap around the image. Here, choosing Right flows the text down the right side of the image. You can increase or decrease the space between the text and the image under **Distance from text**. Then choose **OK**.

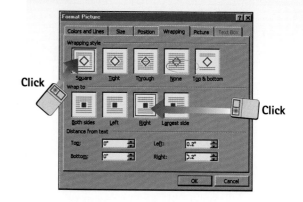

Click

Click

4 Wrapped Text

The text shifts up and wraps to the right of the image.

5 Place an Image Behind Text

To place an image behind your text, follow steps 2 and 3 to set the image's Wrapping style to None, and then drag the image on top of the text. Next, right-click the image, and click **Order**, **Send Behind Text** from the shortcut menu. The tomato image shown here is placed behind the recipe text.

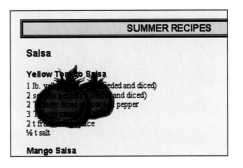

6 Make the Image a Watermark

To lighten an image's colors so that you can easily read the text placed on top of it, you need to create a *watermark*. Select the image, click the **Image Control** button on the Picture toolbar, and click **Watermark**.

Click

7 A Watermark

The tomato image shown here was converted to a watermark after it was sent behind the text.

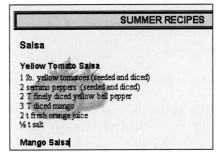

End

How-To Hints

What Do the Options Mean?

To read descriptions of the various options in the **Wrapping** tab of the Format Picture dialog box, click the small question-mark button in the upper-right corner of the dialog box, and then click the option you are curious about. A ScreenTip explains the option. (Click anywhere to hide the ScreenTip.)

What Do the Toolbar Buttons Do?

To figure out what a mysterious button in the toolbar does, choose **Help**, **What's This?**, and then click the button with the question-mark pointer. A ScreenTip explains the button's function.

How to Add Comments to Text

Word enables you to add *comments* that provide extra information without interrupting the flow of the text. The comment is available to readers, but only if they want to see it; otherwise, it's hidden.

Comments are an improvement on Word 95's Annotations. When you point to a Comment, the text of the Comment appears in a ScreenTip. (You don't have to open an extra window at the bottom of the screen to read the Comment text.) If you have a document that you want others to review, Comments are a convenient way for reviewers to tell you what they think at appropriate points in the text.

Begin

1 Insert a Comment

Click in the text where you want to place a Comment, and then choose **Insert**, **Comment**.

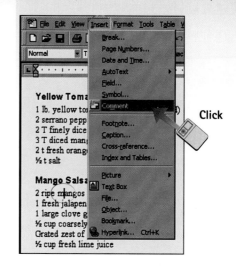

Click

2 A New, Empty Comment Appears

The word nearest the insertion point is shaded yellow, and a small Comment symbol (reviewer initials and a comment number in square brackets) appears at the end of the word.

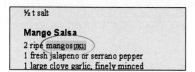

3 Type Your Comment

At the same time, a Comments window opens at the bottom of the screen, and the insertion point appears next to a Comment symbol that matches the Comment symbol just created in the text. Type your comment.

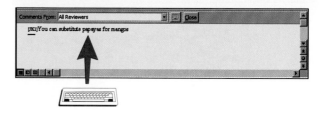

4 Add More Comments

You can add more comments without closing the Comments window. Click in the document window, click to place the next Comment, and then choose **Insert**, **Comment** to add your next Comment. Repeat this step to continue adding Comments until you're finished.

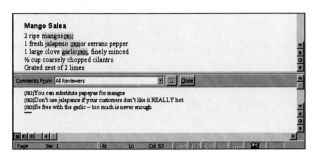

5 Close the Comments Window

To close the Comments window, click **Close**. After you close the Comments window, the Comments symbols in the text are hidden, but the words remain shaded to indicate the location of each Comment.

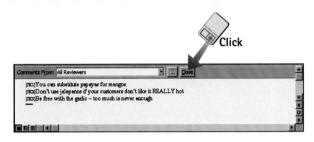

Click

6 Read Comments

To read Comments in the document, point to a shaded word. The Comment appears in a ScreenTip, and the name of the reviewer who made the Comment is included in the ScreenTip. Move the pointer away from the Comment to hide it again.

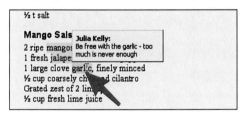

End

How-To Hints

Adjust the Comments Window

To make the Comments window smaller or larger, point at the border between the Comment and document windows. When the pointer becomes a two-headed arrow, drag to raise or lower the window border.

Edit a Comment

To edit a comment, right-click the comment in the document and click **Edit Comment** on the shortcut menu. The Comments window opens; edit the Comment and close the Comments window.

Delete a Comment

To delete a Comment, right-click the comment in the document and click **Delete** on the shortcut menu.

How Did That Name Get There?

The reviewer name that appears in Comments is the username entered in the reviewer's copy of Word. To change your username, choose **Tools**, **Options**, and click the **User Information** tab; change the name in the Name box, and then choose **OK**.

Task

How to Use Excel 97

Microsoft Excel 97 serves as an excellent tool for keeping track of data and crunching numbers. You can use it to perform any kind of mathematical calculation, whether simple or complex, and to organize data in a meaningful and useful manner.

Although at first Excel resembles an accounting spreadsheet, it's much easier to use because you're not always erasing data and rewriting it somewhere else; to reorganize data on a worksheet, you can just drag the data around, or you can instruct Excel to sort or filter data for you. You can chart data to make relationships among the numbers easier to grasp, and you can rearrange the worksheet grid so that the data is easier to read. For visual interest, you can format the characters you enter and the borders around cells with a wide variety of fonts, line widths, and colors.

Excel makes it easy to keep track of lists such as names/addresses or sales volumes; after you grasp the concepts of formulas, functions, and references, you'll find that calculations are as simple as a couple of mouse clicks.

How to Use the Excel Window

When Excel starts, a blank workbook opens. A *workbook* is an Excel file, just as a document is a Word file. A workbook is a container for at least one *worksheet*, which looks like an accountant's spreadsheet divided into a grid of columns and rows. Each little square in the worksheet grid is a *cell*, which holds its own parcel of data that you enter.

Above the worksheet grid is the Formula bar, where the value or formula in a specific cell is displayed with the cell's address. Above the Formula bar are two toolbars and the menu bar: As with all Microsoft programs, the menu bar contains menus of commands and the toolbars contain buttons that help you carry out commands faster.

Begin

1 At the Top of the Screen

The title bar (at the top of the Excel window) shows the program name (Microsoft Excel) and the filename of the active workbook, which is the workbook displayed on the screen. A new workbook will be named Book1 until you save it with a permanent filename.

2 Choose a Menu Command

Below the title bar is the menu bar. Click a menu name to drop the menu list, and click the name of the command you want. If you change your mind about clicking a command, click anywhere in the Excel window to close the menu.

3 Below the Menu Bar

The Standard toolbar (the upper toolbar) and the Formatting toolbar (the lower toolbar) contain buttons for quicker access to many of the commands on the menu bar. If you're not sure about what a button's icon represents, hold your mouse pointer over the button for a moment until a *ScreenTip* appears with the button's name.

4 The Big Picture

This figure shows the entire Excel screen and the names of its important parts.

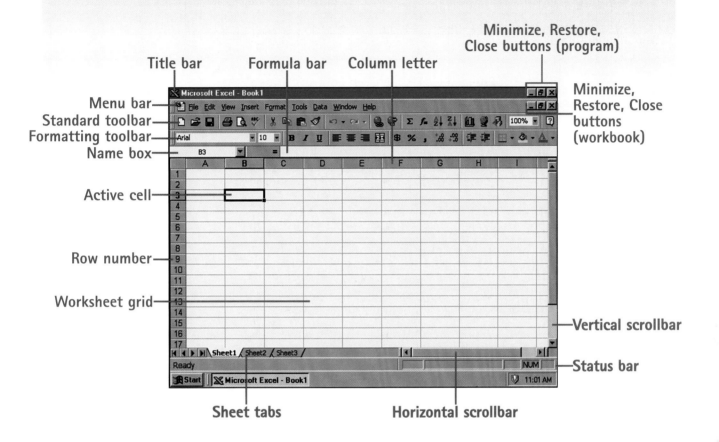

Title bar   Formula bar   Column letter

Minimize, Restore, Close buttons (program)

Menu bar

Standard toolbar

Formatting toolbar

Name box

Active cell

Row number

Worksheet grid

Minimize, Restore, Close buttons (workbook)

Vertical scrollbar

Status bar

Sheet tabs   Horizontal scrollbar

Continues

5 Button Explanations

If seeing the button name doesn't help, choose **Help**, **What's This?**, and click the toolbar button. A bigger ScreenTip appears with an explanation of the button's function.

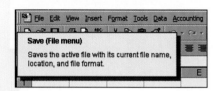

6 Below the Screen

At the bottom of the window, *sheet tabs* tell you the name of the worksheet in which you are working (a workbook contains several worksheets unless you delete them). To select another worksheet, click its sheet tab.

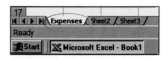

7 Below the Toolbars

The Formula bar, above the worksheet grid, has two main sections. On the left is the Name box, where you'll see the active cell's address; on the right is the formula area, where the content of the active cell is displayed.

8 Rename Sheet Tabs

To rename a worksheet for easier identification, double-click the sheet tab, type a new name, and press Enter.

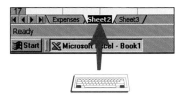

9 A Single Cell, Close Up

The active cell, also called the selected cell, is the cell in which data is entered when you type. This cell has a dark border, and its location, or *cell address*, is the intersection of its column letter and row number. On the worksheet, the mouse pointer appears as a white plus symbol.

10 The Pointer Changes

When you move the mouse pointer over a border of the selected cell, the pointer becomes an arrow symbol.

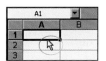

End

How-To Hints

Customize Your Environment

You can customize your Excel environment to suit your preferences. If your toolbars are missing, or if unwanted toolbars are displayed, right-click any toolbar. A shortcut menu appears with multiple toolbar names listed—the toolbars that are displayed have check marks next to them. Simply click a toolbar name to show or hide that toolbar.

The Worksheet Is Bigger Than You Think

The worksheet grid you see is only a small part of the whole worksheet—a worksheet is actually 256 columns wide and 65,536 rows long. You can scroll to the hinterlands of a worksheet with the vertical and horizontal scrollbars. When you scroll past column Z, the columns are labeled AA, AB, and so on; the last column in any worksheet is labeled IV.

How to Enter Data

Data in a worksheet is always entered in cells. To enter data, you click a cell, type the data, and press Enter (or press Tab, or click another cell in the worksheet). You can use lots of tricks for making data entry more efficient, such as entering the same word or number in several cells at the same time or copying an entry from another cell in the same column.

In Task 6, you'll learn how to enter a formula, and in Task 7 you'll learn to use AutoFill to enter lists of data automatically.

Begin

1 Select a Cell

Click the cell in which you want to enter data. The cell you click becomes the active cell and displays a dark border.

2 Enter Data in the Selected Cell

Type your entry (numbers and/or letters), and press Enter. The active cell border moves down one cell, and your characters are entered in the cell where you typed them. If you press Tab after you type, the active cell shifts to the right (which is convenient for typing multicolumn lists).

3 Enter a Multicolumn List

To enter a list, begin at the upper-left corner of the list. As you type the entries, press Tab to move to the right to enter the data for each cell in the row. After you type the last entry in the row, press Enter instead of Tab; the active cell moves to the beginning of the next row—this function is called AutoReturn.

	Jan	Feb	Mar	
Mugs	452	521	352	
Dipping Bowls	225	264	241	
Mixing Bowls	385	334	341	

4 Copy the Cell Above

To copy the entry from the cell above the active cell, press Ctrl+' (press Ctrl and the apostrophe key simultaneously).

	A	B	C
45	7/22/98	Post Office	P.O. box rental (1 yr)
46	7/24/98	US West	business phone
47	8/8/98	Business VISA	interest
48	8/11/98	Northland Times	newspaper - 3rd qtr
49	8/14/98	Office Depot	boxes to move office
50	8/15/98	Mudville Clays	clay
51	8/15/98	Restaurant Supplies. Inc	bulk oils
52	8/16/98	Sprint	long distance charges
53	8/23/98	Sprint	long distance charges
54	8/24/98	US West	business phone
55	8/26/98	Custom Printing	print booklets
56	8/27/98	Custom Printing	copies
57	9/1/98	Custom Printing	
58			
59			

5 AutoComplete an Entry

If you want to repeat an entry from anywhere in the same column (which not only saves time but also prevents typing mistakes), type the first few letters of the entry. A possible match appears in the cell—this function is called *AutoComplete*. If the entry is correct, press Enter. If you don't want that entry, just continue typing.

	A	B	C
45	7/22/98	Post Office	P.O. box rental (1 yr)
46	7/24/98	US West	business phone
47	8/8/98	Business VISA	interest
48	8/11/98	Northland Times	newspaper - 3rd qtr
49	8/14/98	Office Depot	boxes to move office
50	8/15/98	Mudville Clays	clay
51	8/15/98	Restaurant Supplies. Inc	bulk oils
52	8/16/98	Sprint	long distance charges
53	8/23/98	Sprint	long distance charges
54	8/24/98	US West	business phone
55	8/26/98	Custom Printing	print booklets
56	8/27/98	Custom Printing	copies
57	9/1/98	mudville Clays	
58			
59			
60			

6 Pick a Repeated Entry

If you want to repeat an entry that already exists in the column somewhere, you can select it from a list instead of retyping it. Right-click the active cell, and choose **Pick From List**. A list of all the entries in the column appears; click the entry you want.

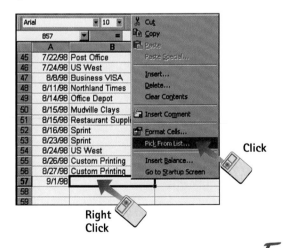

Right Click

Click

How-To Hints

Ways to Move

You can move the active cell using the Arrow, Page Up and Page Down, Home, and End keys. You can jump to the end of a row or column of filled cells or blank cells by pointing to the border of the active cell and then double-clicking when the mouse pointer becomes an arrow. (The border you double-click should be the direction in which the active cell jumps; that is, double-click the top border to jump upward, double-click the right border to jump right, and so on.)

End

How to Edit and Delete Data

After you enter data in a worksheet, you'll want to be able to change the data by editing or deleting it in cells. Sometimes you'll just want to change part of a cell's entry, and sometimes you'll want to replace or delete the entire entry. And if you change your mind about any action you take in a worksheet, you can undo it with the click of a button; in fact, you can undo a whole series of actions with the click of a button.

Begin

1 Edit in a Cell

To edit the data in a cell, double-click the cell to open it for editing, select the characters you want to change, and type new characters or delete the selected characters (just as with editing in Word). When you finish editing, press Enter to keep the changes.

Double Click

	A	B	C
1	**Product**	**Category**	**Price**
2	Redberry Soap	Soap	$3.50
3	Skin Tonic Soap	Soap	$3.50
4	Farmhand Soap	Soap	$3.50
5	Christmas Spice Soap	Soap	$3.50
6	Sea Soap	Soap	$4.50
7	Almond Loofah Soap	Soap	$4.50
8	HoneySuckle Soap	Soap	$4.50
9			

A2 — Redberry Soap

2 Edit in the Formula Bar

You can also edit data in the Formula bar. When you click a cell, its contents appear in the Formula bar, and you can edit here the same way you edit in Word. When you finish editing, press Enter to keep the changes.

Redberry Soap

	A	B	C
1	**Product**	**Category**	**Price**
2	Redberry Soap	Soap	$3.50
3	Skin Tonic Soap	Soap	$3.50
4	Farmhand Soap	Soap	$3.50
5	Christmas Spice Soap	Soap	$3.50
6	Sea Soap	Soap	$4.50
7	Almond Loofah Soap	Soap	$4.50
8	HoneySuckle Soap	Soap	$4.50

3 Replace a Cell Entry

To replace the entry in a cell, select the cell and type the new entry (no need to delete the cell contents first).

A1 — Item

	A	B	C
1	**Item**	**Category**	**Price**
2	Redberry Soap	Soap	$3.50
3	Skin Tonic Soap	Soap	$3.50
4	Farmhand Soap	Soap	$3.50
5	Christmas Spice Soap	Soap	$3.50
6	Sea Soap	Soap	$4.50
7	Almond Loofah Soap	Soap	$4.50
8	HoneySuckle Soap	Soap	$4.50

4 Delete Data

To delete data, select the cell(s) containing the data and press the Delete key.

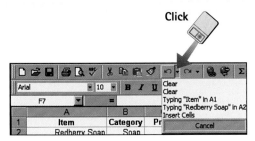

5 Undo a Mistake

If you make a mistake, you can undo it by choosing **Edit**, **Undo** or by pressing Ctrl+Z.

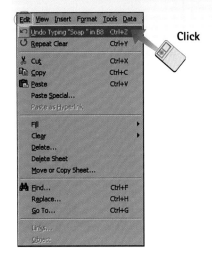

Click

6 Undo Several Mistakes

You can undo several actions by clicking the down arrow next to the **Undo** button on the Standard toolbar; a list of recent actions appears. Click an action to undo all consecutive actions back to that point.

Click

End

How-To Hints

Redo What You Undid

If you undo actions and then wish you hadn't, you can redo what you undid. Choose **Edit**, **Redo**, or click the **Redo** button on the Standard toolbar.

Erase Everything in a Cell

When you delete a cell's contents, only the contents disappear (formatting stays). To erase everything, select the cell(s) and choose **Edit, Clear, All**.

How to Sum Numbers

The most common mathematical calculation in Excel is the sum. You might sum the sales results for several months or the total items in an invoice. Summing is so common that there's a toolbar button that enters a SUM formula for you. You can add the contents of cells by writing a formula such as =A1+B1, but using the SUM function in a formula is faster because Excel does the work for you. You'll learn how to write a formula in Task 6, and you'll learn more about functions (built-in equations) in Task 16; here you learn to enter a fast sum with the AutoSum button.

Begin

1 Enter the Numbers

Enter the numbers you want to sum in a column, row, or rectangular block of cells. If there are any text entries in the *range* of cells (the collection of cells you'll sum), the formula ignores them.

	100	
	200	
	300	
	400	
	500	

2 Select a Location for the Sum

Select the cell where you want the sum result to appear (usually at the end of the row or column of numbers).

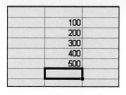

3 Click AutoSum

On the Standard toolbar, click the **AutoSum** button.

Click

4 The SUM Formula Is Entered

The AutoSum button inserts a formula that uses the SUM function, and surrounds the cells being summed with a temporary moving border.

=SUM(D12:D16)		
C	D	E
	100	
	200	
	300	
	400	
	500	
=SUM(D12:D16)		

5 Complete the Entry

If the moving border is surrounding all the cells you want to sum, press Enter to complete the formula; if the surrounded cells are wrong, drag to select the cells you want summed (the moving border surrounds the cells you drag), and press Enter. The result of the formula is displayed in the cell.

		100	
		200	
		300	
		400	
		500	
		1500	

6 See the Formula and the Result

To see the formula and the result, click the cell where you entered the formula. The results appear in the cell, and the formula appears in the Formula bar.

=SUM(D12:D16)		
C	D	E
	100	
	200	
	300	
	400	
	500	
	1500	

End

How-To Hints

Sum a Whole Table at Once

To AutoSum all the columns in a table at once, select all the cells in the row below the table, and click the **AutoSum** button; each column is summed in the cell below the column. To sum all the rows in a table at once, select all the cells in the column next to the table, and click the **AutoSum** button. Each row is summed in the cell at the end of the row.

Put the AutoSum Anywhere

You can place an AutoSum formula anywhere on the worksheet, not just next to the range you're summing. To place the AutoSum formula away from the range of cells, click the cell where you want to display the result, and click the **AutoSum** button. Drag to select the cells you want to sum, and press Enter.

How to Calculate Numbers Quickly

Sometimes you need an immediate calculation but you don't need the formula to be permanently entered in a worksheet cell. *AutoCalculate* is a feature that's always turned on, always out of your way, and available any time you need a quick answer to a simple calculation while you work. For example, if you're entering a column of numbers and you want to know the total of what you've entered so far, all you have to do is select the cells you want to sum and look at the AutoCalculate box. You can also get a quick average, count of cells, or other calculations by changing the AutoCalculate function.

Begin

1 Select Cells

Select the cells you want to calculate.

Telephone Charges	$26.10
Telephone Charges	$14.19
Telephone Charges	$6.48
Telephone Charges	$2.32
Telephone Charges	$14.87
Telephone Charges	$14.87
Telephone Charges	$14.87
Telephone Charges	$16.01
Telephone Charges	$16.47
Telephone Charges	$17.39
Telephone Charges	$18.51

2 Look at AutoCalculate

Look at the AutoCalculate box on the Status bar. The calculation result is displayed for the selected cells.

harges	$2.32	
harges	$14.87	
harges	$14.87	
harges	$14.87	
harges	$16.01	
harges	$16.47	
harges	$17.39	
harges	$18.51	

ist / |◀|

Sum=$112.99

3 See a List of Functions

To change the calculation function, right-click the AutoCalculate box.

Sum=$112.99

Right Click

4 Select a Function

Click a different function, or click **None** to turn it off.

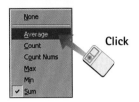

Click

5 Look at the Results

AutoCalculate changes to show the results of your selected function.

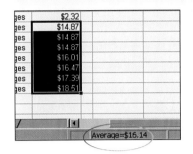

Average=$16.14

End

How-To Hints

If AutoCalculate Isn't There

If AutoCalculate doesn't appear, make sure its calculation is set to a function (not to None) by right-clicking the AutoCalculate box, and make sure a range of cells that contain numbers is selected.

If Your Status Bar Isn't There

If your Status bar is missing, choose **Tools**, **Options**. On the **View** tab, mark the **Status bar** check box, and choose **OK**.

How to Enter a Formula

On paper, we write a formula like this: 2+2=4. In Excel, a *formula* takes a slightly different form: we type =2+2; the answer, 4, is displayed in the cell. All formulas in a worksheet begin with an equal sign (=).

In Excel, you're not limited to writing =2+2; you can type =(*a cell*)+(*another cell*), and the values entered in those cells are added together. If you change the values in those cells, the formula continues to add together their current values. You can also use *mathematical operators* to perform other calculations, such as subtraction (-), multiplication (*), or division (/).

Begin

1 Select a Cell

Click the cell where you want to enter the formula.

C	D	E
10		
20		

2 Type =

Type an equal sign (=).

3 Build the Formula

Click the first of the cells you want to add together, type a plus symbol (+), and then click the next cell you want to add together. As you click each cell, its cell address, or *cell reference*, appears in the formula.

=C13+C14

C	D	E
10		
20	=C13+C14	

4 Complete the Formula

Press Enter to complete the formula. The formula is entered, and the result appears in the formula cell. (The formula is displayed in the Formula bar.)

	B	I	U						
= =C13+C14									

C	D	E
10		
20		
	30	

5 Test the Formula

Now change the values in the cells you referenced in the formula; the formula result changes automatically because the formula adds whatever values are in the cells.

	B	I	U						
=C13+C14									

C	D	E
55		
100		
	155	

End

How-To Hints

Calculate a Large Range

To calculate a large range of cells on a worksheet without entering each cell into the formula separately, you can sum a *range* of cells by including the first and last cell; Excel includes all the cells in between. For example, if you want to sum cells A1, A2, A3, A4, and A5 (the first five cells in column A), a more convenient formula is =SUM(A1:A5). This formula tells Excel to sum all the cells between A1 and A5 (SUM is a specific Excel function; you'll learn more about functions in Task 16).

What's Really in the Cell?

You can't tell by looking at a cell whether the value you see is a simple number or the result of a formula; to find out, select the cell, and look at the Formula bar (what's actually entered in the cell is always displayed in the Formula bar).

Group Operators Within Parentheses

To use different operators in the same formula, use parentheses to divide the formula appropriately. For example, if you want to add 4+6 and divide the result by 2, the formula =4+6/2 gives the wrong answer (7); but the formula =(4+6)/2 gives the right answer (5). Operations within parentheses are performed first.

How to Enter Data Automatically

A feature called *AutoFill* can speed up data entry dramatically by filling in series or duplicate entries for you. AutoFill can fill in lists of day or month names, a series of numbers, or a list of identical text entries by dragging the mouse across the worksheet.

Day and month names, and the standard three-letter abbreviations, are built-in lists in Excel; that's how AutoFill knows what to enter. You can create custom lists—of people or product names, for example—and AutoFill will fill them, also.

Begin

1 Start a Month List

To AutoFill a list of month names, enter a single month name in a cell, and then select that cell.

2 Drag the Fill Handle

Move the mouse pointer over the *fill handle* (the small black square in the lower-right corner of the cell), and click and hold down the left mouse button while you drag across a row or column of cells (you can fill cells in any direction). A ScreenTip shows what's being filled into each cell you drag (so you can tell when you've dragged far enough).

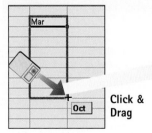

Click & Drag

3 Release the Fill Handle

Release the mouse button at the end of the row or column of cells you want to fill. The series is entered in the cells, in the proper order.

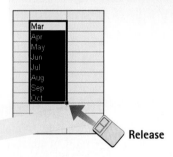

Release

4 Start a Number Series

To fill a number series that increases by 1, start the series by entering **1** and **2**; then select the two cells and drag the fill handle to fill the series.

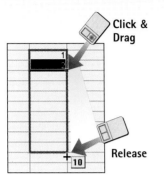

Click & Drag

Release

10

5 Fill a List with a Repeated Entry

To fill a list with a repeated text entry, type the entry, and then select it and drag the fill handle to copy the entry repeatedly.

3/15/98	US West	business phone	Telephone Charges
4/15/98	US West	business phone	Telephone Charges
6/24/98	US West	business phone	Telephone Charges
7/24/98	US West	business phone	Telephone Charges
8/24/98	US West	business phone	Telephone Charges
9/1/98	US West		
10/1/98	US West		
11/1/98	US West		
12/1/98	US West		

Click & Drag

Release

business phone

End

How-To Hints

Copy a Formula with AutoFill

You can use AutoFill to copy a formula down the side or across the bottom of a table; the cell references in the formula adjust so the formula calculates the correct cells (see Task 17 to learn how to use cell references).

Create a Custom List

To create a custom list, enter the entire list in any worksheet. Select the list, and then choose **Tools, Options**. On the **Custom Lists** tab, click **Import**, and choose **OK**. The list is saved in the Custom lists window. You can fill the list in any workbook by typing any entry in the list, and then dragging with the fill handle.

How to Navigate Around Worksheets

Because worksheets are huge (256 columns by 65,536 rows), you need some techniques for moving around in them efficiently. The examples in this book are necessarily small so that I can show you what I'm talking about with minimal confusion. At times, however, you might have a table or list of data that's several screens wide or long, and you might not have the time to spend scrolling back and forth.

Begin

1 Double-click a Cell Border

To jump to the bottom of a list, click a cell in the list to select it. Point to the bottom border of the cell so that your mouse pointer becomes an arrow. Double-click the bottom border of the cell.

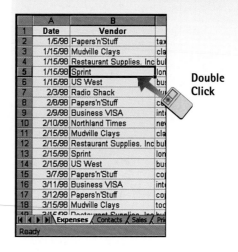

Double Click

2 The Active Cell Jumps

The active cell jumps to the last cell in the column that contains data, which takes you to the bottom of the list. Move back to the top, or from side to side, by double-clicking the top or side borders.

	A	B	
51	8/15/98	Restaurant Supplies. Inc	bulk oils
52	8/16/98	Sprint	long dist
53	8/23/98	Sprint	long dist
54	8/24/98	US West	business
55	8/26/98	Custom Printing	print bod
56	8/27/98	Custom Printing	copies
57	9/1/98	US West	business
58			
59			

3 Jump Home, or Jump to the End

To jump back to the first cell in the worksheet, A1, press Ctrl+Home. To jump to the lower-right corner of the working area of the worksheet (the area you've been working in, not cell IV65536), press Ctrl+End.

	D	E	F
46	Telephone Charges	$17.39	
47	Interest	$51.22	
48	Office Supplies	$32.50	
49	Office Supplies	$42.57	
50	Clay supplies	$355.00	
51	Soap supplies	$200.00	
52	Telephone Charges	$6.48	
53	Telephone Charges	$2.32	
54	Telephone Charges	$18.51	
55	Books/Publications	$314.03	
56	Office Supplies	$3.24	
57	Telephone Charges	$14.87	
58			
59			

4 Jump to the Beginning or End

To jump to the beginning of the row (column A), press Home. To jump to the right-most cell in the row (within the working area of the worksheet), press End, and then press Enter (this instruction is often written as "press End, Enter").

18	Mudville Clays	tools	Clay supplies	$83.14
19	Restaurant Supplies. Inc	bulk oils	Soap supplies	$250.00
20	Sprint	long distance charges	Telephone Charges	$18.90
21	US West	business phone	Telephone Charges	$14.87
22	Business VISA	interest	Interest	$58.59
23	Toshiba	laptop carrying case	Office Equipment	$49.95
24	Mudville Clays	clay	Clay supplies	$125.00

5 Select an Entire Table or List

To select an entire contiguous table or list, click any cell in the list, and then click **Edit, Go To**. In the Go To dialog box, click **Special**. In the Go To Special dialog box, click the **Current region** option, and choose **OK**. When you need to select a really big list for some operation, this is a fast way to do it.

Click

6 Scroll Around and Return Quickly

As you drag a scrollbar, a ScreenTip tells you which row is at the top of the window, or which column is on the left side of the window (it's a fast way to get to a specific row or column). Scrolling doesn't move the active cell, so you can return your view to the active cell quickly by pressing Ctrl+Backspace.

Click
Hold &
Drag

How-To Hints

Jump to the End of the Data

When you double-click a cell border to jump, the active cell jumps to the end of a contiguous block of data, so it jumps to the end of the list and stops short of the first empty cell. If you double-click again, the active cell jumps to the end of the block of empty cells and stops short of the next block of data.

A Useful Custom Toolbar Button

The Customize toolbar button can select the current region for you without using dialog boxes. Right-click any toolbar, and choose **Customize**. In the **Edit** category, on the **Commands** tab, drag the **Select Current Region** command onto a toolbar. Click **Close** to close the dialog box. Now you can click any cell in a table and then click the **Select Current Region** button to select the entire table.

End

How to Insert Columns and Rows

If you need to add a row or column of data into the middle of a table, you could move the existing data by dragging and dropping it to make room for the new row or column. But it's faster to insert a new row or column.

If you're adding an item to an alphabetical list, you don't need to insert it yourself; you type it at the end of the list and tell Excel to sort the list alphabetically (see Task 20 to learn how to sort data). But if you need to add a new row of data above existing subtotal formulas, then you must insert rows and columns.

Begin

1 Select the Row

To insert a row in a list, select the row you want to place below the inserted row (click the row number to select it). Right-click the selected row.

	A	B	C	D	E
1	Sales				
2					
3		Mugs			
4			Jan	$521	
5			Feb	$352	
6			subtotal	$873	
7		Dipping Bowls			
8			Jan	$225	
9			Feb	$264	
10			subtotal	$489	
11		Mixing Bowls			
12			Jan	$385	
13			Feb	$334	
14			subtotal	$719	
15					

Right Click

2 Choose Insert

Choose **Insert** on the shortcut menu.

Click

- Cut
- Copy
- Paste
- Paste Special...
- Insert
- Delete
- Clear Contents
- Format Cells...
- Row Height...
- Hide
- Unhide

3 A New Row Is Inserted

A new row is inserted above the row you selected.

	A	B	C	D	E
1	Sales				
2					
3		Mugs			
4			Jan	$521	
5			Feb	$352	
6					
7			subtotal	$873	
8		Dipping Bowls			
9			Jan	$225	
10			Feb	$264	
11			subtotal	$489	
12		Mixing Bowls			
13			Jan	$385	
14			Feb	$334	
15			subtotal	$719	
16					

4 Select the Column

To insert a column in a list, select the column you want to place on the right of the inserted column (click the column letter to select it). Right-click the selected column.

C	D	E	F
Street	City	State	Zip
5850 W. Mallory Road	Westwood	ID	83899
17200 N. Trails End Road	Westwood	ID	83899
5755 W. Kruger Road	Westwood	ID	83899
PO Box 184	Westwood	ID	83899
5775 W. Mallory Road	Westwood	ID	83899
5980 E. Mallory Road	Westwood	ID	83899
PO Box 150	Lodi	ID	83462
5650 W. Kruger Road	Westwood	ID	83899
5730 W. Mallory Road	Westwood	ID	83899
5775 W. Mallory Road	Westwood	ID	83899
16750 N. Trails End Road	Westwood	ID	83899
16980 N. Trails End Road	Westwood	ID	83899
6195 W. Mallory Road	Westwood	ID	83899
255 N. Trails End Road	Westwood	ID	83899
16105 N. Trails End Road	Westwood	ID	83899
5755 W. Kruger Road	Westwood	ID	83899

Right Click

5 Insert a New Column

Click **Insert** on the shortcut menu. A new column is inserted left of the column you selected.

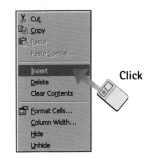

Click

6 Insert Adjacent Rows or Columns

To insert several adjacent rows or columns at one time, select that many rows or columns in the table, right-click the selection, and choose **Insert**. An equal number of rows or columns is inserted.

2			
3	Mugs		
4		Jan	$521
5		Feb	$352
6		Mar	$456
7			
8			
9			
10			
11		subtotal	$1,329
12	Dipping Bowls		
13		Jan	$225
14		Feb	$264
15		subtotal	$489
16	Mixing Bowls		
17		Jan	$385

End

How-To Hints

Formulas Usually Self-Adjust

If you've written formulas that calculate across the table, the formulas adjust themselves automatically after you insert new rows or columns (unless you insert a row immediately above a subtotal; then you'll need to adjust the formula).

Insert a Whole Row or Column

When you insert rows or columns, be sure you select the entire row or column before you click the **Insert** command. If you select only a few cells, Excel tries to insert more cells, which messes up the table completely.

How to Delete Columns and Rows

If you need to remove an entire row or column of data from a table, you could delete the data and then move the remaining data to close the empty space. It's faster, however, to delete the entire row or column because the table closes up the space for you.

If you've written formulas that calculate across the table, the formulas adjust themselves automatically after you delete rows or columns.

Begin

1 Select the Row

To delete a row, select the row you want to delete (click its row number to select it). Right-click the selection.

Right Click

5	Baker	John & Mabel	PO Box 184
6	Balogh	William	5775 W. Mallory Roa
7	Bedrosian	Dick & Annie	5980 E. Mallory Ro.
8	Christensen	Jim	PO Box 150
9	Dandyn	Millard & Mary	5650 W. Kruger R.
10	Deak	Gail A.	5730 W. Mallory R.
11	Domokos	Larry	5775 W. Mallory Ro.

2 Delete the Selected Row

Choose **Delete** on the shortcut menu.

Click

3 Select the Column

To delete a column, select the column you want to delete (click its column letter to select it). Right-click the selected column.

D		
Street2		City
oad	Suite 411	We
		Wes
		Wes
		Wes
	Suite 35	Wes
		Lodi
		Wes
		Wes

Right Click

4 Delete the Selected Column

Choose **Delete** on the shortcut menu.

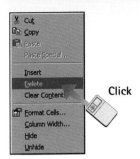

Click

5 Delete Several Adjacent Rows

To delete several adjacent rows at one time, select the adjacent rows in the table, right-click the selection, and choose **Delete** from the shortcut menu.

Right Click

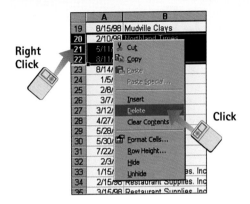

Click

6 Delete Several Adjacent Columns

To delete several adjacent columns at one time, select the adjacent columns in the table, right-click the selection, and choose **Delete** from the shortcut menu.

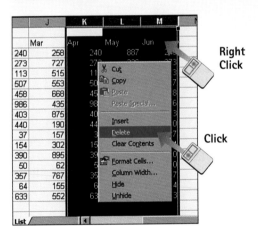

Right Click

Click

End

How to Delete Cells

It's easy to delete data from cells—you select the cells and press Delete. But sometimes you'll want to remove the actual cells. For example, you might want to remove a row of data from a table, but there's another table next to it from which you don't want to remove the data. If you delete the data by deleting the row from the worksheet, you'll affect the second table because the row will be deleted all the way across the worksheet.

However, if you delete the cells in the first table, the table closes up the space where the cells were, and the table next to it is unaffected.

Begin

1 Select the Cells

Select the cells you want to delete. Right-click the selected cells.

	Item	Price		Item	Price
25					
26	**Item**	**Price**		**Item**	**Price**
27	HoneySuckle Soap	$3.50		Mixing Bowls	$20.00
28	Sea Soap	$3.50		Butter Crock	$5.00
29	Blueberry Soap	$3.50		Coffee Mug	$4.00
30	Christmas Spice Soap	$3.50		Soup Tureen	$25.00
31	Farmhand Soap	.50		Lidded Casserole	$30.00
32	Skin Tonic Soap	$3.5		Dutch Oven	$40.00
33	Almond Loofah Soap	$3.50			
34					
35					
36					
37					

Right
Click

2 Choose Delete

Choose **Delete** from the shortcut menu.

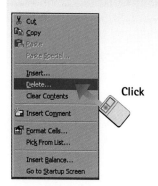

Click

3 Shift Replacement Cells Up

In the Delete dialog box, click the **Shift cells up** option, and choose **OK**.

Click

4 Replacement Cells Move

The cells are removed from the worksheet, and the cells below move up to fill in the empty space; the cells on either side of the deleted cells are unaffected.

26		Item	Price		Item	Price
27		HoneySuckle Soap	$3.50		Mixing Bowls	$20.00
28		Sea Soap	$3.50		Butter Crock	$5.00
29		Blueberry Soap	$3.50		Coffee Mug	$4.00
30		Farmhand Soap	$3.50		Soup Tureen	$25.00
31		Skin Tonic Soap	$3.50		Lidded Casserole	$30.00
32		Almond Loofah Soap	$3.50		Dutch Oven	$40.00
33						
34						
35						
36						

5 If You Shift Cells Left...

If you select the **Shift cells left** option in the Delete dialog box (in step 3), cells on the right side of the deleted cells move over, and cells above and below the deleted cells are unaffected.

26		Item	Price		Item	Price
27		HoneySuckle Soap	$3.50		Mixing Bowls	$20.00
28		Sea Soap	$3.50		Butter Crock	$5.00
29		Blueberry Soap	$3.50		Coffee Mug	$4.00
30		Soup Tureen	$25.00			
31		Farmhand Soap	$3.50		Lidded Casserole	$30.00
32		Skin Tonic Soap	$3.50		Dutch Oven	$40.00
33		Almond Loofah Soap	$3.50			
34						
35						
36						

6 Clear the Formatting

If you don't want to delete the cells but you want to remove their formatting (cell borders and colors) without affecting the data, select the cells and choose **Edit**, **Clear**, **Formats**.

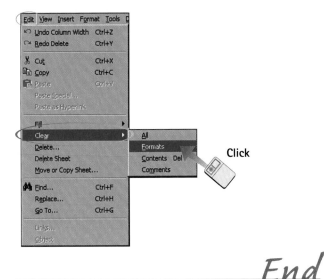

Click

End

How to Move or Copy Data with Drag and Drop

If you need to move or copy data to another location on a worksheet and the new location is only a short distance from the original location, the easiest way is to drag it and drop it with the mouse.

1 Select Cells to Move

To move cells, select the range of cells you want to move, and point to any border of the selected range so that the mouse pointer becomes an arrow. Drag the range to a new location.

Item	Price		Item	Price
HoneySuckle Soap	$3.50		Mixing Bowls	$20.00
Sea Soap	$3.50		Butter Crock	$5.00
Blueberry Soap	$3.50		Coffee Mug	$4.00
Christmas Spice Soap	$3.50		Soup Tureen	$25.00
Farmhand Soap	$3.50		Lidded Casserole	$30.00
Skin Tonic Soap	$3.50		Dutch Oven	$40.00
Almond Loofah Soap	$3.50			

Click & Drag

2 Drop the Cells

While you drag, an outline of the range moves across the worksheet, and a ScreenTip tells you the reference of the range location. When the range border is where you want it, drop the data by releasing the mouse button.

Item	Price		Item	Price
HoneySuckle Soap	$3.50		Mixing Bowls	$20.00
Sea Soap	$3.50		Butter Crock	$5.00
Blueberry Soap	$3.50		Coffee Mug	$4.00
Christmas Spice Soap	$3.50		Soup Tureen	$25.00
Farmhand Soap	$3.50		Lidded Casserole	$30.00
Skin Tonic Soap	$3.50		Dutch Oven	$40.00
Almond Loofah Soap	$3.50			

B34:C39

Release

3 The Range Moves

The range moves to its new location.

Item	Price		Item	Price
HoneySuckle Soap	$3.50			
Sea Soap	$3.50			
Blueberry Soap	$3.50			
Christmas Spice Soap	$3.50			
Farmhand Soap	$3.50			
Skin Tonic Soap	$3.50			
Almond Loofah Soap	$3.50			
Mixing Bowls	$20.00			
Butter Crock	$5.00			
Coffee Mug	$4.00			
Soup Tureen	$25.00			
Lidded Casserole	$30.00			
Dutch Oven	$40.00			

4 Select Cells to Copy

To copy cells, select the range of cells you want to copy, and point to any border of the selected range so that the mouse pointer becomes an arrow. Drag the range to a new location.

Item	Price		Item	Price
HoneySuckle Soap	$3.50			
Sea Soap	$3.50			
Blueberry Soap	$3.50			
Christmas Spice Soap	$3.50			
Farmhand Soap	$3.50			
Skin Tonic Soap	$3.50			
Almond Loofah Soap	$3.50			
Mixing Bowls	$20.00			
Butter Crock	$5.00			
Coffee Mug	$4.00			
Soup Tureen	$25.00			
Lidded Casserole	$30.00			
Dutch Oven	$40.00			

Click & Drag

5 Drag the Cells

While you drag, an outline of the range moves across the worksheet, and a ScreenTip tells you the reference of the range location.

Item	Price		Item	Price
HoneySuckle Soap	$3.50			
Sea Soap	$3.50			
Blueberry Soap	$3.50			E27:F32
Christmas Spice Soap	$3.50			
Farmhand Soap	$3.50			
Skin Tonic Soap	$3.50			
Almond Loofah Soap	$3.50			
Mixing Bowls	$20.00			
Butter Crock	$5.00			
Coffee Mug	$4.00			
Soup Tureen	$25.00			
Lidded Casserole	$30.00			
Dutch Oven	$40.00			

6 Press Ctrl and Drop the Cells

When the range border is where you want it, press and hold down Ctrl, and then drop the data by releasing the mouse button. When you press Ctrl, the mouse pointer acquires a small plus symbol that tells you it's copying. A copy of the data is dropped in the new location.

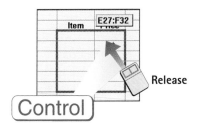

Item | E27:F32

Release

Control

End

How-To Hints

Press Ctrl Only When You Drop

Lots of books will tell you that you must hold down Ctrl while you drag a range you want to copy—not so. You must press and hold down Ctrl *while you release the mouse button*; it doesn't matter whether you press Ctrl while you drag. This is true of any drag-and-drop copy operation in any Microsoft software.

Drag with the Right Mouse Button

You can drag data with the right mouse button, and then choose a command—choose from several Move and Copy commands—on the shortcut menu that appears when you drop the data in its new location.

How to Move or Copy Data with the Clipboard

If you need to move or copy data over a long distance or to another worksheet or workbook (or even to another Office program, such as Word), it's easier to cut or copy the text to the Windows Clipboard, and then paste it where you want it.

The *Windows Clipboard* is a temporary holding area in Windows 95 for data you've cut or copied in any of the Office programs; data on the Clipboard can be pasted repeatedly and is kept on the Clipboard until you cut or copy another chunk of data, or until you close Windows 95.

Begin

1 Select the Data to Move

To move data, you'll use the cut and paste commands. Select the data you want to move, right-click the selected cells.

Right Click

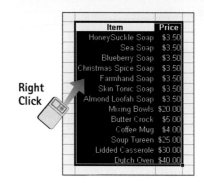

2 Cut the Selected Data

Choose the **Cut** command on the shortcut menu. The selected data will have a moving border around it that disappears when you paste it somewhere else.

Click

3 Paste the Cut Data

Right-click the upper-left cell of the range where you want to paste the data, and choose **Paste** on the shortcut menu. The data is pasted into its new location and disappears from its original location.

Right Click

Click

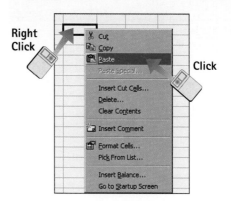

4 Select the Data to Copy

To copy data, you'll use the Copy and Paste commands. Select the data you want to copy. Right-click the selected cells.

Right Click

5 Copy the Selected Data

Choose the **Copy** command on the shortcut menu. The selected data will have a moving border around it.

Click

6 Paste the Copied Data

Right-click the upper-left cell of the range where you want to paste the copied data, and choose **Paste** on the shortcut menu. The data is pasted into its new location (the moving border remains around the copied data until you begin typing in another cell, or until you press Enter or Esc).

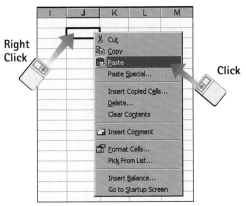

Right Click

Click

End

How-To Hints

Icons Are the Same Everywhere

The icons next to the commands on the shortcut menu and Edit menu are the same icons as on the toolbar buttons; between the command icons and the button ScreenTips, you should be able to figure out which toolbar buttons are Cut, Copy, and Paste.

Keystrokes

You can also cut data with the keystroke Ctrl+X; copy with the keystroke Ctrl+C; and paste with the keystroke Ctrl+V.

Paste with Enter

You can also paste cut or copied data by pressing Enter. If you press Enter to paste data, the data is removed from the Clipboard and is not available for more pasting.

Undo a Mistake

If you make a mistake, click the **Undo** button on the Standard toolbar; choose **Edit**, **Undo**; or press Ctrl+Z to undo the mistake.

How to Adjust Column Width

Often an entry is much too long to fit in the cells in a new worksheet. If the long entry is a text entry, the text flows over into the cell to the right, until you enter data in the cell on the right; then the wide entry is cut off at the cell border (it's all there, but it's hidden). If it's a number entry, it won't flow over; instead it appears as ######## in the cell.

You can adjust column widths to whatever measurement you want.

1 Point at the Column's Border

Point at the right border of the column letter for the column you want to widen. The mouse pointer becomes a two-headed arrow.

2 Drag to Resize

Hold down the left mouse button and drag the border in either direction to adjust the column width. Release the mouse button when the column is the width you want.

Click Hold & Drag

3 Double-click to Best-fit

To make the column fit its widest entry exactly (even if you don't know which entry is widest because the list is really long), point at the right border of the column letter and double-click the two-headed arrow. This is called a "best-fit."

Double Click

④ Resize Multiple Columns

To make several columns exactly the same width, select all the columns by dragging over their column letters. Adjust the width for any one of them while they're all selected, and they all adjust to the same width.

Click Hold & Drag

⑤ Best-fit Multiple Columns

To make several columns best-fit their own entries in one action, select all the columns and then double-click the right border of any one of them.

Double Click

⑥ Use Menu Commands

You can also set column width with menu commands. Click a cell in the column, and then choose **Format**, **Column**. A submenu appears with several commands. **Width** opens a dialog box where you can type an exact measurement, **AutoFit Selection** best-fits the column, and **Standard Width** resets the width of all the unadjusted columns in the worksheet to a new default width that you choose.

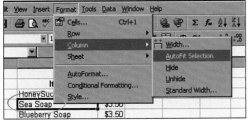

End

How-To Hints

Numbers Don't Print?

Occasionally numbers that seem to fit the column onscreen don't fit on the printed page; if that happens, just widen the column a bit more.

Multiple Non-adjacent Columns

You can adjust non-adjacent columns to the same width the same way as you adjust adjacent columns (in step 4). To select non-adjacent columns, select the first column, and press and hold Ctrl while you select the rest. Release Ctrl after you've selected all the columns you want to resize.

How Wide?

When you drag to resize a column, a ScreenTip shows you the width of the column (the width is measured as the number of characters in default font that fit in the column). You can use this or ignore it—it's not quick and easy to set a specific measurement by dragging.

How to Format Numbers in Cells

When you enter a number, it's displayed the way you type it. After you perform a few calculations, the results can have long strings of decimal places because of Excel's precision; and if you're calculating something such as money, a half-dozen decimal places look confusing. You can change the number display, without affecting the calculated value, by changing the cell's number format.

What you see in a cell is the displayed value, which can be quite different from the actual value because of formatting. To see the actual value that Excel is calculating, select the cell and look at the Formula bar.

Begin

1 Select the Cell or Range

Select the cell or range where you want to change the number format.

B *I* U			$ % ,	
= 12345.1234				
J	K	L	M	N
	12345.1234			

2 Click Currency

To change a format to accounting format (which adds a $, rounds the number to two decimal places, and spaces the $ in the column so that all the $s in the column are aligned), click the **Currency Style** button on the Formatting toolbar.

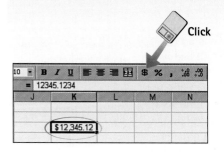
Click

10	B *I* U			$ % ,	
= 12345.1234					
J	K	L	M	N	
	$12,345.12				

3 Click Percent

To change a format to percent format (which adds a % and changes the number from a fraction or integer to a percentage value), click the **Percent Style** button on the Formatting toolbar. (Remember, percent means hundredths, so 0.12 is displayed as 12%, but 12 is displayed as 1200%.)

Click

10	B *I* U			$ % ,	
= 1234512.34%					
J	K	L	M	N	
	1234512%				

4 Click Comma

To apply comma format (which rounds the number to two decimal places and adds a comma at each thousands mark), click the **Comma Style** button on the Formatting toolbar.

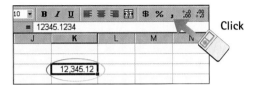

Click

5 Use the Format Cells Dialog Box

To apply different formats that aren't on the Formatting toolbar, choose **Format**, **Cells**, and select a format from the list on the **Number** tab. When you click a format in the **Category** list, your selected number is displayed with that format in the **Sample** box. Choose **OK**.

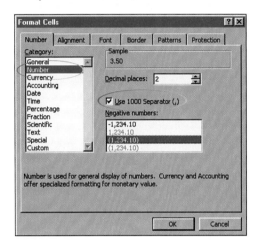

6 Set Format Options

Different formats in the Format Cells dialog box offer different options; select a **Category**, and set the options for that format. A description of the selected category appears at the bottom of the dialog box.

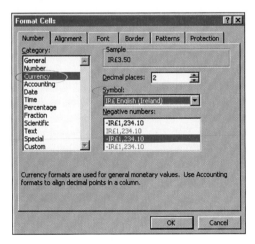

End

How-To Hints

Automatic Formatting

If you type a number with $ or %, the Currency or Percent formatting is applied automatically.

Currency Isn't Really Currency

Even though the toolbar button is named Currency Style, it doesn't apply Currency format; it applies Accounting format. In this format, your numbers, decimals, and dollar signs won't line up the same way.

If You Can't Locate a Formatting Problem

To remove number formatting, select the cell or range and use the Format Cells dialog box to apply the General format. If you have trouble with formatting somewhere on a worksheet, start over again by selecting the entire worksheet (press Ctrl+A), and apply the General format to the entire worksheet; then reapply your number formats.

How to Use Functions in Formulas

Task 6 showed you how to write formulas and briefly mentioned functions. A *function* is a built-in formula with a name that Excel recognizes; a function saves you time you would have spent setting up the math yourself.

To use a function, write a formula that includes the function name, the cells you want calculated, and sometimes other information (called *arguments*) that the particular function needs. In Task 4, you learned how to use AutoSum to automatically create a SUM formula; the formula consisted of an equal sign (=), the function name (SUM), and the cells you wanted summed (in parentheses).

Begin

1 Type =

Click the cell where you want to write the formula, and type an equal sign (=). On the Formula bar, click the down arrow next to the Name box. The Name box becomes a list of common function names.

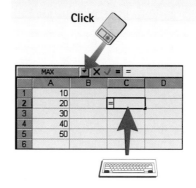

Click

2 Select a Function

Click a function name—I'll demonstrate with the AVERAGE function. The AVERAGE function is better than a manual adding-and-dividing-cells formula because it ignores empty cells, which give an incorrect result.

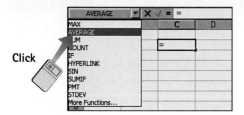

Click

3 Move the Formula Palette

The Formula palette appears. The palette may guess which cells you want to average, but you'll replace those cells to be sure you're calculating what you want. Drag the Formula palette away if you need to uncover cells.

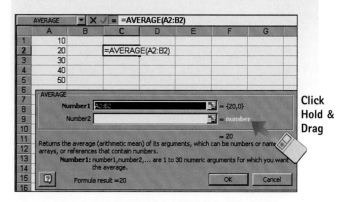

Click Hold & Drag

4 Drag the Cells to Be Calculated

Be sure the **Number1** argument box is highlighted (if it's not, drag over the cell references to highlight them), and drag across the cells you want to calculate. A moving border appears around the cells, and the cell references appear in the Formula palette's **Number1** argument box. Ignore the other argument boxes; they're for including other ranges in the calculation.

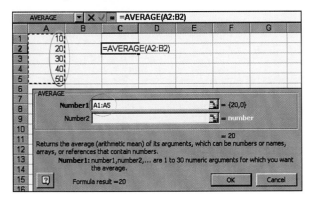

5 Complete the Formula

Choose **OK** to complete the formula. The palette disappears, and the formula result appears in the worksheet.

	A	B	C	D	E
C2			=AVERAGE(A1:A5)		
1	10				
2	20		30		
3	30				
4	40				
5	50				
6					

6 Try the Other Functions

The MIN, MAX, and COUNT functions work the same way as the AVERAGE and SUM functions. Shown here are the results of each of these formulas for the same range of cells. If you don't see the function you want on the Functions list, click **More Functions**, and find the function in the Paste Function dialog box.

	A	B	C	D
C5			=SUM(A1:A5)	
1	10	Average:	30	
2	20	Min:	10	
3	30	Max:	50	
4	40	Count:	5	
5	50	Sum:	150	
6				

End

How-To Hints

Write Your Own Formulas

You can write formulas yourself by simply typing them. When you type a function name in a formula, it must be spelled correctly. Type the name in lowercase letters; Excel converts the name to uppercase letters if it's spelled correctly.

Minimize and Maximize the Palette

If the Formula palette is so large that you can't drag it out of the way, minimize it temporarily by clicking the button on the right end of the argument box you want to fill (the small button looks like a busy grid with a little red arrow). After you drag the cells, click the button on the end of the minimized palette to return it to full size.

Learn More About Functions

To learn more about using functions, check out *Using Excel 97, 3rd Edition*, by Julia Kelly.

How to Work with Cell References

Cell references are the worksheet addresses of cells. Three types exist: relative, absolute, and mixed. *Relative references* give a cell's location relative to the active cell, as in "two cells left and one cell up." *Absolute references* give an address that's unchanging, such as "the intersection of row 3 and column B." *Mixed references* return a mixture of the two; for example, "two cells below the active cell, in column D." Mostly you'll want to use the default relative references.

The difference between types is that a relative reference looks like A1; an absolute reference looks like $A$1; and a mixed reference looks like A$1 or $A1.

Begin

1 Enter a Formula

To demonstrate the difference between relative and absolute references, enter a formula that sums the two cells left of the formula. Shown here, the cells in columns C and D are summed in column E.

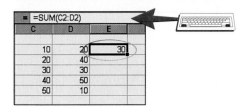

2 AutoFill the Formula

Copy the formula down the column using AutoFill. The formula for each cell adjusts to sum the two cells to its left. Usually, this is exactly what you want.

3 Rewrite the Formula

Now delete the formulas, and rewrite the original so it multiplies the cell to its left by the value in cell F2.

4 AutoFill the Formula

Use AutoFill to copy the formula down the column again—the results are wrong because relative references tell each formula to multiply the cell to its left by the cell on its right (instead of the value in F2). You need to change the F2 reference to an absolute reference so that each formula multiplies the cell on its left by the value in cell F2.

= =D6*F6			
C	D	E	F
10	20	2000	100
20	40	0	
30	30	0	
40	50	0	
50	10	0	

5 Change the Reference Type

To change the reference type, click the cell that contains the original formula. In the Formula bar, click the reference F2, and press F4. (Pressing F4 cycles the reference type repeatedly through all the reference types). When the reference in the Formula bar reads $F$2, press Enter to complete the formula.

= =D2*$F$2			
C	D	E	F
10	20	=D2*$F$2	100
20	40		
30	30		
40	50		
50	10		

F4

6 AutoFill the Formula

Use AutoFill to copy the formula down the column again. Now each formula multiplies the cell on its left by the value in cell F2.

# =D6*$F$2				
C	D	E	F	G
10	20	2000	100	
20	40	4000		
30	30	3000		
40	50	5000		
50	10	1000		

End

How to Name Cells and Ranges

When you refer to cells in a formula, you can use a reference, but you risk a couple of potential problems: You occasionally have to mess with relative versus absolute references; and a formula such as =B20+B21 is not very intuitive. But you can name cells and ranges, and then refer to those names in formulas. Unlike =B20+B21, the formula =Subtotal+Tax is clear.

Names are always defined with absolute references, and they work like absolute references. The only difference is that when you move named cells, they take their names with them. Any formulas that refer to named cells can always find them.

Begin

1 Click in the Name Box

To name a cell, click the cell to select it, and then click in the Name box. The cell address in the Name box is highlighted.

Click

	B	C	D	E	F
12	Coffee Mug	$4.00			
13	Soup Tureen	$25.00			
14	Lidded Casserole	$30.00			
15	Dutch Oven	$40.00			
16					
17		Subtotal			
18					
19					

2 Type a Name and Press Enter

Type a name for the cell, and press Enter. The name appears in place of the cell address when the cell is selected. Names can only be one word long and cannot be existing cell addresses (for example, TotalSales is allowable, but FY1998 isn't). Names must begin with a letter or an underscore (_); all other characters can be letters, numbers, periods, and underscores.

SubTotal			=	
	B	C	D	E
12	Coffee Mug	$4.00		
13	Soup Tureen	$25.00		
14	Lidded Casserole	$30.00		
15	Dutch Oven	$40.00		
16				
17		Subtotal		
18				

3 Click the Cell from the Name Box

To jump to the cell from anywhere in the workbook, click the arrow next to the Name box, and click the cell name on the list.

Click

4 Use the Cell Name in a Formula

To use the name in a formula, write the formula and click the cell to include it; the cell's name appears in the formula instead of the cell's reference.

	=SubTotal+Tax		
C	D	E	F
Subtotal		$49.00	
Tax		$3.92	
Total		$52.92	

5 Name a Range

To name a range, select the range. Click in the Name box, type a name, and press Enter.

Contacts	▼	=	Last	
A	B	C	D
Last	First	Street	City
Abovian	Julia	5850 W. Mallory Road	Westwood
Andersen	George D	17200 N. Trails End Road	Westwood
	Robin	5755 W. Kruger Road	Westwood
5 Baker	John & Mabel	PO Box 184	Westwood
6 Balogh	William	5775 W. Mallory Road	Westwood
7 Bedrosian	Dick & Annie	5980 E. Mallory Road	Westwood
8 Christensen	Jim	PO Box 150	Lodi
9 Dandyn	Millard & Mary	5650 W. Kruger Road	Westwood
10 Deak	Gail A	5730 W. Mallory Road	Westwood
11 Domokos	Larry	5775 W. Mallory Road	Westwood
12 Dyhr	Richard & Tami	16750 N. Trails End Road	Westwood
13 Fabin	Leo & Gail	16980 N. Trails End Road	Westwood
14 Fairfax	Colleen	6195 W. Mallory Road	Westwood

6 Create Several Names at Once

If a worksheet contains labels, you can name the cells they refer to all at once. Select the label cells and the cells to which they refer. Choose **Insert**, **Name**, **Create**. In the Create Names dialog box, click the check boxes for the labels you want to use, and choose **OK**. All the cells are named with their worksheet labels in one step.

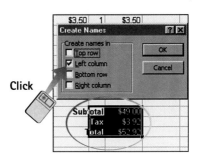

Click

End

How-To Hints

Delete a Name

To delete a name, open the worksheet that contains the named cell or range. Choose **Insert**, **Name**, **Define**. In the Define Names dialog box, select the name and click **Delete**, and then choose **OK**.

Not Case-Sensitive

Names are not case-sensitive; if you create the name TotalSales, Excel reads it and the names TOTALSALES and totalsales as the same name.

How to Search for Data

As in Microsoft Word, you can search for and replace any character in a worksheet. You can find or replace text strings, such as a company or employee name, and you can find or replace numbers, either single digits or strings of numbers. You can also choose to search for characters in cell values, formulas, and worksheet comments.

If you've used Microsoft Word, you'll discover that Find and Replace procedures are almost identical in the two programs. If you're new to the procedure, I'll teach you how to use them in Excel, and you'll know how to use them in Word.

Begin

1 Choose Edit, Find

To search for a word or number in a worksheet, choose **Edit, Find**.

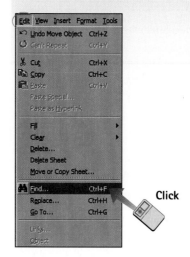

Click

2 Search for Characters

In the Find dialog box, in the **Find what** box, type the characters (numbers, text, symbols) you want to search for. In the **Look in** box, select what you want to search. Then click **Find Next** to find the first cell containing your search characters. Click **Find Next** repeatedly to find each occurrence of the character string.

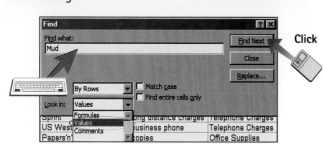

Click

3 Search in Displayed Values

To search displayed values for number or text characters, select **Values** from the **Look in** box. Values searches both constant values and the results of formulas—anything displayed in a cell. Shown is the result of a search for the word "jar."

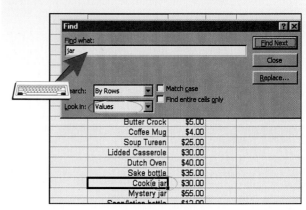

4 Search in Formulas

To search in formulas for numbers, cell names, function names, mathematical operators, or anything that's part of the formula, select **Formulas** in the **Look in** box, and then click **Find Next**. Shown is the result of a search for the cell name "products."

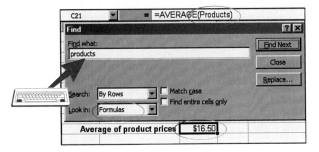

5 Search in Worksheet Comments

To search in cell Comments for a text string, select **Comments** in the **Look in** box, and then click **Find Next**. Shown is the result of a search for the word "discontinued." (A comment is extra information added to a worksheet that doesn't appear in cells; a cell with a comment has a red triangle in its upper-right corner.)

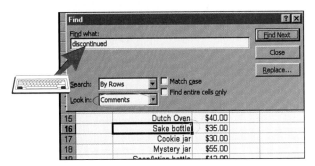

6 Replace Characters

To replace a character string, click **Replace** in the Find dialog box. In the Replace dialog box, type the old characters in the **Find what** box; type the replacement characters in the **Replace with** box. Click **Find Next** to find the first occurrence, and then click **Replace**. Click **Replace** repeatedly to replace strings one at a time; click **Replace All** to replace all occurrences at once.

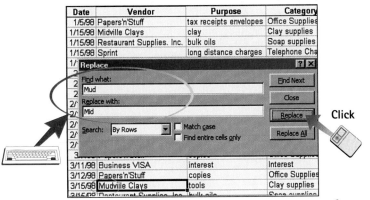

Click

End

How-To Hints

Keyboard Shortcuts

The keyboard shortcut for Edit, Find is Ctrl+F; the shortcut for Edit, Replace is Ctrl+H. You can open the Replace dialog box without first opening the Find dialog box.

Narrow Your Search

To limit your search to text with specific capitalization, mark the **Match case** text box. To limit your search to complete entries instead of including partial entries (for example, if you want to search for 100 and not find 1,000 or 20,100), mark the **Find entire cells only** check box.

Speed Up the Search

In a large table, the search is sometimes faster if you select **By Rows** or **By Columns** in the **Search** box, especially if you start by selecting a cell in the specific row or column you want to search. In a small table, it makes no difference what's selected in the **Search** box.

How to Sort Data

Sorting data is the most basic procedure in organizing data. For example, you can sort a list to see product names in alphabetical order, and then sort the list to see product prices from highest to lowest. When you add new products, type them at the end of the list, and then sort the list to position the new products.

When you sort a list, the entire list is sorted and each record (row) in the list retains its integrity; other tables on the same worksheet are not affected by the sort.

Begin

1 Click in the Sort Key Column

To sort by a single key, or column, click on any cell in that column.

Click

	A	B	C	D
1	Date	Vendor	Purpose	Category
2	1/5/98	Papers'n'Stuff	tax receipts envelopes	Office Supplies
3	1/15/98	Midville Clays	clay	Clay supplies
4	1/15/9	Restaurant Supplies. Inc.	bulk oils	Soap supplies
5	1/15/98	Sprint	long distance charges	Telephone Charges
6	1/ /98	US West	business phone	Telephone Charges
7	/98	Radio Shack	duplex jack for fax line	Office Equipment
8	/98	Papers'n'Stuff	copies	Office Supplies
9	2/9/98	Business VISA	interest	Interest
10	2/10/98	Northland Times	newspaper - 1st qtr	Office Supplies
11	2/15/98	Midville Clays	clay	Clay supplies
12	2/15/98	Restaurant Supplies. Inc.	bulk oils	Soap supplies
13	2/15/98	Sprint	long distance charges	Telephone Charges
14	2/15/98	US West	business phone	Telephone Charges
15	3/7/98	Papers'n'Stuff	copies	Office Supplies

2 Sort in Ascending Order

To sort the list in alphabetical order (A-Z) or in lowest-to-highest numerical order, click the **Sort Ascending** button on the Standard toolbar. To sort the list in reverse alphabetical order (Z-A) or in highest-to-lowest numerical order, click the **Sort Descending** button on the Standard toolbar.

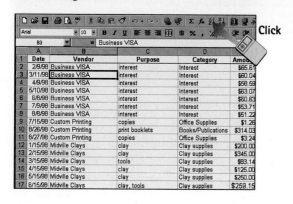

Click

3 Set Up a Multi-Key Sort

To run a multiple-key sort, click anywhere in the list and then choose **Data**, **Sort**.

Click

4 Set the First Key

In the Sort dialog box, in the **Sort by** box, select the column you want for your major sort (shown here, Category in a product list). Next to the column heading, click the sort order option you want (**Ascending** or **Descending**).

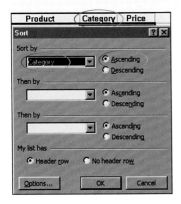

5 Set the Second Key

For the second key in the sort, select the column in the first **Then by** box (shown here, by Product within Category) and click a sort order option. To sort by a third key within the second key, use the second **Then by** box. Choose **OK** to run the sort.

6 Results of a Multi-Key Sort

Shown here is the result of the two-key sort, by Category and then by Product.

Product	Category	Price
Butter Crock	Pottery	$5.00
Coffee Mug	Pottery	$4.00
Cookie jar	Pottery	$30.00
Dutch Oven	Pottery	$40.00
Lidded Casserole	Pottery	$30.00
Mixing Bowls	Pottery	$20.00
Mystery jar	Pottery	$55.00
Sake bottle	Pottery	$35.00
Soap/lotion bottle	Pottery	$12.00
Soup Tureen	Pottery	$25.00
Almond Loofah Soap	Soap	$3.50
Blueberry Soap	Soap	$3.50
Christmas Spice Soap	Soap	$3.50
Farmhand Soap	Soap	$3.50
HoneySuckle Soap	Soap	$3.50
Sea Soap	Soap	$3.50
Skin Tonic Soap	Soap	$3.50

End

How-To Hints

Sort One Column, Not the Whole List

If you want to sort a single column within a list but not sort the rest of the list with that column, select all the cells in the table column that you want to sort; only the cells in that column are sorted.

Lose Your Headings?

If your columns headings are similar enough to the data in your list that Excel doesn't guess that they're headings, they may get sorted into the data. To fix that, click the **Undo** button to undo the sort. Choose **Data, Sort.** In the Sort dialog box, click the **Header row** option before you run the sort.

Sort Day or Month Names

If you sort day or month names, they'll be sorted in alphabetical order, not calendar order; to sort them in calendar order, use the Sort dialog box. Click the **Options** button at the bottom. In the Sort Options dialog box, select the appropriate list from the list box, and choose **OK**. Choose **OK** in the Sort dialog box to run the sort.

How to Filter Data

Filtering shows only the records you want to see and hides the rest. Records aren't removed; they're just temporarily hidden.

Filtering is based on *criteria*, data that's shared by all the records you want to see. For example, if you filter a list of contacts to show only those whose city is Poughkeepsie, your criteria is "Poughkeepsie" in the City column.

You don't have to sort a list before you filter, and you can have blank cells in the list; but the top row should contain column headings or labels, and the list should contain no completely blank rows.

Begin

1 Click a Cell

Click any cell in the list or table.

Product	Category	Price
Lidded Casserole	Pottery	$30.00
Mystery jar	Pottery	$55.00
Blueberry Soap	Soap	$3.50
Dutch Oven	Pottery	$40.00
Sea Soap	Soap	$4.50
Skin Tonic Soap	Soap	$3.50
Sake bottle	Pottery	$35.00
Coffee Mug	Pottery	
Soap/lotion bottle	Pottery	$12
Farmhand Soap	Soap	$3.50
Cookie jar	Pottery	$30.00
Almond Loofah Soap	Soap	$4.50
Mixing Bowls	Pottery	$20.00
Butter Crock	Pottery	$5.00
Christmas Spice Soap	Soap	$3.50
HoneySuckle Soap	Soap	$4.50
Soup Tureen	Pottery	$25.00

Click

2 Click the Filter Command

Choose **Data, Filter, AutoFilter**.

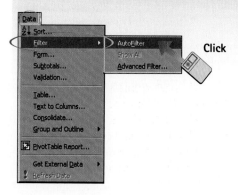

Click

3 Click a Filter Arrow

Filter arrows appear in each column label cell. In the column that contains your criteria, click the filter arrow to drop a list of all the values in the column.

Product	Catego	Price
Lidded Casse	(All)	$30.00
Mystery	(Top 10...)	
Blueberry S	(Custom...) Pottery	$
Dutch O	Soap	$40.00
Sea Soap	Soap	$4.50
Skin Tonic Soap	Soap	$3.50
Sake bottle	Pottery	$35.00

Click

4 Click Filter Criteria

Click the criteria you want. All records that don't share that criteria are hidden. The filter arrow where you set the criteria turns blue, and the row numbers where records are hidden turn blue.

Product	Catego	Price
Lidded Casserole	Pottery	$30.00
Mystery jar	Pottery	$55.00
Dutch Oven	Pottery	$40.00
Sake bottle	Pottery	$35.00
Coffee Mug	Pottery	$4.00
Soap/lotion bottle	Pottery	$12.00
Cookie jar	Pottery	$30.00
Mixing Bowls	Pottery	$20.00
Butter Crock	Pottery	$5.00
Soup Tureen	Pottery	$25.00

5 Set Multiple Criteria

To set multiple criteria, set criteria in multiple columns (repeat steps 1-4). Shown is a list filtered to show all soaps that are priced at $4.50.

Product	Catego	Price
Sea Soap	Soap	$4.50
Almond Loofah Soap	Soap	$4.50
HoneySuckle Soap	Soap	$4.50

6 Remove the Filter

To remove the filter and show all the records in the list, either click the filter arrow where you set the criteria and click **(All)**, or choose **Data**, **Filter**, **AutoFilter** to turn AutoFilter off.

Product	Catego	Price
Blueberry S	(All)	$3.50
Sea S	(Top 10...)	$4.50
Skin Tonic S	(Custom...)	
Farmhand S	Pottery Soap	
Almond Loofah Soap	Soap	$4.50
Christmas Spice Soap	Soap	$3.50
HoneySuckle Soap	Soap	$4.50

Click

End

How-To Hints

Field or Column?

The terms "column" and "field" are used interchangeably in Excel (and in Access, Word, and Outlook); *field* is a database term that refers to a column in a table.

Top 10

To filter the top (or bottom) 10 (or another number) number of items in a list, select the **Top 10** filter criteria. Select **Top** or **Bottom**, select a number, select **Items** or **Percent**, and choose **OK**.

Comparison Criteria

To set complex criteria such as "prices greater than $4," click the filter arrow in the column where you want to set the criteria, and click **(Custom...)**. In the Custom AutoFilter dialog box, select comparison operators in the list box on the left, and type or select criteria in the list box on the right; then choose **OK**.

How to Create a Chart

A chart turns boring numbers into an instantly accessible, persuasive visual presentation. This task tells you how to create charts from your worksheet data.

The *ChartWizard* builds the chart for you and asks for your input along the way. After the chart is built you can resize it, rearrange it, recolor it, and personalize it so that it doesn't look like every other Excel chart in the computer world.

Begin

1 Select Data

Select the table or list of data you want to chart. Include headings and labels, but don't include subtotals or totals.

		Jan	Feb
HoneyS	ckle Soap	$125	$138
	Sea Soap	$350	$275
Blue	erry Soap	$225	$248
Christmas S	pice Soap	$185	$204
Farm	and Soap	$120	$132
Skin	onic Soap	$155	$171
Almond L	ofah Soap	$190	$209
	Total	**$1,250**	**$1,377**

2 Start the ChartWizard

On the Standard toolbar, click the **ChartWizard** button. The ChartWizard starts. Click the **Chart type** you want on the left and the **Chart sub-type** you want on the right, and then click **Next**.

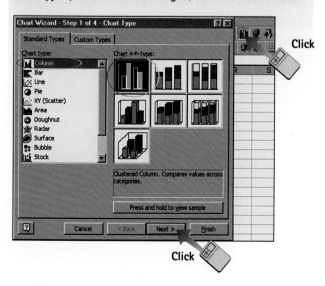

Click

Click

3 Check the Data Range

In Step 2, check the **Data range** to be sure it's correct. Click the two **Series in** options (**Rows** and **Columns**) to see which layout is best, and then click **Next**.

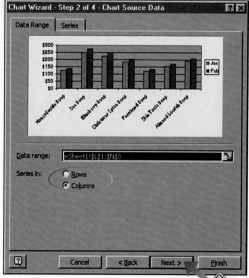

Click

4 Set Chart Features

In step 3, type a **Chart title** and **axis** titles, if you want them, on the **Titles** tab. You can reposition or turn off the legend on the **Legend** tab, and append a data table to the bottom of the chart by clicking the **Show data table** check box on the **Data Table** tab. Click **Next**.

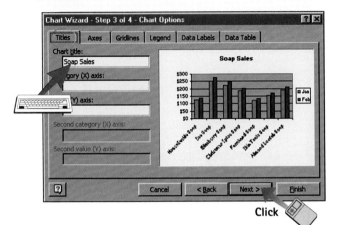

Click

5 Choose a Location and Finish

In step 4, choose a location for the chart; the **As object in** option creates an embedded chart object on the worksheet you select from the **As object in** drop-down list. The **As new sheet** option creates a separate *chart sheet* (this is similar to a worksheet, but it holds only a big chart) in the workbook. Then click **Finish**.

Click

6 Resize and Move the Chart

To resize a chart object on a worksheet, click it and drag one of the handles that appears around its edges. To resize a chart without stretching it out of proportion, hold down **Shift** while you drag a corner handle. To move the chart, click anywhere near its edge and drag it. To deselect the chart and return to the worksheet, click in the worksheet.

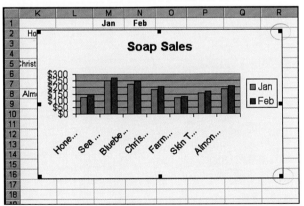

End

How-To Hints

Finish Fast

To create a chart quickly using all the default chart settings, click **Finish** in step 2.

TASK *23*

How to Change the Chart Type

When you create a chart, you have lots of options for the *chart type*. Standard chart types use columns or bars, lines and points, or a sliced-up pie. It's probably best to stick to standard chart types. If you use a chart type that your audience isn't used to seeing, they may have difficulty deciphering it, and the data may lose its impact.

After you've created a chart, you can easily change the chart type without having to re-create the chart, so you can try out different chart types to see what you like best.

Begin

1 Select the Chart

Click the chart to select it. If the chart is on a chart sheet, it is automatically selected when you click its sheet tab.

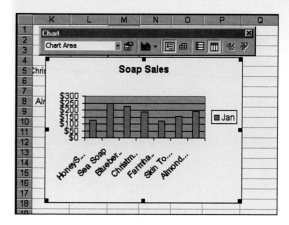

2 Click the Chart Type Button

On the Chart toolbar, click the down arrow on the **Chart Type** button. Click a chart type icon on the button's list.

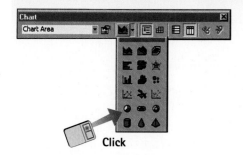

Click

3 The New Chart Type Is Applied

The chart type changes to the type you select (shown is the same column chart changed to a pie chart).

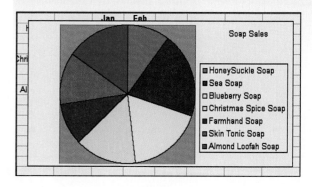

4 Use the Chart Type Command

With the chart selected, choose **Chart**, **Chart Type**. On the Chart Types dialog box, select a **Chart type** and **Chart sub-type**, and then choose **OK** (shown is the same chart changed to a 3D bar chart).

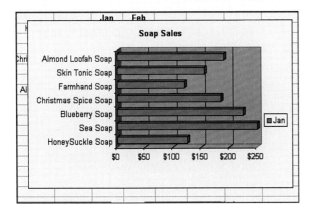

5 Change a Single Series' Markers

To change the chart type for a single series in a multiseries chart, right-click one of the data markers in the series, and then choose **Chart Type**.

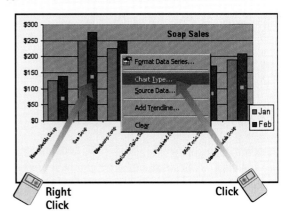

Right Click

Click

6 Select a Different Marker Type

On the Chart Types dialog box, select a new chart type for the selected series, and then choose **OK**. Shown here, one series in a column chart is changed to a line chart type.

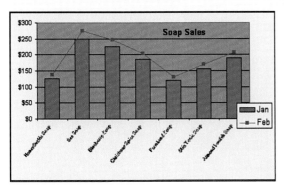

End

How-To Hints

Change Colors

To change the color of any element in the chart (data series, gridlines, axes, plot area, and so on), click the element to select it. Click the down arrow on the **Fill Color** button on the Formatting toolbar, and click a different color.

Change Font Size for the Chart

When you resize a chart, the axis and title characters may be too big or too small; to change the font size, click near the edge of the chart to select the **Chart Area**, and select a new size in the Font Size box on the Formatting toolbar.

How to Work with Chart and Axis Titles

You don't need to spend a lot of time deciding on titles for your chart when you first create it because you can add, change, move, and delete titles at any time.

1 Move a Title

To move a title, click it to select it, and then drag its border.

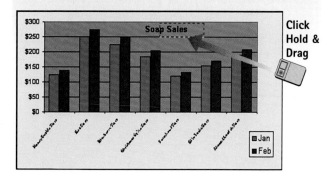

Click Hold & Drag

2 Change a Title's Text

Click the title to select it; when you point at the title text, the mouse pointer becomes a cursor. Drag to select the characters you want to change or delete, or click to place the insertion point within the title and type new characters (when you click or drag within the title text, the title's border disappears). Click anywhere outside the title to finish.

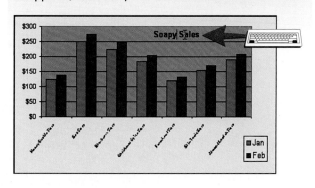

3 Delete a Title

To delete a title, click the title to select it, and then press Delete. You can also right-click the title and choose **Clear**.

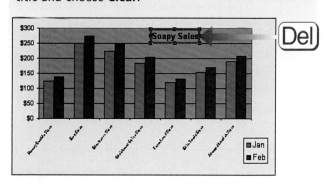

Del

4 Add a Title

To add a new chart title, choose **Chart**, **Chart Options**. On the **Titles** tab of the Chart Options dialog box, type your title(s) and choose **OK**.

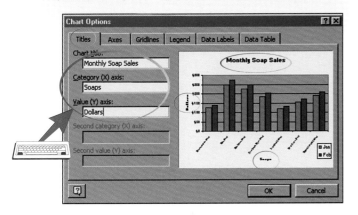

5 Use a Text Box

To add a text box as a title, select the chart, type your title text, and press Enter. When you type, the text appears in the Formula bar; after you press Enter, the text box appears on the chart. Move the text box by dragging its border. Text boxes are similar to titles except that you can resize a text box.

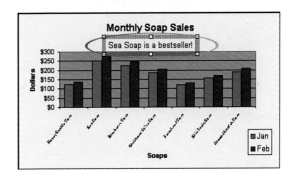

6 Change Colors

To format the colors in either a title or a text box, select the object and choose colors from the **Fill Color** and **Font Color** buttons on the Formatting toolbar; or right-click the object, choose **Format Chart Title** or **Format Text Box**, and set formatting details in the dialog boxes.

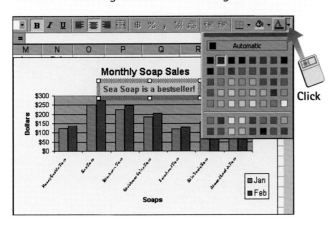

7 Change the Font or Font Size

To change the font or font size in either a title or a text box, select the object and then drag to select the characters you want to change. Make changes in the Font and Font Size boxes on the Formatting toolbar; or right-click the object, click **Format Chart Title** or **Format Text Box**, and set formatting details in the dialog boxes.

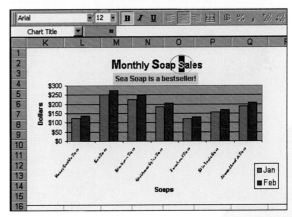

End

How to Change the Chart Data

If you delete a column or row of data from a chart's source data table, the chart adjusts automatically. But if you add data to the source table (for example, if you add another month's sales figures), you need to add the new data to the chart. You can add expanded data to a chart in several quick ways.

If you've already created a highly formatted chart and you want to use it to display a different source data table (instead of creating a new chart), you can change the chart's source data range in the ChartWizard.

Begin

1 Drag the Source Range Border

Click the chart to select it. The source data is surrounded by a colored border; drag the corner handle of the colored border to expand (or reduce) the source data range.

	Jan	Feb	Mar
HoneySuckle Soap	$125	$138	$151
Sea Soap	$250	$275	$303
Blueberry Soap	$225	$248	$272
Christmas Spice Soap	$185	$204	$224
Farmhand Soap	$120	$132	$145
Skin Tonic Soap	$155	$171	$188
Almond Loofah Soap	$190	$209	$230
Total	$1,250	$1,377	$1,513

Monthly Soap Sales

Click Hold & Drag

2 Drag and Drop Data

Select the new data on the worksheet, and drag the range border onto the chart and drop it. When you drag the mouse pointer onto the chart, it acquires a small plus symbol; release the mouse pointer to add the data to the chart.

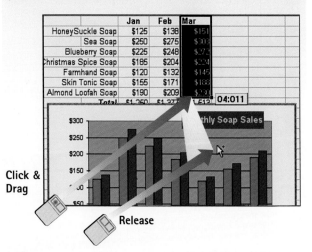

Click & Drag

Release

3 Use the Add Data Command

Select the chart, and choose **Chart**, **Add Data**. The Add Data dialog box appears.

Add Data

Select the new data you wish to add to the chart.

Include the cells containing row or column labels if you want those labels to appear on the chart.

Range:

OK

Cancel

4 Drag the New Data

Drag to select the data on the worksheet you want to add (the added range appears in the Add Data dialog box), and choose **OK**.

1		Jan	Feb	Mar
2	HoneySuckle Soap	$125	$138	$151
3	Sea Soap	$250	$275	$303
4	Blueberry Soap	$225	$248	$272
5	Christmas Spice Soap	$185	$204	$224
6	Farmhand Soap	$120	$132	$145
7	Skin Tonic Soap	$155	$171	$188
8	Almond Loofah Soap	$190	$209	$230

Add Data

Select the new data you wish to add to the chart.

Include the cells containing row or column labels if you want those labels to appear on the chart.

Range: `=Sheet1!$O$1:$O$8`

OK　Cancel

5 Use the Source Data Command

Use this method if you want to completely change the source range. Right-click in the chart area, and choose **Source Data**.

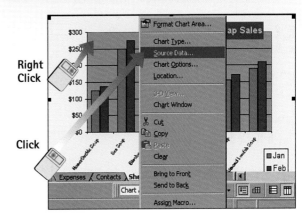

Right Click

Click

6 Drag the New Range

On the worksheet, drag to select the entire range you want the chart to display. The dragged range references appear in the **Data range** box in the Source Data dialog box. Choose **OK**.

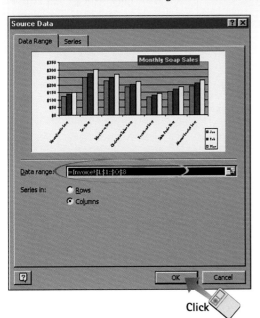

Click

End

How to Draw Shapes on a Chart or Worksheet

You can grab a reader's attention by adding drawn graphical objects to a worksheet or a chart. The Excel 97 Drawing toolbar has buttons for a tremendous variety of shapes, so you don't have to be a tremendously talented computer artist.

To draw shapes on a worksheet, click the worksheet and then click a button on the Drawing toolbar. To draw shapes on a chart, click the chart to select it, and then click a button on the Drawing toolbar.

Begin

1 Show the Drawing Toolbar

Right-click any toolbar, and choose **Drawing**. The Drawing toolbar appears, usually at the bottom of your screen.

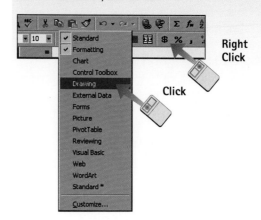

2 Draw Simple Objects

To draw lines, arrows, rectangles, or ovals, click the appropriate button on the toolbar, and then drag across the screen to draw the shape. To resize or reshape an object, click to select it, and then drag one of its handles. To draw a perfect square or circle, hold down Shift while you draw a rectangle or oval.

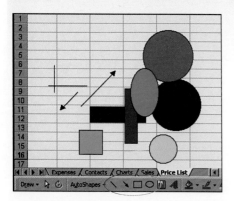

3 Draw AutoShapes

Use this method to draw complex shapes: On the Drawing toolbar, click **AutoShapes**, point to a shape category, and click a shape.

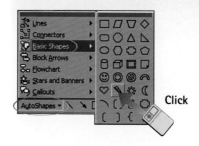

4 Click to Create an AutoShape

After you click an AutoShape button, click the worksheet or chart. A default shape appears, and you can resize it (using its handles) and move it wherever you want it.

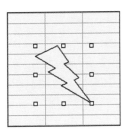

5 Drag to Create an AutoShape

After you click an AutoShape button, drag the crosshair pointer across the worksheet or chart to draw the shape the size you want. Hold down Shift while you drag to keep the shape's original proportions.

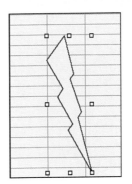

6 Customize a Shape

To resize a shape, click it and drag a handle. To format a shape's colors, right-click the shape and choose **Format AutoShape**. Select details in the Format AutoShape dialog box and choose **OK**.

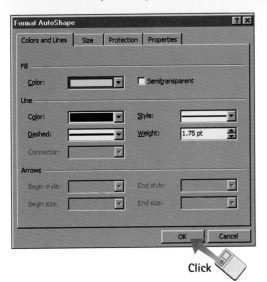

Click

End

How-To Hints

Delete a Shape

To delete a shape (or any other graphical object), click the object to select it, and press Delete.

Reorder Shapes

To overlap separate shapes on top of one another, you must tell Excel which goes in front or in back. Right-click the shape you want to rearrange, choose **Order**, and click a command to change the object's position in the stack of overlapped objects.

How to Use Multiple Worksheets

Multiple worksheets in a workbook act like extra pages in a binder; they're interactive and inter-related, and they always stay together in the same file. Their advantage is that you can keep several tables in the same file but not have to scroll to Timbuktu to find them. An efficient use for multiple worksheets might be monthly revenue and expenses, on separate month worksheets, all in the same file so they open together.

You can delete extra worksheets, add more worksheets, and move between them easily. You can also rename worksheets and reposition them in a workbook or make copies.

Begin

1 Move Between Worksheets

To move from one sheet to another, click the sheet *tab* for the sheet to which you want to move. The selected sheet, the *active* sheet, is the one with the bright white-and-black sheet tab; sheets that aren't selected have sheet tabs that are gray and black.

Click

2 Rename a Worksheet

Double-click the sheet tab; the sheet name is highlighted. Type a new name, and press Enter or click a cell in the worksheet.

Double Click

3 Delete a Worksheet

Right-click the sheet tab for the work-sheet you want to delete, and choose **Delete**.

Click

Right Click

4 Add Another Worksheet

Right-click a sheet tab and choose **Insert**. In the Insert dialog box, on the **General** tab, double-click the **Worksheet** icon. The new worksheet is inserted on the left side of the sheet tab you initially right-clicked.

Double Click

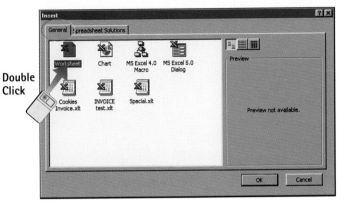

5 Move a Worksheet

To move a worksheet within a workbook, drag its sheet tab. While you drag, the mouse pointer acquires a sheet-of-paper symbol, and a small black triangle points to the position where the sheet will be moved.

6 Copy a Worksheet

To make a copy of a worksheet within a workbook, drag its sheet tab. While you drag, the mouse pointer acquires a sheet-of-paper symbol, and a small black triangle points to the position where the sheet will be copied. Before you release the mouse button, press Ctrl (the pointer will show a small plus symbol on its sheet-of-paper, which indicates a copy).

End

Task

4

How to Use Outlook 98

*O*utlook is a desktop information manager that helps you organize and manage your daily activities. It's extremely versatile; you can schedule and track daily appointments, build and maintain a database of contacts, create "to do" lists for projects and track each item's status, jot down electronic notes, and more.

You can also manage your email correspondence, whether you're emailing colleagues on a corporate intranet or users on the global Internet. Outlook's email features include composing and sending messages, forwarding messages, and attaching files. The email features are well-integrated with the other Outlook components; for example, you can automatically record your email messages in the Journal, or quickly add a message address to your Contacts database.

Although Outlook 97 is part of the Office 97 suite of programs, Outlook 98 is now available. If you have taken time to learn Outlook 97, you won't have trouble learning Outlook 98, and it's worth the upgrade. Outlook 98 loads faster, performs more efficiently, and closes more quickly than Outlook 97. Also, Microsoft has improved the command structure in the menus and dialog boxes to make Outlook easier to use.

This chapter covers the basic features of Outlook 98, including each of Outlook's components, such as Calendar, Contacts, Tasks, and Notes. ●

How to Get Around the Outlook 98 Window

The Outlook window features the familiar title bar, menu bar, toolbar, and status bar used in other Office 97 programs. In addition, you see the Outlook Bar on the left side of the window. Use the Outlook Bar to access each Outlook component. Outlook's components are organized into folders, represented by icons on the Outlook Bar. When you click a component, such as Inbox, the appropriate folder opens in the work area.

Because the Outlook 98 window differs in appearance from the other Office program windows, take a few minutes to acclimate yourself to the window elements.

Begin

1 The Profile Box

When you start Outlook 98, a Choose Profile dialog box appears. For now, click **OK** to continue. You can always set up a personalized profile later. (To set a personalized profile, click the **New** button and set up a new profile.)

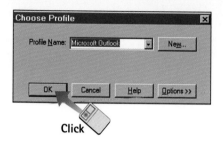

Click

2 Using the Menu Bar

To display an Outlook menu, click the menu name. The menu drops down to reveal a list of commands. Select the command you want to use.

Click

3 Using the Toolbar

Outlook's toolbar buttons change to reflect the component or task you're working on. To activate a toolbar button, just click it. To learn more about what a button does, hover your mouse pointer over the button to reveal a ScreenTip.

4 Viewing the Outlook Window

The Outlook window contains many of the same program elements used in other Office 97 programs. Use the Minimize, Maximize, and Close buttons at the far right end of the title bar to manipulate the Outlook 98 window.

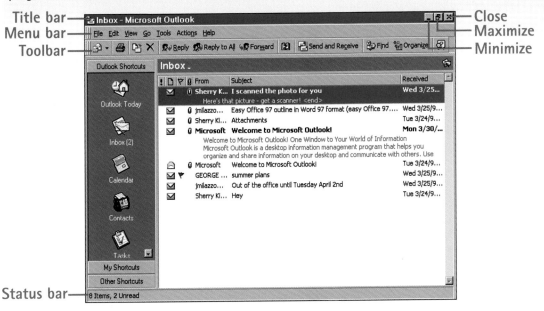

Title bar
Menu bar
Toolbar
Close
Maximize
Minimize
Status bar

5 Using Group Buttons

The Outlook Bar has three group buttons that organize your folders and shortcuts: Outlook Shortcuts (which hold all the Outlook components), My Shortcuts (which hold various folders for sent messages, drafts, and more), and Other Shortcuts (lets you access My Computer, the My Documents and Favorites folders). To display a new folder group, click the appropriate group button.

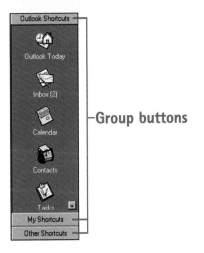

Group buttons

6 Changing Folders

Each Outlook component has its own folder, represented by an icon on the Outlook Bar in the Outlook Shortcuts group. To open another Outlook component, click the appropriate icon in the Outlook Bar. To open the Calendar feature, for example, click the **Calendar** icon. Use the scroll button to view more icons on the Outlook Bar.

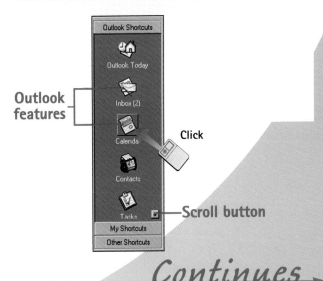

Outlook features
Click
Scroll button

Continues

7 Display the Folder List

Another way to view Outlook's components is with the Folder List. Open the **View** menu and select **Folder List**, or click the **Folder** drop-down arrow in the work area. The Folder List displays each

Outlook folder, including any you add to organize Outlook items you create. (Click the **Pushpin** icon to keep the Folder List open onscreen.)

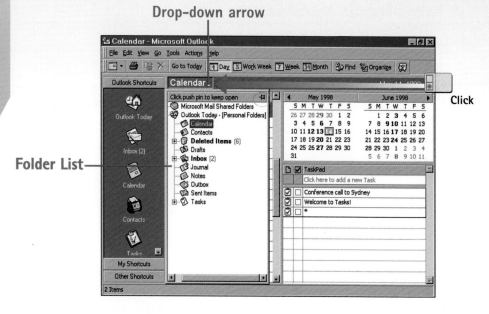

Drop-down arrow

Folder List

Click

8 Changing Views

Some of the Outlook components let you change your view of the information presented. Calendar, for example, lets you see your schedule by

Day, Work Week, Week, and Month. To change a view, use the **View** menu or click the appropriate view button on the toolbar.

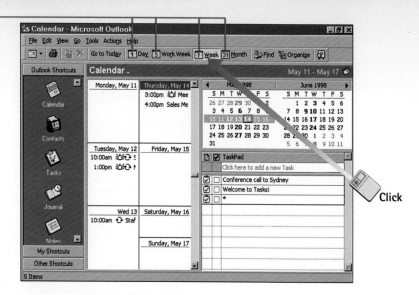

View Buttons

Click

9 Using Outlook Today View

A new feature in Outlook 98 is the Outlook Today folder (click the **Outlook Today** icon on the Outlook Bar to open). This lets you see your day's schedule and projects at a glance. The items displayed are actually hyperlinks to other Outlook items. Click an appointment, for example, to open the Appointment window that has details about the appointment.

Link

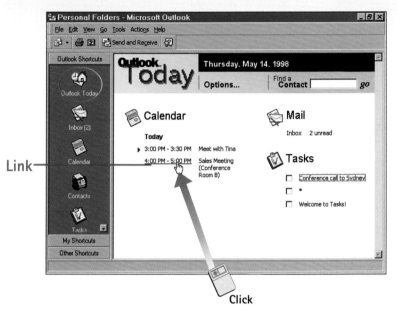

Click

10 Finding Outlook Contacts

Use the **Find a Contact** tool at the top of the Outlook Today display to quickly look up a name in your Contacts database (learn more about adding contacts in Task 9. Click inside the text box and type the person's name. Press Enter, and Outlook displays the Contact form with details about the person.

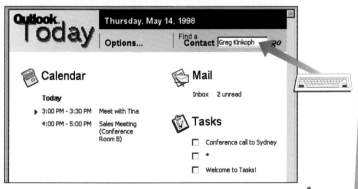

How-To Hints

Customizing Outlook Today

By default, Outlook 98 opens with the Inbox displayed. However, you may want to customize Outlook to start with the Outlook Today feature displayed. That way, you can always see your day's events and tasks at a glance. To do this, click the **Options** link on the Outlook Today display. This opens another display page with several options. Click the **When starting, go directly to Outlook Today** check box. You can also customize how appointments and tasks appear. Click the **Back to Outlook Today** link to return to the previous display page.

End

How to Schedule an Appointment

Use Outlook's Calendar feature to keep track of appointments, events, and any other special engagements. When you open the Calendar folder, Outlook displays your daily schedule in the schedule pane, along with a monthly calendar pane and a miniaturized version of your TaskPad (learn more about creating Outlook tasks in Task 6.

You can easily add appointments to your calendar and set reminder alarms to let you know of imminent appointments. To open Calendar, click the Calendar icon on the Outlook Bar.

Begin

1 Choose a Date

In the monthly calendar pane, select the month and date for the appointment. Click the date and the schedule pane changes to reflect that date.

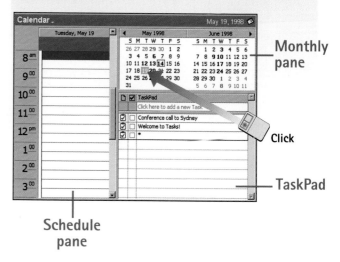

Monthly pane

Click

TaskPad

Schedule pane

2 Choose a Time

On the schedule pane, double-click the time slot for which you want to schedule an appointment. This opens the Appointment window.

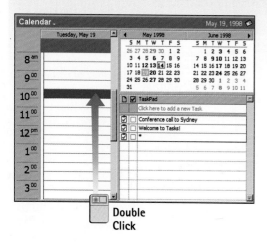

Double Click

3 Fill Out the Form

The Appointment window is actually a form you can use to enter details about the appointment. Fill out the **Subject** and **Location** text boxes. Enter the name of the person you're meeting with, for example, and the place where you're meeting, if needed. Click inside the text boxes, or use the Tab key to move from field to field.

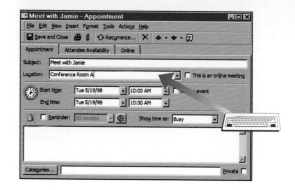

4 Enter Appointment Details

Use the **Start time** and **End time** drop-down arrows to set or change the date, time, and length of the appointment. By default, Outlook schedules your appointments in 30-minute increments, but you can easily set a longer time increment.

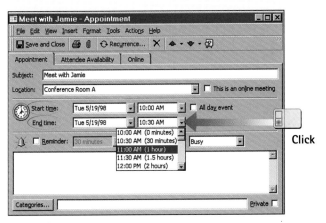

Click

5 Need a Reminder?

Select the **Reminder** check box if you want Outlook to remind you about the appointment with a prompt box and an audible beep. Specify the amount of time before the appointment for which you want to be reminded.

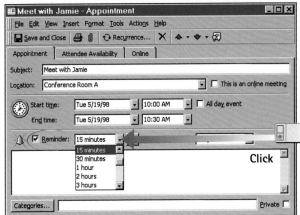

Click

6 Save and Close

When you have finished filling in all the details you want to include with the appointment, click the **Save and Close** button on the Appointment window's toolbar to exit the form and return to Calendar.

Click

End

How-To Hints

Reminder Prompt

If you select the Reminder check box, Outlook reminds you about the appointment with a prompt box and a beep. However, this works only if Outlook is running at the time of the reminder prompt. You can minimize Outlook so it's a button on the Windows taskbar. This way, you can work with other programs, but Outlook can still remind you of imminent appointments.

Block Your Time

If you're using Outlook on a network, use the **Show time as** drop-down list on the Appointment form to determine how others see the appointment on your calendar.

How to Set a Recurring Appointment

If your schedule is prone to recurring appointments, Outlook's Recurring Appointment features can help. For example, perhaps you have a weekly staff meeting. Rather than schedule each meeting separately, set the meeting as a recurring appointment. Outlook will automatically add the meeting to each week's calendar for you.

With the Recurring Appointment feature, you can indicate the recurrence pattern to tell Outlook how often the meeting occurs (Daily, Weekly, Monthly, or Yearly), which day of the week it falls on, and other related options.

Begin

1 Open the Dialog Box

To schedule a recurring appointment from the Calendar folder, first open the Appointment Recurrence dialog box. Display the **Actions** menu and select **New Recurring Appointment**.

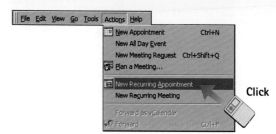

Click

2 Enter a Time

Use the **Start**, **End**, or **Duration** drop-down lists to set the appointment start and end times and designate how long the appointment lasts.

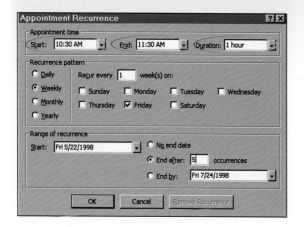

3 Enter a Recurrence Pattern

Under **Recurrence Pattern**, select the frequency of the appointment and the day on which the appointment falls. Depending on your selection, the remaining recurrence options will vary. If you select **Weekly**, for example, you can specify every week or every other week.

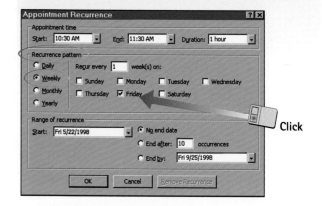

Click

4 Range of Recurrence

Use the **Range of recurrence** options to enter any limits to the recurring appointment. You may need to schedule five doctor visits over the next five months, for example; after that, you no longer need the appointment. Use the **End after** option to set such a range.

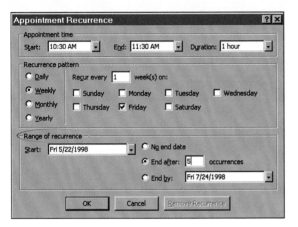

5 Fill in the Details

Click **OK** to close the Appointment Recurrence window and display the Appointment form. Now you can fill in any details about the appointment. Click the **Save and Close** button when you're finished.

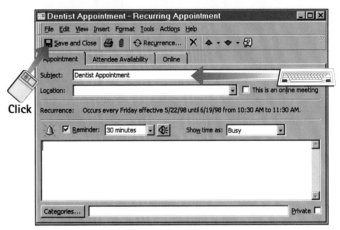

6 The Appointment Is Set

The recurring appointment now appears on your calendar with a double arrow icon to indicate it's a recurring appointment.

End

How-To Hints

Add a Reminder

Use the **Reminder** check box in the Appointment form to add a reminder alarm to your recurring appointment.

Edit Appointments

To edit a recurring appointment or any other appointment, double-click the appointment in your schedule. This opens the Appointment form where you can make any changes.

Other Recurring Ideas

You might also use recurring appointments to mark birthdays, anniversaries, and other special occasions on your calendar. This may keep you from forgetting them from year to year.

How to Schedule an Event

Not all items you add to your schedule are appointments. Some items are events. A calendar event is any activity that lasts the entire day, such as an anniversary, conference, trade show, or birthday. Use events in your daily calendar to block off larger time slots than appointments. Events appear as banners at the top of the Daily schedule.

Begin

1 Open the Event Window

To schedule an event, open the **Actions** menu and choose **New All Day Event**. This opens the Event window.

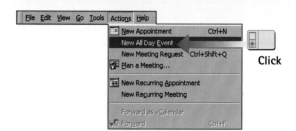

Click

2 Enter the Event Title

The Event window looks like the Appointment window. Fill in the details pertaining to the event. Start by filling in a title for the event in the **Subject** text box and entering a location in the **Location** text box.

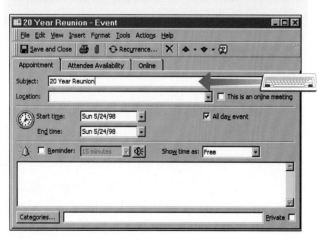

3 Enter Start and End Times

Use the **Start time** and **End time** drop-down lists to specify a time frame for the event.

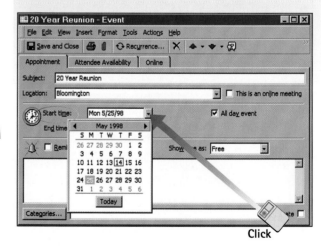

Click

4 Set the All Day Event Option

Be sure to select the **All Day Event** check box (this option is what makes an event different from a regular appointment).

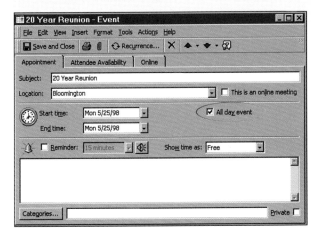

5 Save and Close

When you have finished filling in the Event details, click the **Save and Close** button to exit the Event window.

Click

6 The Event Is Saved

The event now appears as a banner at the beginning of the day in the schedule pane (use Day view to see it).

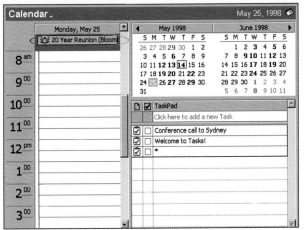

How-To Hints

Edit Events

To edit an event, double-click the event on your calendar. This reopens the Event form and you can make the necessary changes.

Event Reminder

Use the Reminder check box to assign a reminder alarm to alert you about the event.

Recurring Events

To schedule a recurring event on your calendar, click the **Recurrence** button on the Event window's toolbar.

End

How to Plan a Meeting

If you're using Outlook 98 on a network, you can utilize the Plan a Meeting feature to schedule meetings with others. The feature also lets you designate any resources needed for the meeting, such as a conference room or equipment.

The Plan a Meeting feature lets you invite attendees via email messages and track their responses. To get started, open the Calendar folder; click the **Calendar** icon on the Outlook Bar.

Begin

1 Open the Plan a Meeting Feature

From the Calendar folder, open the **Actions** menu and select **Plan a Meeting**. This opens the Plan a Meeting window.

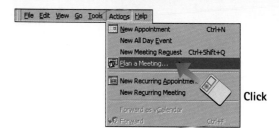

Click

2 Enter the Attendees

Enter the names of the attendees in the **All Attendees** list. Click **Type Attendee name Here** and enter the first person's name. Continue entering names on each line, as many attendees as you need.

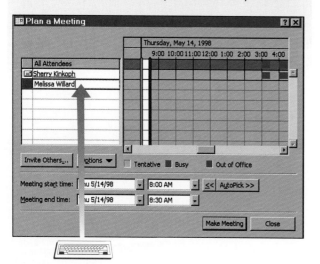

3 Set a Date

Click the **Meeting start time** drop-down arrows and choose a date and time for the meeting. Use the **Meeting end time** drop-down arrows to specify an end date and time for the meeting.

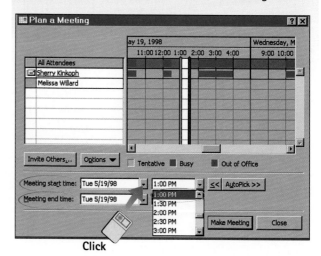

Click

4 Or Drag a Time

Alternatively, you can drag the green bar in the schedule area to set a start time for the meeting, and drag the red bar to set an end time. (It's difficult to distinguish the colors on some monitors; just remember that the bar to the left of the time increment starts the time and the right bar sets an end time.)

Start time bar   End time bar

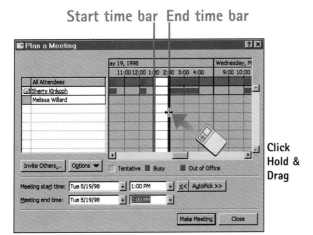

Click Hold & Drag

5 Fill in Meeting Details

When you have finished planning the meeting attendees and times, click the **Make Meeting** button. This opens the Meeting window, which resembles the Appointment form. Refine the meeting details as needed.

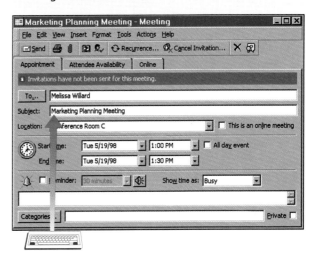

6 Send the Invitations

When you have finished filling out the meeting details, click **Send** to send email invitations to the attendees. Click the **Close** button to exit the Meeting window.

Click

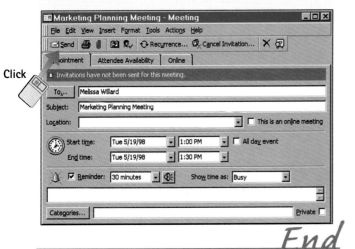

End

How-To Hints

Track Your Responses

To see how the attendees are responding to your meeting invitation, click the **Show attendee status** option in the **Attendee Availability** tab of the Meeting window.

How to Create a New Task

Use Outlook's Tasks folder to keep track of things you need to do, such as steps for completing a project or arranging an event. Tasks can be as complex as a year-long project or as simple as a shopping list you need to fill in on the way home. A task list can include things such as writing a letter, making a phone call, or distributing a memo.

After you create a task list, you can keep track of the tasks and check them off as you complete them. You can choose to view your task list in the Tasks folder or in the Calendar folder. To open the Tasks folder, click the **Tasks** icon in the Outlook Bar.

Begin

1 Open the Task Dialog Box

From the Tasks folder, open the **Actions** menu and select **New Task**, or click the **New Task** button on the toolbar.

Click

2 Enter a Title

The Task window, like the Appointment window, is a form you can fill out detailing the task. With the **Task** tab displayed, enter the subject or title of the task in the **Subject** text box.

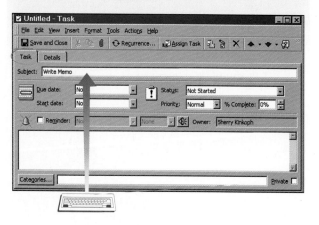

3 Enter a Due Date

If the task has a due date, click the **Due date** drop-down arrow and choose a due date from the calendar. (You can also enter a start date, if needed.)

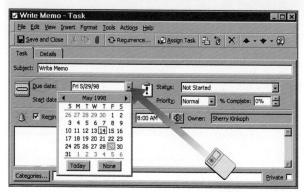

Click

4 Select a Status Setting

Use the **Status** drop-down list to select a status setting for the project: Not Started, In Progress, Completed, Waiting on Someone Else, or Deferred. As you manage your task list, you can update the status as needed.

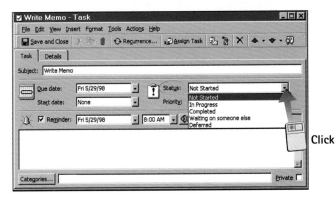

Click

5 Set a Priority

Use the **Priority** drop-down list to give the task a priority level: Normal, Low, or High. Use the **% Complete** box to specify a percentage of completeness, if needed.

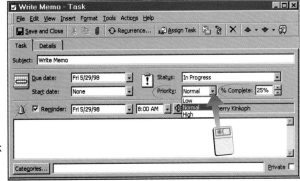

Click

6 Enter Notes

Use the Notes box to enter any notes about the task. When you have finished filling out the Task form, click the **Save and Close** button. The task is now added to your Tasks folder's task list, as shown in this figure.

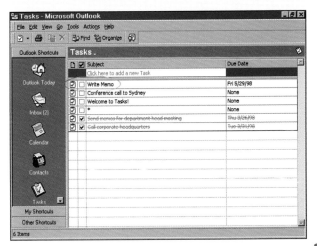

End

How-To Hints

Managing Tasks

To edit a task, double-click the task in the task list. To mark a task as complete, right-click the task and choose **Mark Complete**. To delete a task, right-click and choose **Delete**.

Recording Statistics

To record statistics about a task, such as billable time, contacts, or mileage, double-click the task and display the **Details** tab of the Task form.

Working with the TaskPad

The TaskPad that appears in Calendar shows your current tasks. To quickly open a task from the TaskPad, double-click the task name.

How to Create a New Contact

Use Outlook's Contacts folder to build a database of people you contact the most. A contact can be any person you communicate with, such as a coworker, relative, vendor, or client. You can enter all kinds of information about a contact, including addresses, phone numbers, email addresses, birthdays, and Web pages.

After you enter a contact, you will always have access to information about that person. You can quickly fire off an email message, for example, or have your modem dial the phone number for you. To begin entering contacts, first open the Contacts folder; click the **Contacts** icon on the Outlook Bar.

Begin

1 Open the Contact Form

From the Contacts folder, open the **Action** menu and select **New Contact**, or click the **New Contact** button on the toolbar. This opens the Contact window.

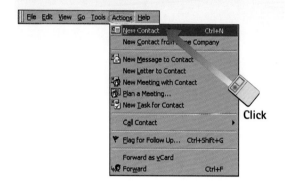

Click

2 Using the General Tab

From the **General** tab in the Contact form, you can begin filling in information about the contact. Click inside each text box and fill in the appropriate information. To move from field to field, press Tab.

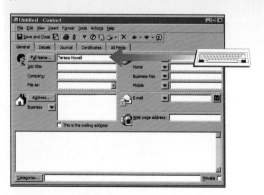

3 The File As List

Click the **File as** drop-down arrow and choose how you want to file your contact—by last name or first name. The default setting is to file the contacts by last name first.

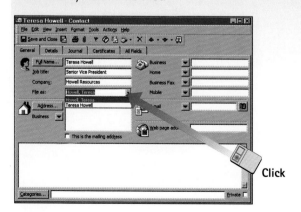

Click

4 Enter Phone Numbers

Outlook gives you the option of entering numerous phone numbers for the contact, including business and home numbers, fax numbers, and cell phone numbers.

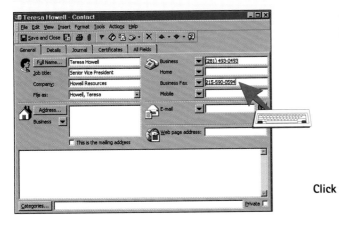

5 Enter an Address

Enter the contact's address in the **Address** box. Use the drop-down arrow to designate a Business, Home, or Other address. (Use the **Address** button to enter address information in separate fields.)

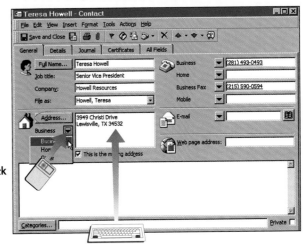

Click

6 Save the Contact

After filling out all the pertinent information (don't forget to enter an email address), click the **Save and Close** button, and the contact is added to your database. To keep entering more contacts, click the **Save and New** button to open another Contact form.

Save and New

Click

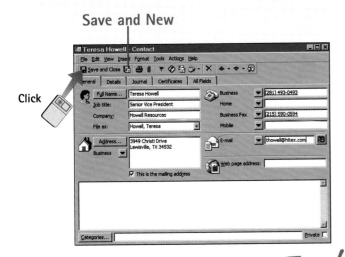

How-To Hints

More Details

Use the **Details** tab in the Contact form to enter information such as spouse name, birthdays, anniversary, and other details.

Editing Contacts

To edit a contact, double-click the contact's name in the Contacts folder. This reopens the Contact form where you can make changes to the data.

End

How to Import Contact Data

If you already have a contacts database in another program, whether it's an Office program such as Excel or Access, or a non-Microsoft program such as Lotus Organizer, you can import the database into Outlook. Use Outlook's Import and Export Wizard to walk you through the steps.

Begin

1 Select Import and Export Wizard

Open the **File** menu and select **Import and Export**.

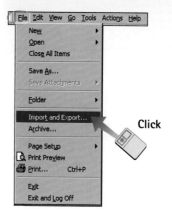

Click

2 Choose an Action

In the first Wizard dialog box, choose an import or export action. Because you are importing addresses, choose **Import from another program or file**, and then click **Next** to continue.

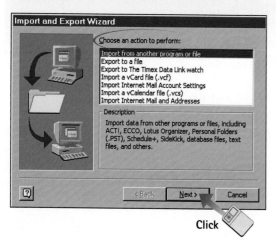

Click

3 Choose a File Type

In the next wizard dialog box, choose the type of address file you want to import. Scroll through the list and make your selection; then click **Next**.

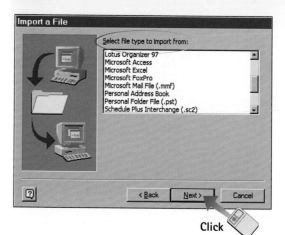

Click

4 Locate the File

If you know the path of the file you want to import, type it into the text box. If you don't know for sure, use the **Browse** button to locate the exact file to import. Make your selection and click **Next**.

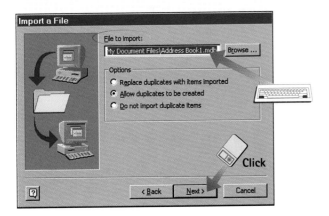

Click

5 Choose a Destination Folder

Select a destination folder to hold the imported data. If you're importing addresses, consider placing them in the Contacts folder. Click **Next** to continue.

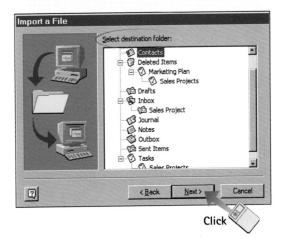

Click

6 Select an Import Action

In the final wizard box, select the import action to perform, and then click **Finish**. Outlook imports your address data as specified.

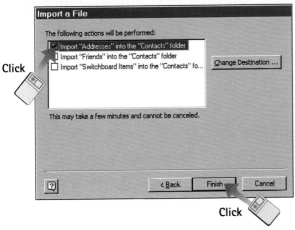

Click

Click

End

How-To Hints

Copying and Pasting Outlook Items

Not only can you import and export with Outlook 98, you can also copy and paste Outlook items between the Office programs using the Copy and Paste commands.

How to Phone a Contact

If your computer has a modem, you can use it to dial the phone numbers of contacts in your Contacts list. Of course, after the number is dialed, you will have to pick up the receiver to start talking. However, rather than waste time trying to find a phone number or memorizing it yourself, let Outlook take care of it.

Begin

1 Select the Contact

From the Contacts folder, select the contact you want to call.

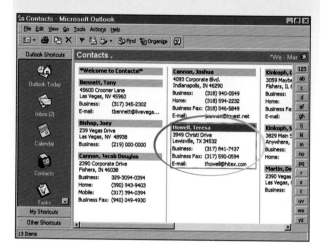

2 Use AutoDialer

Click the **AutoDialer** button on the Outlook toolbar to open the New Call dialog box.

Click

3 Choose the Number

Click the **Number** drop-down arrow and select which number you want to dial (such as business, home, or mobile).

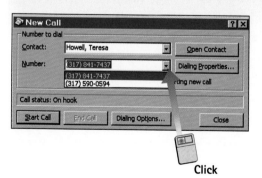

Click

4 Dial the Number

Click the **Start Call** button to have your modem dial the number.

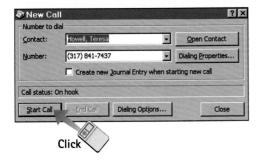

Click

5 Pick Up Prompt

When prompted, pick up the receiver and click **Talk** to begin talking to the contact.

Click

6 End the Call

When you're finished with the call, click **End Call**; then click **Close** to close the dialog box.

Click

End

How-To Hints

Create a Journal Entry

To help you track your calls, use Outlook's Journal feature to create a journal entry that documents the call. Before dialing the number, click the **Create new Journal Entry when starting new call** check box.

10

How to Create a Journal Entry

Outlook's Journal feature can help you track chronological events, such as when you completed a job-related task or placed a call. Logging journal entries can help you track past happenings, but only if you're consistent in logging entries. Outlook can help by automatically logging entries for email messages, faxes, meeting requests, and tasks you assign to others. One of the most useful aspects of the Journal is to log phone calls you make, especially when you need to note details about conversations.

In this task, you will learn how to manually create a Journal entry. Open the Journal folder by clicking the **Journal** icon on the Outlook Bar.

Begin

1 Start a Journal Entry

To create a manual entry, open the **Actions** menu and choose **New Journal Entry** or click the **New Journal** button on the toolbar. This opens the Journal Entry window.

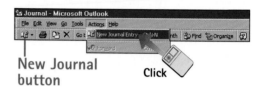

New Journal button   Click

2 Fill in the Form

Like the other windows used in Outlook, the Journal Entry window acts like a form; it has fields you can to fill in with information about the entry. Start by clicking in the **Subject** text box and entering a title for the entry.

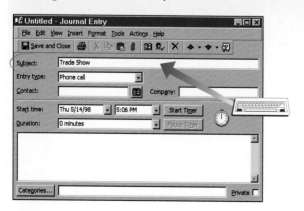

3 Select the Entry Type

Click the **Entry type** drop-down arrow and choose an entry type from the list, such as Phone call.

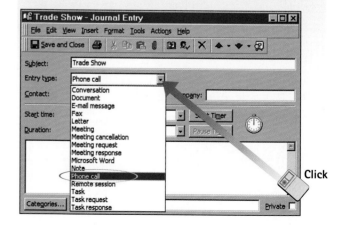

Click

4 Enter the Contact

If the entry is about a particular contact or company, enter the names in the **Contact** and **Company** text boxes.

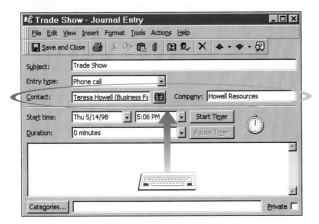

5 Record the Time

Use the **Duration** drop-down list to specify the amount of time spent on the journal activity. To let Outlook track the time (logging a phone call), click the **Start Timer** button.

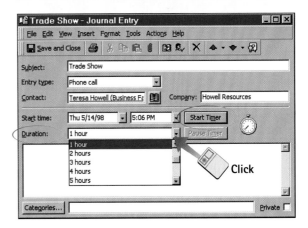

6 Finish Details and Exit

Use the bottom text box to enter notes about the activity (such as logging notes about a telephone conversation). Click **Save and Close** to exit the Journal form and add it to the Journal time-line, as shown in this figure.

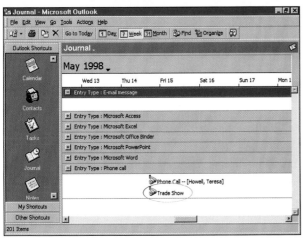

End

How-To Hints

Automatic Entries

To set Outlook to automatically log activities for you, open the **Tools** menu and select **Options**. Select the **Preferences** tab, click the **Journal Options** button, and select which types of items to record in your Journal. Click **OK** twice to exit.

Changing Views

Be sure to check out the different view options for viewing journal entries. Click the **Day**, **Week**, or **Month** buttons on the toolbar and choose a different view of the Journal time line.

How to Create a Note

Outlook's Notes feature is the electronic version of sticky notes, those yellow notes you stick onto your desk or computer to remind you of things. Use Outlook's Notes to do the same. You can attach a note to a contact to remind you to call them, or you can drag a note onto the Windows desktop to remind you of an important task. You can also drag notes into other Office 97 programs.

To work with Outlook notes, open the Notes folder and click the **Notes** icon on the Outlook Bar.

Begin

1 Start a New Note

To create a note, open the **Actions** menu and select **New Note**, or click the **New Note** button on the toolbar. This opens a small, yellow, note box.

New Note   Click

2 Enter Note Text

Notice the note already has the current date and time entered. Enter your note text.

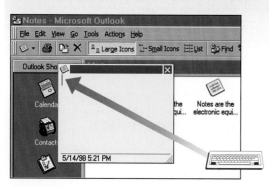

3 Resize the Note

Drag any edge of the note to resize it. When you hover your mouse pointer over an edge, it becomes a two-sided arrow. Click and drag the edge to resize the note box.

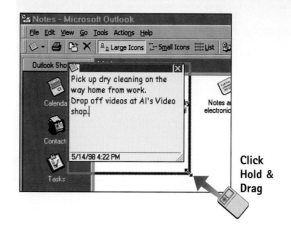

Click
Hold &
Drag

4 Change the Note Color

If you prefer a color other than the default yellow, click the upper-left icon in the note and select **Color**; then choose another color to use.

Click

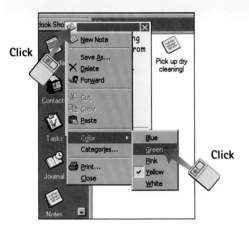

Click

5 Close the Note

To close a note, click anywhere outside the note, or click the note's **Close** button. To drag a note elsewhere on the desktop, click and drag the note's blue bar (located at the top of the note box).

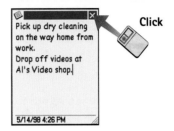

Click

End

How-To Hints

Save as a File

You can save a note as a file. Click the icon in the upper-left corner of the note and select **Save As**. Assign a name to the note and designate which folder to save it in; then click **Save**.

Print a Note

To print a note, first click the icon in the upper-left corner of the note and select **Print**. This opens the Print dialog box where you can change any print settings before printing.

How to Create a New Folder

Outlook saves items you create in folders and sub-folders. Email messages are saved in the Inbox folder, notes are saved in the Notes folder, and so forth. When managing the many items you create, you may want to organize items into different folders. For example, you may want to store all the Outlook items related to a particular project in one folder. You can easily create new folders and move Outlook items into them as needed.

Begin

1 Open the Folder List

To see all the available folders that come with Outlook, open the Folder List. Click the **Folder name** drop-down arrow; then click the **Pushpin** icon in the upper-right corner of the list to keep the list open onscreen.

Click

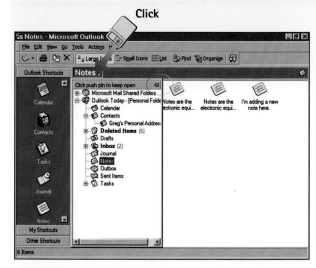

2 Choose a Parent Folder

To create a new subfolder, first select the parent folder (the folder to hold the subfolder). You may want a Sales Project folder, for example, to be stored in the Tasks folder. First, select the **Tasks** folder.

Click

3 Open the Create New Folder Box

Right-click the folder to display a short-cut menu, and then select **New Folder**. This opens the Create New Folder dialog box.

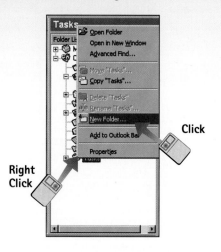

Click

Right Click

4 Enter a Folder Name

Enter a name for the new folder in the **Name** box.

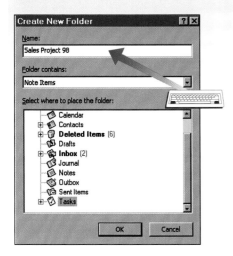

5 Select Items

Choose which items you want to store in the folder using the **Folder contains** drop-down list. Click **OK** to exit the dialog box and create the folder.

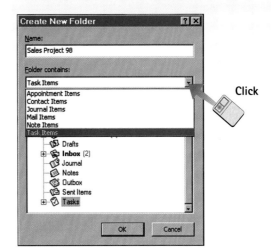

Click

6 The Folder is Saved

A prompt box asks if you want to save the folder as an icon on the Outlook Bar. Click **No**. The folder name is now added to the Folder List.

How-To Hints

Subfolders in Subfolders

You can create subfolders within subfolders. You might have a subfolder in the Inbox folder named Vendor Mail, for example, and additional folders within that folder named Suppliers and Printers.

End

How to Move Items to Folders

After you create your own folders, you will want to move Outlook items into the folders. You may want to keep all your email correspondence from a particular client in one folder, for example, so you can easily retrieve old messages. Or you might want to keep personal messages separate from business messages. Outlook makes it easy to move items from one folder to another.

Begin

1 Open the Folder List

To see your folders, open the Folder List. Click the **Folder name** drop-down arrow, or open the **View** menu and choose **Folder List**.

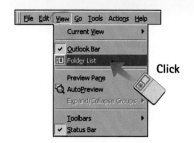

2 Select the Item

Open the folder containing the item you want to move and select the item.

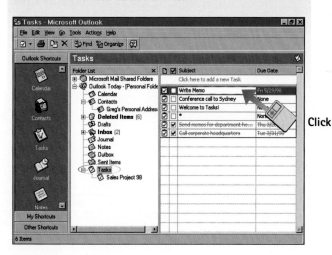

3 Use the Move Command

Open the **Edit** menu and select the **Move to Folder** command. This opens the Move Items dialog box.

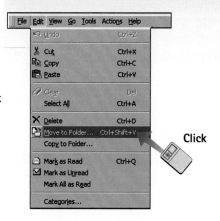

4 Choose a Folder

Choose the folder where you want to move the selected item and click **OK**.

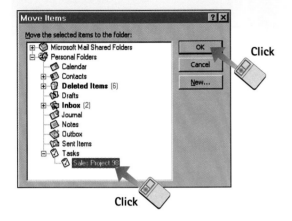

Click

Click

5 Or Use Click and Drag

Another method of moving items between folders is to click and drag them. Select the item you want to move, and then hold down the left mouse button and drag the item to the new folder name.

Click & Drag

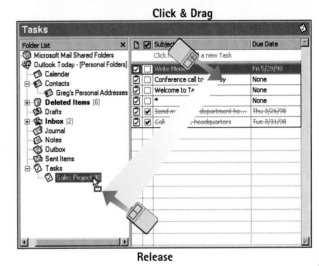

Release

End

How-To Hints

Drag and Drop

You can also drag and drop items from open folders into any folder on the Outlook Bar. Select the item and drag and drop it into the appropriate folder.

TASK *14*

How to Delete Items

Items you delete in Outlook don't disappear entirely. Instead, they're held in Outlook's Deleted Items folder. To truly delete them, you must empty the folder. This works the same as the Windows Recycle Bin. Items you delete from your Windows desktop are held in the Recycle Bin until you remove them.

It's a good idea to clear your Deleted Items folder before exiting Outlook. If you forget, the items tend to stack up and take up space on your hard drive.

Begin

1 Open the Deleted Items Folder

To empty your deleted items, first open the Deleted Items folder. Click its icon on the Outlook Bar. Use the Scroll arrow button to locate the icon.

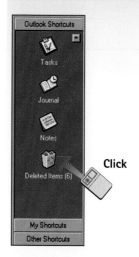

2 Choose the Items to Delete

To permanently erase an Outlook item from your system, select the item from the Deleted Items folder. To select more than one item, hold down the Ctrl key while clicking items.

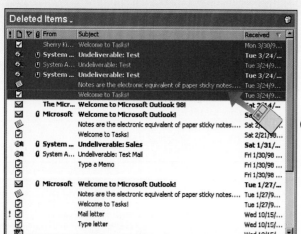

3 Click the Delete Button

Click the **Delete** button on the Outlook toolbar.

4 Confirm the Deletion

A confirmation box appears asking you if you really want to delete the item. Click **Yes**.

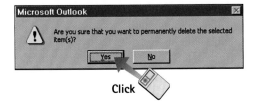

Click

5 Undeleting Items

If you have sent Outlook items to the Deleted Items folder but change your mind about deleting them, you can retrieve them. Select the item and drag it to any folder in the Outlook bar.

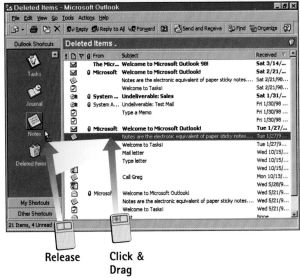

Release   Click & Drag

End

How-To Hints

Automatic Delete

You can set up Outlook so it automatically deletes items from the Deleted Items folder whenever you exit the program. Open the **Tools** menu and select **Options**. Display the **Other** tab and select the **Empty the Deleted Items Folder upon exiting** option and click **OK**.

How to Compose and Send a Message

Provided you have the correct email address, you can use Outlook to send a message to anyone with an email account. Like the other Outlook components, the email portion features a message form you can fill out. If you know the recipient uses Outlook, too, you can even add formatting to your message.

Before you can use Outlook's email options, however, you must have a modem and an email account, whether through a service provider, a network connection, or a commercial service. The easiest way to track and send messages is through the Inbox folder; click the **Inbox** icon on the Outlook Bar to open the folder.

Begin

1 Open a New Message Form

From the Outlook Inbox folder, open the **Actions** menu and select **New Mail Message**, or click the **New Mail Message** button on the toolbar. This opens the Message window.

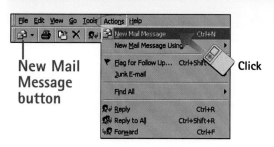

New Mail Message button

Click

2 Enter a Recipient Address

The Message window resembles a form. Fill out the form, using Tab to move from field to field. Click inside the **To** text box and type the name of the recipient. (To use an address in an Address Book, click the **To** button and select the recipient from your list.

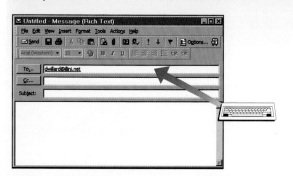

3 Carbon Copy

If you want to send the message to multiple recipients, enter the other recipients' addresses in the **Cc** text box.

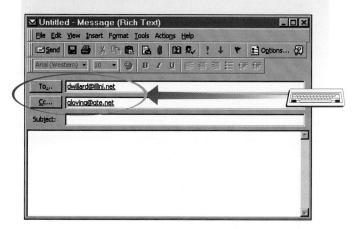

4 Enter the Subject

Click inside the **Subject** text box and enter a title or phrase to identify the content or purpose of your message.

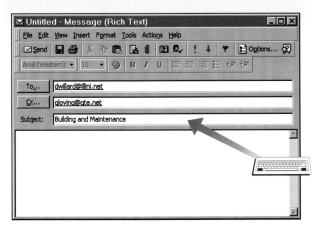

5 Type Your Message

Click inside the message box and type your message text. Outlook automatically wraps the text for you. Use the Delete and Backspace keys to fix mistakes, just as you would in a Word document.

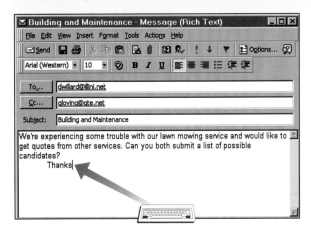

6 Send the Message

To send the message, click the **Send** button. If you're offline (not connected to the Internet or network), the message waits in the Outbox until the next time you go online to collect your mail.

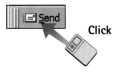

Click

End

How-To Hints

Spell Check

You can spell check your email messages before sending them. Open the **Tools** menu and select **Spelling**.

Message Options

Use Outlook's **Options** button on the Message form's toolbar to assign options such as priority levels or tracking options. Be sure to check out the variety of available options.

How to Add an Address to Your Personal Address Book

The Personal Address Book is one of two address sources you have in Outlook. The other address book is your Contacts list. Unlike the Contacts list, the Personal Address Book enables you to create Personal Distribution Lists, which are address groups that enable you to send a message to a large group of recipients without accidentally forgetting to include a name.

If you've used Microsoft Exchange for email, all your addresses are stored in the Exchange Personal Address Book; Outlook and Exchange share the same Personal Address Book, so all those addresses are available in Outlook, too.

Begin

1 Open the Personal Address Book

From the Inbox folder, open the **Tools** menu and select **Address Book,** or click the **Address Book** button on the toolbar to open the Address Book window.

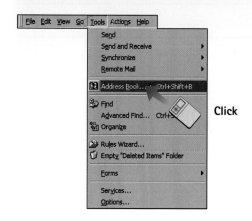

Click

2 Click New Entry

Click the **New Entry** button on the Address Book toolbar to open the New Entry window.

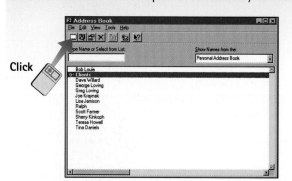

Click

3 Choose an Email Type

From the **Select the entry type** list box, choose the type of email address you're adding and click **OK**. To add an Internet email address, for example, click **Internet Mail Address**.

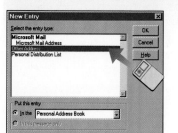

Click

4 Fill in the Information

Use the various tabs to enter information about the email recipient. Enter the **Display name** (the name that appears on your messages), the **Email address** (the actual email address), and the **Email type** (usually **SMTP**). Choose **OK**.

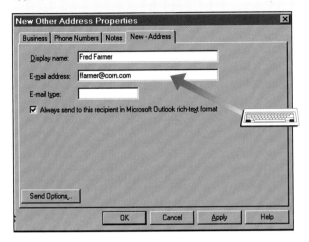

5 Exit

When you're finished adding new entries, exit the Address Book window. Click the **Close** button or select **File**, **Close**.

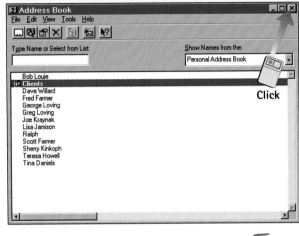

End

How-To Hints

Can't Find Your Personal Address Book?

If Outlook didn't pick up your Personal Address Book when it was installed, choose **Tools**, **Services**; in the Services dialog box, click **Add** (the Add Service to Profile dialog box appears). Click **Personal Address Book** and **Outlook Address Book**; then choose **OK** to close both dialog boxes. Close Outlook and restart it.

Create a Personal Distribution List

In the Address Book window, choose **File**, **New Entry**. Double-click **Personal Distribution List**. Type a **Name** for the list; then click **Add/Remove Members**. Double-click each name you want to add, choose **OK** twice, and then choose **File**, **Close** to exit.

How to Read an Incoming Message

Use the Inbox to see messages you receive in Outlook. The Inbox displays each message as a single line with a **From** field that tells you who sent it, a **Subject** field that gives you a clue as to what's in the message, and a **Date** field that tells you when it was received. The symbol columns at the left of the Inbox provide important information about each message, such as priority level or whether it has a file attachment.

Use the AutoPreview feature to screen new messages by showing you the first three lines of a message before you open it. If AutoPreview isn't turned on, choose **View**, **AutoPreview** to turn it on.

Begin

1 Check for New Mail

To check for new messages from the Inbox folder, click the **Send and Receive** button on the Outlook toolbar to go online to pick up mail. Your new messages appear in your Inbox.

Click

2 Open a Message

Double-click a message you want to open and read.

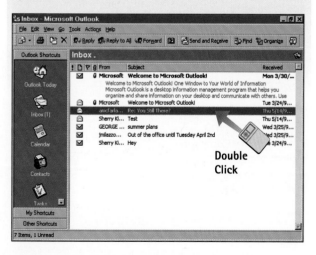

Double Click

3 Read a Message

The message opens for you to read. If it's a long message, use the scrollbars to scroll through the message. If you want to print the message, click the **Print** button on the message toolbar.

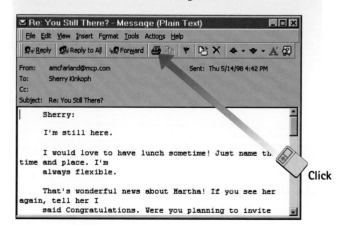

Click

4 Read the Next Message

To continue reading new mail messages without returning to the Inbox, click the **Next Item** button on the message toolbar. To return to the previous message, click the **Previous Item** button.

Previous Item   Next Item

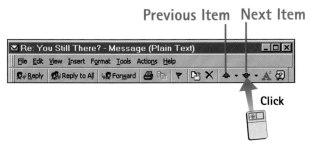

Click

5 Delete a Message

If you don't need to keep a message, click the **Delete** button in the message toolbar.

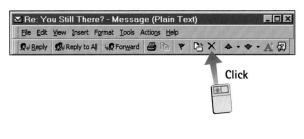

Click

6 Close a Message

When you're finished reading a message, and you want to keep it, click the **Close** button in the upper-right corner of the message. If you want to reply to the message or forward it to someone else, see Task 18, "How to Reply to or Forward a Message," (don't close the message; replying and forwarding close it automatically).

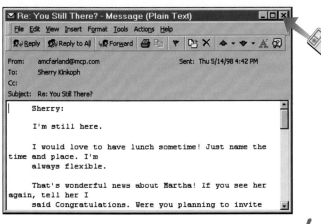

Click

End

How-To Hints

Read and Unread

You can mark messages in the Inbox as read or unread. By default, Outlook marks messages as read after you open them. If you want to remember to read the message again later, close it, and then right-click the message line in Inbox and click **Mark as Unread**. The message returns to unread-mail status.

Deleting Messages

If you're cleaning out your Inbox, delete old messages by selecting the message and then clicking the **Delete** button on the Outlook toolbar.

Creating an Address Book Entry

When you receive a message, the sender's name and address are always included in the **From** line of the message form. To transfer the name and address directly into your Personal Address Book, right-click the sender name, and then click **Add to Personal Address Book**.

TASK *18*

How to Reply to or Forward a Message

You can quickly reply to or forward any message immediately after opening and reading the message. A reply, of course, is an answer to a message sent to you, and a forward is a message you have received that you send on to others. Outlook creates a reply or forward message that includes all the original text. When you reply or forward a message, the action and the date are recorded in the original message (and copies of your replies and forwards are kept in the Sent Items folder).

Begin

1 Click Reply

To reply to an open message, click the **Reply** button to open a Reply Message window. If the message you received has names in **Cc** box, you can send your reply to all the recipients by clicking **Reply to All** instead.

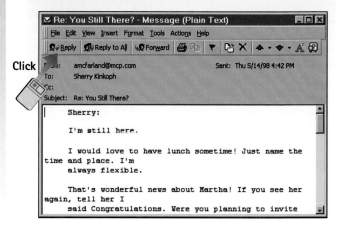

2 Enter Your Reply

The Reply Message window includes the original text with the sender's name in the **To** text box. Select and delete any text you don't need to include. Type your response to the message (Text you type in the reply area is blue, and if your correspondent reads your message in Outlook or Windows Exchange, he will see your response in blue).

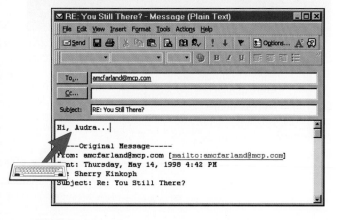

3 Send Your Reply

When your reply is ready, click the **Send** button on the message window's toolbar.

Click

168 CHAPTER 4: HOW TO USE OUTLOOK 98

4 Or Forward the Message

To forward an open message to others, click **Forward** in the original message window. This opens a new copy of the message.

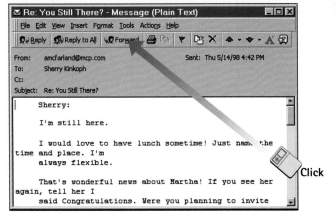

Click

5 Enter the Forwardee's Address

Fill in the **To** box with the address of the person you're forwarding the message to. Add a note at the top of the message (it appears in blue to anyone reading it in Outlook or Windows Exchange), and select and delete any text you don't want to include in the forwarded message.

6 Send It Forward

When the message is ready to be forwarded, click the **Send** button on the message window's toolbar.

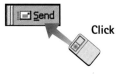

Click

End

How-To Hints

What About Attachments?

If the message contains attachments, they will be forwarded; if you want to delete the attachments, click each one and press **Delete**.

How to Attach a File to a Message

You can attach files of any type to Outlook messages. You can send your boss the latest sales figures from your Excel worksheet, for example, or pass along your Word report to your colleague on the Internet. You can also attach other Outlook items, such as a contact or note.

When you attach a file to a message, it appears as an icon on the message. The recipient can open the file from within the message or save the file to open later. Keep in mind, however, that the recipient *must* have the appropriate program to view the file. If you send a PowerPoint presentation to a coworker, for example, he must have PowerPoint installed to view the file.

Begin

1 Click Insert File

After you compose the message, click the **Insert File** button on the message toolbar. This opens the Insert File dialog box.

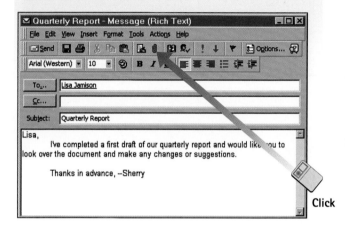

Click

2 Locate the File

Use the **Look in** drop-down list to locate the folder or drive where the file is stored.

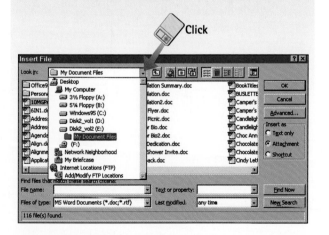

Click

3 Select the File

From the list box, select the file you want to attach and click **OK**.

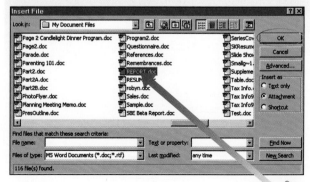

Click

4 The File Is Attached

The file appears as an icon in your message text. You can now send the message.

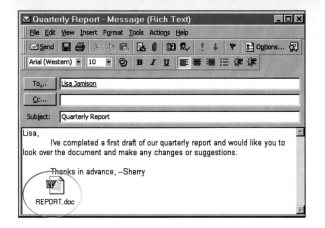

5 Attaching Outlook Items

To attach an Outlook item to a message, open the **Insert** menu and select **Item**. This opens the Insert Item dialog box.

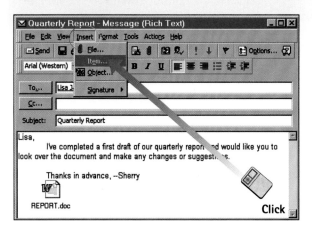

6 Locate the Item

Open the folder in which the item is stored, and then select the item. In the **Insert As** area, choose **Attachment**. Click **OK** and send the message.

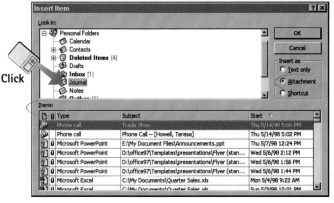

How-To Hints

Receiving Attachments

If you receive a message that contains an attached file, you will notice a paper clip symbol in the Attachments field in your Inbox. Open the message, and you will see an icon in it that represents the attached file. To view the file, double-click the attachment icon.

End

How to Archive an Email Message

Use Outlook's AutoArchive feature to automatically archive old email messages as well as other Outlook items. If unchecked, your Outlook Inbox will continue to grow as more and more email messages are added to the folder. To help remove clutter and restore disk space, archive items you no longer need to access.

You can archive old items manually or use AutoArchive to do it for you. When you archive items, they are removed from their current folder and copied to an archive file.

Begin

1 Open the Options Dialog Box

Open the **Tools** menu and select **Options**. This opens the Options dialog box.

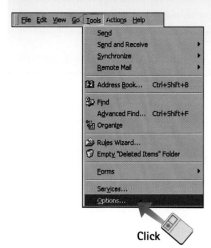

Click

2 Display the Other Tab

Next, click the **Other** tab and click the **AutoArchive** button. This opens the AutoArchive dialog box.

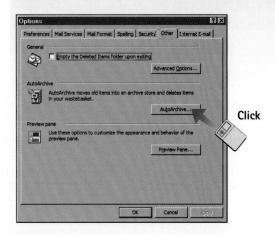

Click

3 Turn AutoArchive On

Select the **AutoArchive every** check box. You can now specify the number of days between archives, or you can set up each folder's properties to archive differently (proceed to step 4 to learn how). Click **OK** twice to exit the dialog boxes.

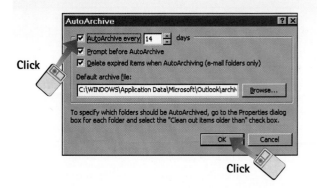

Click

Click

4 Open the Properties Dialog Box

You can set the AutoArchive properties for each Outlook 98 folder, including the Inbox. To display the Properties dialog box for a folder, right-click the folder in the Outlook Bar and select **Properties** from the shortcut menu.

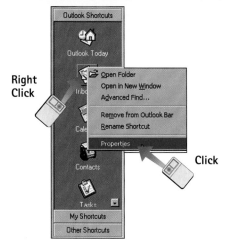

Right Click

Click

5 Set Archive Options

Click the **AutoArchive** tab and select the **Clean out items older than** check box. Designate the value in months when items are to be automatically archived.

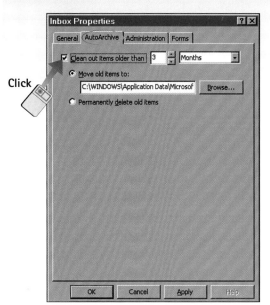

Click

6 Set an Archive Folder

Outlook stores the archived items in a default archive folder, but you can choose another folder, if needed. Click the **Browse** button and select another archive folder. Click **OK** to exit the dialog box and the AutoArchive properties are set.

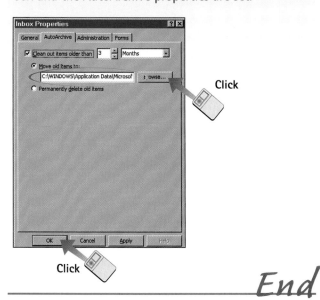

Click

Click

How-To Hints

Manual Archive

To manually archive an Outlook item, such as an email message, open the **File** menu and choose **Archive**. To archive all the folders, choose **Archive all folders according to their AutoArchive settings**. To archive one folder, choose **Archive this folder and all subfolders**, and then select the folder. Use the **Archive items older than** option to set a limit to the archive items; items dated before the date specified will be automatically archived. Click **OK** to exit.

End

Task

How to Use Publisher 98

Publisher 98 is an easy-to-use yet full-featured program for desktop publishing. With it, you can create a tremendous variety of printed material and convert your printable pages into Web pages for online marketing.

Some documents—such as one-page flyers—are often easier to create using Word, but other documents—such as business cards, booklets, and tri-fold brochures—are much easier to create using Publisher. Publisher doesn't work quite the same way as a word processing program (unlike Word, you can't type directly onto the page), but after you get accustomed to working with text and image boxes, you'll find Publisher easy and fun.

How to Use the Publisher Command Bar

On the left side of the Publisher window is the Command bar, a toolbar that contains buttons for creating *objects* and frames on a Publisher page. In Publisher, the buttons on the Command bar are called tools.

When you use the wizards, they'll create documents with fill-in-the-blanks text and picture frames. But you can still customize a wizard-created document by adding your own frames with the tools on the Command bar.

Begin

1 Use the Text Frame Tool

Click the Text Frame tool to place text on a page; then drag the crosshair-pointer on the page to draw a rectangular frame. You can type text in the frame as soon as you release the mouse button.

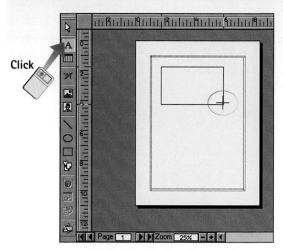

Click

2 Zoom to See the Text

If you can't read the text, press F9 to zoom in or out. You can also click the **Zoom** box at the bottom of the window, and then click **Actual Size** or **Zoom to Selection**; click **Full Page** to see the whole page layout again. See Tasks 3, 4, 9, 10, and 11 to learn more about using text frames.

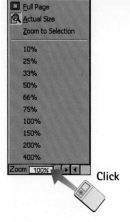

Click

3 Use the Picture Frame Tool

To place a graphics object on the page, click the Picture Frame tool, and then drag to draw a rectangular frame on the page. Right-click in the frame; then choose **Change Picture**, **Picture**, **Clipart** to open the ClipArt Gallery and select a picture. See Tasks 7 and 8 to learn more about using clip art.

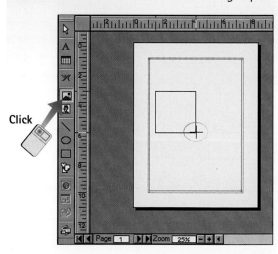

Click

4 Use the Table Frame Tool

To create a table on a page, click the Table Frame tool, and then drag to draw a frame for the table. When you release the mouse button, the Create Table dialog box appears; set up your table by selecting a number of rows, a number of columns, and a table format, and then choose **OK**.

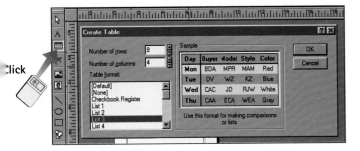

Click

5 Create WordArt

To add a decorative title to a page, click the WordArt Frame tool, and then draw a frame. In the Enter Your Text Here dialog box, type your text; then click **Update Display**. In the WordArt toolbar at the top of the window, use the list boxes to change the shape, font, and size of the WordArt title, and click away from the frame when you finish.

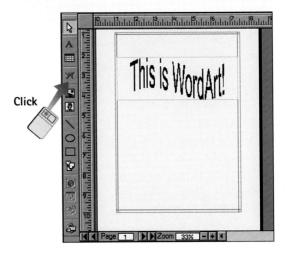

Click

6 Create Shapes

To create a shape, click the appropriate shape tool, and then drag to draw the shape on the page. See Task 18 to learn more about shapes.

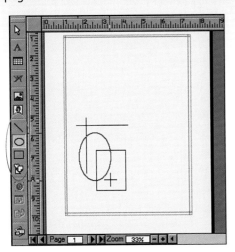

End

How-To Hints

Working in a Publisher Table

In a Publisher table, you can move to different cells by pressing Tab or clicking in the cell you want. Select rows and columns by clicking the gray row and column selectors. If your data is already in an Excel worksheet, copy the Excel table and paste it into a Publisher picture frame.

Delete a Frame

To delete any kind of frame, right-click in the frame and choose **Delete Object**.

More on WordArt

To change a WordArt object, double-click the WordArt frame. Make your changes, and click away from the frame to finish.

How to Use a Page Wizard

The Page Wizard creates a publication from a template you choose. The template has graphics, colorful objects, and pictures and text frames already in place, so it can save you considerable time over creating a publication from scratch. A wizard-created publication is also a good place to look for inspiration for your custom publications.

When you start Publisher, the Catalog dialog box appears. Here you'll find all the Page Wizards. If you've been working in Publisher and the Catalog is closed, you can easily open it to select a wizard and create a new publication.

Begin

1 Open the Catalog

To open the Catalog, choose **File**, **New**.

Click

2 Pick a Publication

On the **Publications by Wizard** tab, click a category and subcategory in the **Wizards** pane. In the right pane, scroll through the template sketches until you find one you like.

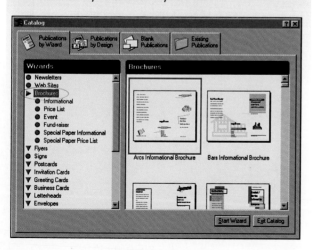

3 Start the Wizard

Click the template sketch you want; then click **Start Wizard**. (Publisher can open only one publication at a time, so if you have another publication open, you'll be prompted to save it so Publisher can close it.)

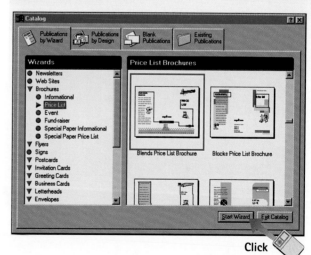

Click

4 Follow the Wizard

In each step, select different options and view the results in the sample. When you like what you see, click **Next** to move to the next step. (To finish quickly and accept all the wizard's default choices, click **Finish**.)

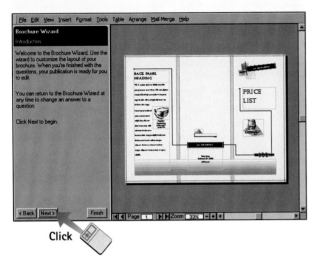

Click

5 Change the Color Scheme

Most wizards enable you to change the color scheme of the publication at some step in the wizard process. The advantage of using color schemes is that the colors in the publication are coordinated for you; and if you're creating several related publications, you can keep them color-coordinated by using the same color scheme in each.

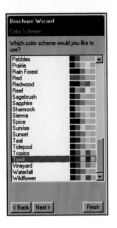

6 Make More Changes

When the wizard finishes, you can make changes by choosing a wizard step in the left pane, or you can work directly in the publication by clicking a text or picture frame. To close the wizard and gain more room to work in the publication, click **Hide Wizard**.

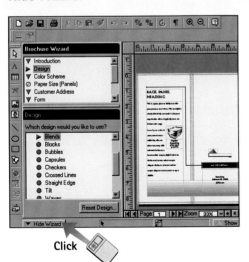

Click

How-To Hints

Save Your Publication

You can save your publication using normal save methods, just as in Word and Excel. Choose **File**, **Save**, and then navigate to a folder. Type a filename, and click **Save**.

Don't Use a Wizard

If you don't want to use a wizard, you can start with a blank page. In the Catalog, click **Exit Catalog** to close the Catalog and begin on a blank single page, or click the **Blank Publications** tab and create a new publication with preset dimensions.

End

How to Create a Text Frame

All the text in a publication resides in *text frames*. Many text frames can exist on a page, each to hold a discrete chunk of text; for example, you can use separate text frames for a title, subtitles, and separate small stories in a newsletter.

Text frames are drawn with the Text Frame tool and then can be moved and resized to fit both your text and your page layout.

Whether you're working in a wizard-created publication or a blank page, you can add, move, and resize text frames.

Begin

1 Click the Text Frame Tool

On the Command bar, click the Text Frame tool. Your mouse pointer becomes a crosshair symbol.

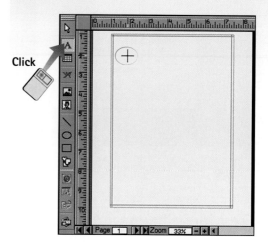

Click

2 Draw the Text Frame

On the page, drag the crosshair pointer to draw a rectangular frame. When you release the mouse button, you can type text (see Task 4 to learn more about adding text).

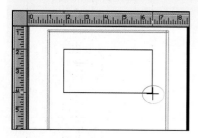

3 Move the Text Frame

To move the frame, click the frame to select it, and then point to a border (but not to a handle). When the mouse pointer becomes a little moving van, press the mouse button and drag the frame to a new location. Release the mouse button to drop the frame.

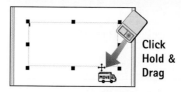

Click
Hold &
Drag

4 Resize the Text Frame

To resize the frame, click the frame to select it, and then point to a handle. When the mouse pointer becomes a two-headed resize arrow, drag to change the size or shape of the frame.

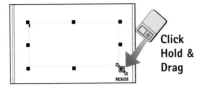

Click
Hold &
Drag

5 Resize Proportionally

To resize a text frame proportionally, hold down Shift while you drag a corner handle.

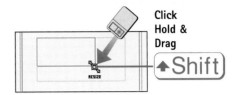

Click
Hold &
Drag

⬆Shift

6 Resize in Two Directions

To resize a frame in two opposite directions at once (for example, to resize both sides equally at the same time), hold down Ctrl while you drag any handle.

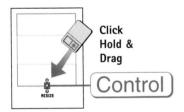

Click
Hold &
Drag

Control

End

How-To Hints

Format the Frame

You can change the border of a text frame to different line styles, colors, and even repeated pictures; you can also fill the frame with color behind the text. See Tasks 10, 11, and 12 to learn how to do all these things.

How to Add Text to a Text Frame

You can type text, copy and paste it from another file, or import it from another file.

If your text doesn't fit in the text frame, you can resize the frame to fit the text, or create a frame on another page and "flow" the text into the new frame. Flowing text to another frame is useful if you're creating a newsletter and need to break a story into smaller pieces.

To read and edit the text, you'll need to zoom in on the text; zoom back out to check the page layout.

Begin

1 Type Your Text

Click the text frame to select it, and then type your text. Unless you zoom in close, you won't be able to read what you type; press F9 to zoom in to actual size, and press F9 again to zoom back out to the previous magnification.

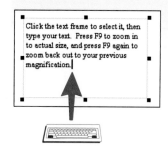

2 Copy and Paste Text

If you want to use a bit of text from another file, open that file and use that program's commands to copy the text to the Clipboard. Then switch to Publisher, select the text frame, and choose **Edit, Paste** to paste the copied text.

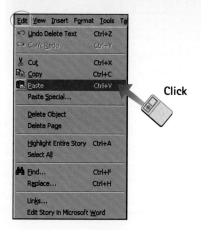

Click

3 Import Text

If your text is in another file, you can import the entire file. Right-click the text frame; then choose **Change Text**, **Text File**. In the Insert Text File dialog box, locate and click the filename; then choose **OK**. Publisher converts the file and asks you whether you want to use AutoFlow. Click **No** to flow the text yourself.

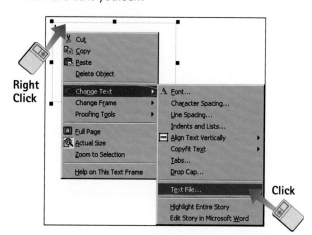

Right Click

Click

4 Make Room for Overflow

If there's too much text for the frame, a Text in Overflow symbol appears. You can resize the frame larger until the symbol disappears, or you can add a new text frame and then flow the remaining text into the new text frame.

Stony Keep Soap & Pottery

- Great thanks to all our customers at the Annual Exhibit and Sale for making the Sale a huge success!
As you know, 50% of our revenue from this annual sale is

5 Add a New Frame

Draw a new text frame, and then click the first text frame (the frame with the text).

6 Flow Text to a New Frame

Choose **Tools, Text Frame Connecting**. On the Connect Frames toolbar that appears, click the **Connect Text Frames** button (the mouse pointer becomes a mug symbol). Click the new text frame; the overflow text flows into the second frame (see Task 9 to learn more).

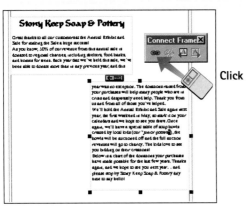

Click

End

How-To Hints

Zoom In and Out

You can select specific magnifications by clicking the **Zoom** box and then clicking a magnification, or by clicking the plus and minus buttons next to the **Zoom** box.

Break the Flow Between Frames

To disconnect text boxes that have text flowed between them, select the text frame that the text flows from, and then click the **Disconnect Text Frames** button on the Connect Frames toolbar.

How to Format Text

As in Word, you can format characters and paragraphs in a variety of ways, and you can add great visual effects to selected text. When you make changes that increase the space needed by your text, you'll have to resize the text frame.

Begin

1 Select the Text

If you're changing font or paragraph formatting, drag to select the text you want to format. If you're changing text frame margins or other properties, click the text frame to select it.

previous year, and this year was no exception. The donations raised from your purchases will help many people who are in crisis and desperately need help. Thank you from us and from all of those you've helped.

We'll hold the Annual Exhibit and Sale again next year, the first weekend in May, so mark it on your calendars and we hope to see you there. Once again, we'll have a special table of soup bowls created by local kids (our "junior potters"); the bowls will be auctioned off and the full auction revenues will go to charity. The kids love to see you bidding on their creations!

Thanks again, and we hope to see you next year... and please stop by Stony Keep Soap & Pottery any time to say hello!

2 Change the Font

To change the font of selected text, choose **Format, Font**. In the Font dialog box, select a different font in the **Font** list box, and select other general font characteristics under **General**.

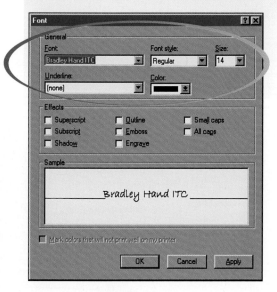

3 Add Font Effects

Under **Effects**, click check boxes to apply special effects. Check the results in the **Sample** box. Most effects look better when the font is a large size. When you like what you see, choose **OK**.

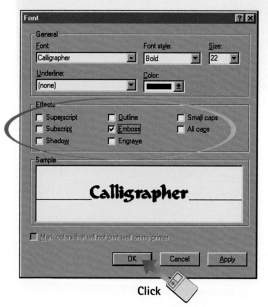

Click

4 Change the Text Frame Margins

If it seems the text is too close to the frame borders, or not close enough, you can change the frame margins. Select the frame; then choose **Format**, **Text Frame Properties**, and change the **Margins** settings. You can also break the text in a frame into **Columns**. Choose **OK**.

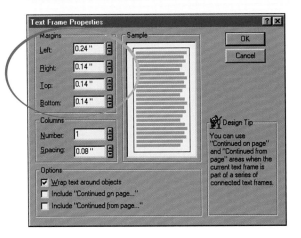

5 Change Paragraph Formatting

Select the paragraphs you want to change, and then choose **Format**, **Indents and Lists**. Set indentation under **Indents**. To change the spacing above and below paragraphs, click **Line Spacing**. Choose **OK** to close each dialog box.

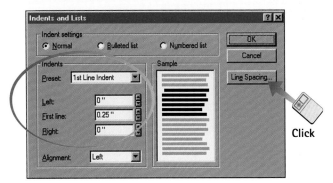

Click

6 Change Vertical Position

You can align the text vertically in a frame so that it hugs the top, sits on the bottom, or hangs in the center of the frame, no matter how big the frame is. Select the text frame; then choose **Format**, **Align Text Vertically**, and click an alignment command.

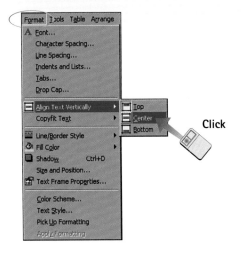

Click

How-To Hints

Look at All the Great Fonts!

Publisher gives you lots of fonts, but for a readable, professional publication you'll want to limit your fonts to perhaps three in a single publication. It's a better design approach to use very few fonts, but be creative with font sizes, bold, italic, and so forth within a font.

End

How to Insert and Navigate Through Pages

If you're creating a publication of any great length, you'll probably need to add pages. You can simply add new blank pages, or you can add pages that duplicate all the objects on an existing page. You can also insert new pages within a multipage document rather than adding them at the end.

When you have more than one page in a publication, you need to be able to navigate among the pages—and if you're creating a book-type publication, it's helpful to see the facing pages two at a time so you can get a view of what the opened book will look like.

Begin

1 Navigate Among Pages

To move from page to page in a publication, click the arrows next to the **Page** box at the bottom of the screen. The arrows jump to the First Page, Previous Page, Next Page, and Last Page in the publication (point to an arrow to see its ScreenTip). The number of the displayed page is shown in the **Page** box.

2 Add a New Page

To add a new page at the end of a publication, navigate to the last page, and then click the Next Page or the Last Page button. You'll be asked if you want to insert a new page; choose **OK**.

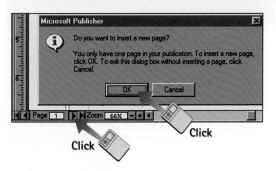

Click

Click

3 Add Duplicate Pages

If you want to use the same element on several pages, such as a title or a graphics object, create the page you want to duplicate. Then choose **Insert, Page**. In the Insert Page dialog box, type the **Number of new pages** you want to create, click the **Duplicate all objects on page** check box, and type the page number. Choose **OK**.

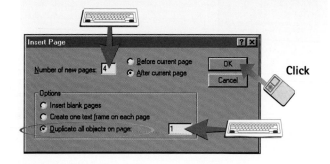

Click

4 Work in Duplicated Pages

The duplicated page(s) are added to the publication, and you can add individual objects to each one. Duplicating pages saves a lot of time.

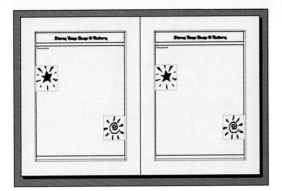

5 Switch Between Views

In a booklet or a four-page newsletter, you'll want to see what the facing pages look like. To switch between single-page and two-page views, choose **View**, **Two-Page Spread**. (If you're on the first or last page, you'll see only one page on your screen.)

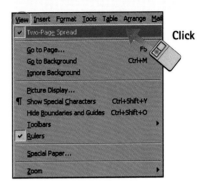

Click

6 Insert Pages in the Middle

If you want to insert pages somewhere within your publication rather than at the end, display the pages where you want to insert new pages, and then choose **Insert**, **Page**. In the Insert Page dialog box, specify the **Number of new pages**, click an option for where they should be inserted, and choose **OK**. (See Task 15 to learn how to insert page numbers.)

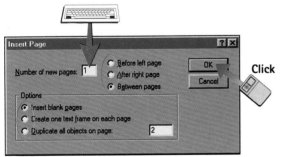

Click

How-To Hints

Delete Pages

To delete a page from a publication, navigate to the page, and then choose **Edit**, **Delete Page**. If you're in single-page view, the page is deleted. If you're in two-page view, you'll be asked whether you want to delete both pages, the left page, or the right page. Make your choice and choose **OK**.

End

How to Use Clip Art

Wizard-created publications always have good graphics, but you can make your own publications just as eye-catching with clip art. Publisher comes with countless clip art graphics on its CD, and if that's not enough for you, check out Task 6 in Chapter 7, "How to Use Internet Explorer 4," to learn how to find more clip art on the Internet.

For this task, we'll use the clip art on the Microsoft Office Small Business Edition CD. After you learn how to insert clip art in a picture frame, you can move it around on the page and resize it to fit in your layout.

Begin

1 Create a Picture Frame

Click the **Clip Gallery Tool**, and then drag to draw a frame on the page.

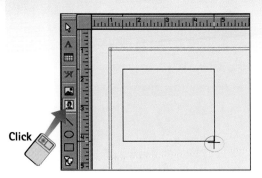

Click

2 Insert a Clip Art Graphic

Because you used the Clip Gallery Tool instead of the Picture Frame Tool, the Microsoft Clip Gallery 4.0 dialog box opens automatically. Select a category on the left, and then peruse the thumbnail sketches. Click a sketch you like, and then click **Insert**. (If you choose a graphic that's on the CD, you'll be asked to insert the CD.)

Click

3 Replace a Graphic

If you decide you want a different graphic, right-click the graphic and choose **Change Object**, **Microsoft Clip Gallery**, **Replace**. Select another graphic from the Gallery, and click **Insert**.

Right Click

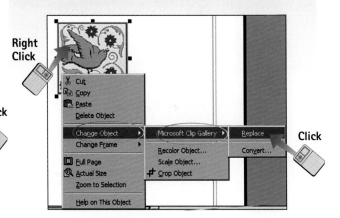

Click

4 Move a Picture

You can move a picture to wherever you want it on the page. Click the graphic to select it, and then point to a border (but not to a handle). When the pointer becomes a moving van symbol, drag the picture frame to a new location. Release the mouse button to drop it.

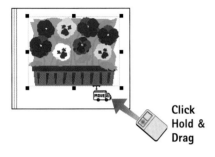

Click
Hold &
Drag

5 Resize a Picture

You can resize a graphic to fit within your text (or to fill space when you don't have enough text). Click the graphic to select it, and then point to a handle. When the pointer becomes a two-headed resize arrow, drag to change the size or shape of the picture.

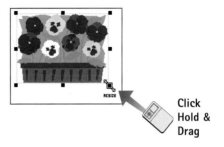

Click
Hold &
Drag

6 Crop a Picture

Sometimes you need only part of a graphic. By cropping a picture, you can cut off the parts you don't want. Click the graphic, and then click **Crop Picture** on the Picture toolbar (which appears when a graphic is selected). Point to a handle; when the pointer becomes a cropping symbol, drag to cut off what you don't want. Click **Crop Picture** again to turn it off.

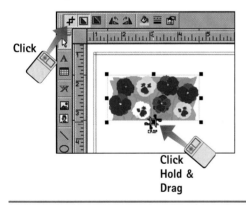

Click

Click
Hold &
Drag

End

How-To Hints

Resize the Picture

Unlike a text frame, dragging a corner handle in a picture frame resizes the frame proportionally. To reshape a picture, hold down Shift while you drag a corner handle.

Resize the Picture in Two Directions

To resize a picture in two opposite directions at once (for example, to resize the top and bottom equally at the same time), hold down Ctrl while you drag any handle.

Rotate a Frame

To rotate a frame, press Alt and point to a handle. When the pointer reads "Rotate," continue to press Alt and drag the handle to rotate the frame.

Oops! Undo a Resize

If you accidentally stretch a picture out of shape while resizing it, choose **Edit, Undo Resize** before you perform any more actions.

How to Wrap Text Around Clip Art

Pages that use graphics like islands in the middle of a lake of text are much more visually interesting than straight text. You can wrap text around either the rectangular picture frame or the picture within the frame.

One thing to keep in mind is the reader's comfort. If the eye has to jump over a graphic in the middle of a line, it's harder to read the text. It's a good idea to keep graphics on the side of a text block or between two columns so that the graphic doesn't break lines of text.

Begin

1 Set Up Your Text Frames

Create the text frames for the page, and enter the text.

2 Create a Picture Frame

Click the **Picture Frame Tool**, and then drag to draw a picture frame in the text. (You may need to resize the text frame after the picture frame is inserted—see Tasks 3 and 4 to learn how.)

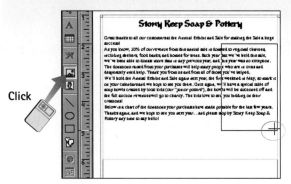

Click

3 Insert Clip Art

Right-click the picture frame, and then choose **Change Picture**, **Picture**, **Clip Art**. In the **Microsoft Clip Gallery 4.0** dialog box, click a picture, and then click **Insert**.

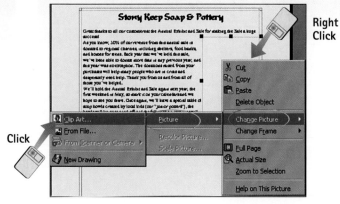

Right Click

Click

4 Drag the Frame into Position

Move the picture frame so that it's against the side of the text frame—you want your page to be easy to read as well as visually interesting.

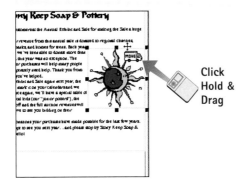

Click
Hold &
Drag

5 Wrap Text Around the Frame

By default, text wraps around the rectangular frame, but if you've previously wrapped the text around the picture, follow this procedure to wrap around the frame. Right-click the picture and choose **Change Frame**, **Object Frame Properties**. In the Object Frame Properties dialog box, click the **Entire frame** option, and choose **OK**.

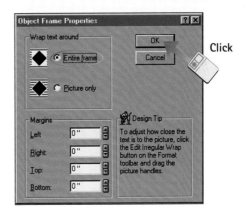

Click

6 Wrap Text Around the Picture

To wrap text around the picture, right-click the picture and choose **Change Frame**, **Object Frame Properties**. In the Object Frame Properties dialog box, click the **Picture only** option, and choose **OK**. You can make the text wrap closer to or farther from the frame or picture by changing the **Margins** settings.

End

How-To Hints

Use Toolbar Buttons

Whenever you have a picture frame selected, you can use toolbar buttons for **Wrap Text to Frame** and **Wrap Text to Picture** instead of the Object Frame Properties dialog box. Point at the buttons and read the ScreenTips to figure out which ones they are.

Hide Boundaries and Guides

To see what your page looks like without the boundaries, guidelines, and frame lines (in other words, for a print preview), choose **View, Hide Boundaries and Guides**. To show the lines again (because they make work easier), choose **View, Show Boundaries and Guides**.

How to Flow Text Between Text Frames

When text is too long to fit in the frame you created and there's no room on the page to enlarge the frame, you need to create another frame to hold the overflow. Flowing the same chunk of text into a second (or third) connected frame is more efficient than copying and pasting separate chunks of text into separate frames because you can change the shapes of the text frames and the text will flow between the frames to wherever it fits.

Begin

1 Check the Overflow Symbol

When there's too much text to fit within the frame, you'll see an overflow symbol on the lower-right border of the selected frame. The text is there, but it's hidden because there's not enough room to display it.

2 Create a New Text Frame

Create a new page if you need to (refer to Task 6), and then draw a new text frame (refer to Task 3). You can also divide a text block into separate frames by drawing another frame on the same page (the new text frame doesn't have to be on a different page).

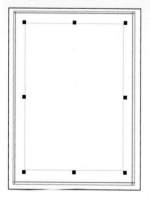

3 Show the Connect Frames Toolbar

Choose **Tools, Text Frame Connecting**. The Connect Frames toolbar appears, and will continue to appear whenever you select a text frame until you close it.

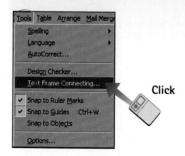

Click

4 Connect the Frames

Click the first text frame (the frame with the overflow text in it). On the Connect Frames toolbar, click the **Connect Text Frames** button. The mouse pointer becomes a mug symbol.

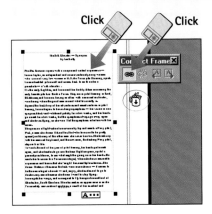

5 Flow the Text

Click in the new text frame; the overflow text flows into the new frame. To jump between connected frames, click the **Go to Previous Frame** button or the **Go to Next Frame** button (these buttons are on the Connect Frames toolbar and also on the text frames).

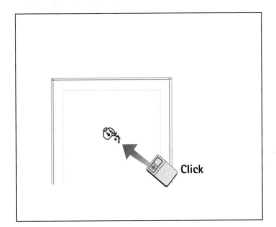

6 Continue to the Next Frame

If your text flows to a frame on another page, you can place automatic "continued on" instructions at the top and bottom of the connected frames. Right-click each of the connected frames, and choose **Change Frame, Text Frame Properties**. In the Text Frame Properties dialog box, under **Options**, click the **Include "Continued on page"** and **Include "Continued from page"** check boxes, and choose **OK**.

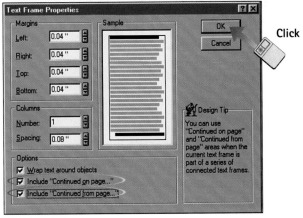

How-To Hints

Disconnect Text Frames

To disconnect text frames, select the frame the text flows from (not the frame it flows into). On the Connect Frames toolbar, click the **Disconnect Text Frames** button.

Where's the Continuation Page?

When you add "continued on page" directions, the page numbers will automatically be correct, but you may want to add page numbers to your pages so your readers can find the continuation. See Task 15 to learn how.

End

How to Recolor and Add a Drop Shadow to Frames

Any frame, whether text or picture, can be enlivened with colors, drop shadows, or border art. Lively frames are a good way to call the reader's attention to a particular item. Be judicious with border art, though—if you get carried away, your page will look too busy and will lose its impact.

Begin

1 Select the Frame

Begin by selecting the frame for which you want to create a border; this can be a text frame or a picture frame.

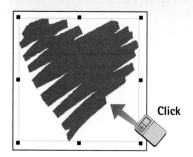

Click

2 Create a Plain Border

Right-click inside the frame, choose **Change Frame**, **Line/Border Style**, and click a black borderline.

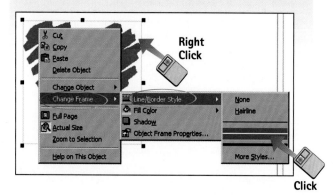

Right Click

Click

3 Create a Color Border

Right-click inside the frame, and choose **Change Frame**, **Line/Border Style**, **More Styles**. In the Border Style dialog box, click the **Color** drop-down list. You can also set a different line thickness under **Choose a thickness**. Then choose **OK**.

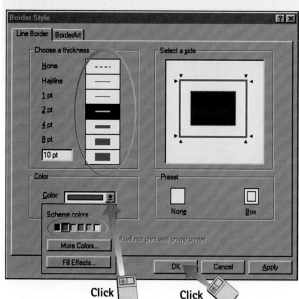

Click   Click

4 Choose from More Colors

In the Border Style dialog box, click the **Color** drop-down list, and click **More Colors**.

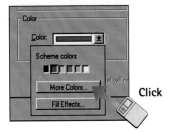

Click

5 Choose the Perfect Color

In the Colors dialog box, select a color from the palette, and choose **OK**. Choose **OK** again to close the Border Style dialog box.

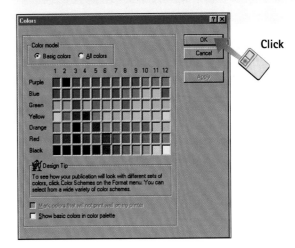

Click

6 Create a Shadow

To add a shadow to a selected frame, right-click inside the frame, and choose **Change Frame**, **Shadow**. A color-coordinated shadow is added to the frame. To remove the shadow, click **Change Frame**, **Shadow** again.

How-To Hints

More Borders

You can also add shadows and colorful borders to rectangles, ovals, and other drawn shapes. Use the techniques in this task to enliven the borders of any shape you draw; see Task 18 to learn about drawing shapes, and see Task 11 to learn how to add a colorful border around an entire page.

End

How to Add an Art Border to a Frame

You can frame any text or picture, or even a whole page, with a border that reflects the mood of the publication. In this task I'll show you how to frame a page, but border art can also be applied to text and picture frames.

Begin

1 Frame the Page

Click the **Rectangle** tool, and then drag to draw a rectangle around the entire page.

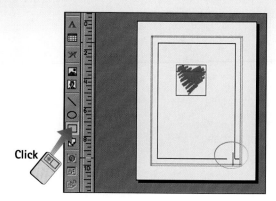

Click

2 Open the Border Style Dialog Box

Right-click the rectangle, and choose **Change Rectangle, Line/Border Style, More Styles.**

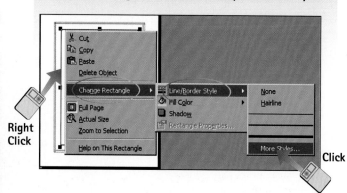

Right Click

Click

3 Find the BorderArt

In the Border Style dialog box, click the **BorderArt** tab.

Click

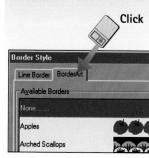

4 Select a Border

Scroll through the borders and find one you like. When you click a border, you'll see a sample in the **Preview** box.

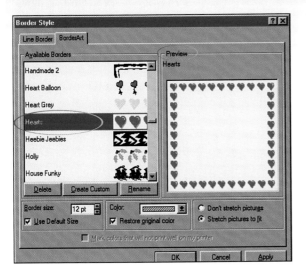

5 Change the Border Size

To make an art border thicker or thinner, change the number in the **Border size** box. To reset the border to its original size, click the **Use Default Size** check box. Choose **OK** to finish.

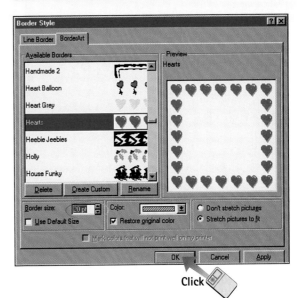

Click

6 Take a Look

Art borders can really enliven a page!

End

How-To Hints

Remove the Page Border

A page border is nothing more than a fancy rectangle. To remove it, click to select it and press Delete.

Add the Border to Every Page

You can draw and format the page-border rectangle once but have it appear on every page in your publication if you draw it in the *background*. To learn more about placing objects in the background so they'll appear on every page, see Task 15, where you learn how to place page numbers in the background.

12

How to Use Gradient Fills and Patterns

Add even more zest to the appearance of your publication by using splashes of color to illuminate your message. Publisher provides a way to fill objects with color and color patterns. Used judiciously—and with taste and common sense—this can make your publication extra special.

A pattern puts texture into a color and makes it busier; a gradient fill changes hue gradually within a frame, which adds an extra visual dimension. These are great for titles, but they also work behind text if the effect is kept subtle.

Begin

1 Create and Select the Frame

I'll demonstrate this task with text frames, but you can use these techniques to fill in behind clip art in picture frames, too.

2 Click the Fill Color Button

Whether you've selected a picture frame, a text frame, or a graphics object such as a rectangle, the Fill Color button will appear on the toolbar. Click the **Fill Color** button.

Click

3 Click Fill Effects

The Fill Color button drops a list of colors and buttons; click **Fill Effects**.

Click

4 Create a Pattern

In the Fill Effects dialog box, click the **Patterns** option; then click a pattern. If your printer is black and white, stick with the black-and-white patterns; but if you have a color printer, try changing the **Base color** and **Color 2** under **Colors**. Choose **Apply** to apply color experiments without closing the dialog box; choose **OK** to close the dialog box.

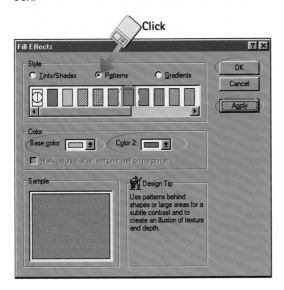

5 Create a Gradient Fill

In the Fill Effects dialog box, click the **Gradients** option. Try different **Base color** and **Color 2** pairs, and experiment with different gradients. Choose **Apply** to apply effects without closing the dialog box; choose **OK** to close the dialog box.

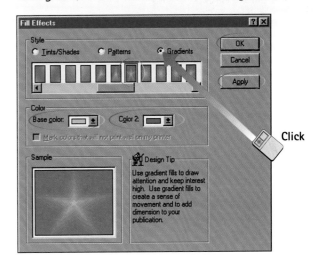

6 Add a Frame of Pure Color

To add pure color to a page, draw a frame (text, picture, or shape), and then fill it with a color gradient. This is a nice way to balance a page that has lots of empty space.

How-To Hints

Easy Does It

Be judicious with your colors if you want a readable, professional publication. Too many colors make it tough for any individual item to stand out (and if you're printing the publication commercially, they make it very expensive). See Task 27 to learn more about commercial printing.

End

13

How to Layer Pictures for Special Effects

Layering is the process of placing one object over another so that there's some overlap. For both objects to be seen, you don't want to cover either object completely; instead, you want to overlap them in such a way as to create an interesting effect. You can layer graphics on graphics, or text on graphics (for example, you can place text in a colorful oval, or on top of a clip art item).

Begin

1 Create Both Frames

To layer items, create them in separate frames on the same page.

2 Layer Items

Use the Move pointer to move items into layered positions by dragging items on top of one another (see Task 3 or 7 to learn how).

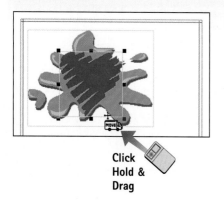

Click Hold & Drag

3 Move an Item in Front or Behind

If an item is on top and it should be underneath, click the **Send to Back** button on the Standard toolbar; to bring an item to the top of the stack, click the **Bring to Front** button.

4 Change the Order of Items

You can layer several items, but you'll probably end up needing to rearrange them more precisely than "on top" or "on the bottom." To move a layered item through a stack one layer at a time, click the item, and then choose **Arrange**, **Bring Forward** or **Arrange**, **Send Backward**.

Click

5 Place Text on a Picture

Text on a picture is a great way to highlight the text. Create the picture; then draw a text frame on top of the picture and enter your text (or create the two frames separately and drag the text frame onto the picture frame). (Refer to Tasks 3 and 4 to learn about text frames.)

6 Hide the Text Background

A text frame usually looks odd on top of a picture unless you make the background transparent. As a shortcut to a transparent background, click the text frame, and press Ctrl+T. (You can also click the **Fill Color** button on the Formatting toolbar, and click **No Fill**.)

End

How-To Hints

It Looks Like There's Still a Border

If you make a layered frame's background transparent with no border, but it looks like there's still a border, you're looking at a boundary, not a border. To see what will print, choose **View**, **Hide Boundaries and Guides** to make the boundary disappear.

How to Group and Ungroup Objects

When you create several separate objects on a page, you may want them to retain their positions relative to one another; for example, you may have layered objects, as in Task 13, or you might want to keep a title firmly attached to its following body text. You can group items so that they can be selected, moved, or copied only as a group, which saves a lot of time because none of the items are ever accidentally shifted out of position.

Begin

1 Create and Position the Frames

Position the text and picture frames the way you want to keep them.

2 Select Objects One at a Time

To select the objects one at a time, click one, and then hold down Shift while you click the remaining objects. You may need to use this technique if there are objects nearby that you don't want to include in the group.

3 Select All the Objects at Once

The fast way to select objects is to lasso them with a big selection rectangle. Be sure the **Pointer** tool is clicked; then drag to draw a big rectangle that completely surrounds all the objects. Only objects that are completely surrounded get included in the group.

Click

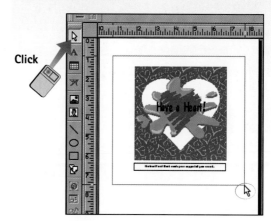

4 Group the Objects

After you select multiple objects, a **Group Objects** button appears in the lower-right corner of the group. Click it to group the objects (when you click it, the puzzle pieces fit together and it becomes an **Ungroup Objects** button).

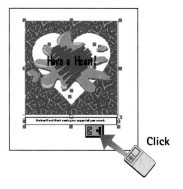

Click

5 Manipulate Objects as a Group

The objects no longer function separately. If you apply formatting, it's applied to all the objects in the group. If you resize the group, all the objects are resized relative to one another. And if you move or copy the group, you get the whole group.

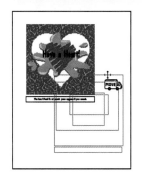

6 Ungroup Objects

If you need to make a change to one of the objects in the group (to change a border or a fill color, perhaps), you'll need to ungroup the objects before you can select and change the one object. Click the group to select it, and then click the **Ungroup Objects** button.

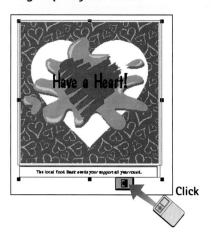

Click

End

How-To Hints

Is This Important?

If you're new to the art of laying out publications, the idea of grouping objects may not seem important yet; but the first time you create your own masthead or logo from multiple text and picture frames, and then need to move it to make room for another element on the page, you'll understand how convenient grouped objects are. Also, if you create a great layered object and then decide to rotate the finished picture, grouping the objects is the only way to keep the picture intact when you rotate it. (Refer to the How-To Hints in Task 7 to learn how to rotate an object.)

How to Insert Automatic Page Numbers and Dates

Publications such as newsletters need dates, and multipage publications such as booklets usually need page numbers. Publisher can keep track of the dates and page numbers for you so they're always current and correct.

The most efficient way to add automatic page numbers is to add them to the page background. The background is identical for every page in the publication, so you can create a page number frame once, in the background, and be done with it. You can add a date frame to the background if you want it on every page, or just create a text frame on the first page and insert an automatic date in it.

Begin

1 Switch to the Background

The page numbers appear on every page, so create them in the page background. Choose **View, Go to Background**. All the objects that might have been on your page disappear because only those objects that appear on every page are visible in the Background. (A small black-and-red symbol on the Status bar indicates Background view.)

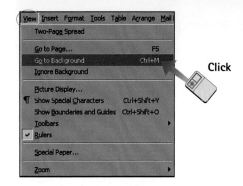

Click

2 Draw the Text Frame

Draw a text frame where you want the page number to appear (refer to Task 3 to learn how to create a text frame). Enter any text you want to appear with the number, such as "Page" or "p.", and enter a space after the text.

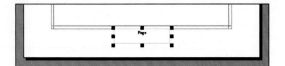

3 Insert the Page Number

Choose **Insert, Page Numbers**. If you want to format the text, do that while you're in the Background. Align the text in the center (click **Center** on the Formatting toolbar) to better fit the text frame. A **#** symbol is the page number placeholder.

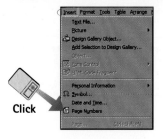

Click

4 Switch to the Foreground

Choose **View**, **Go to Foreground** to switch back to the Foreground. Each page in your publication has its own page number. When you add text and picture frames in the foreground, they don't make room for the background objects, so leave the page numbers uncovered and visible.

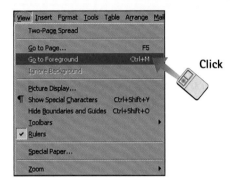

Click

5 Create a Date Text Frame

In the Foreground (perhaps on the first page), create a text frame, and then choose **Insert**, **Date and Time**.

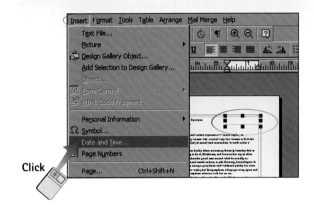

Click

6 Insert an Automatic Date

In the Date and Time dialog box, click a date or time format. Click the **Update automatically** option to ensure that the date is always current; click the **Insert as plain text** option to insert the current date without automatic updating. Then choose **OK**.

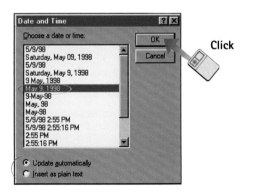

Click

End

How-To Hints

Don't Number the First Page

Most professional publications don't put a page number on page 1 (because it's pretty obvious from the masthead that it's the first page). To start page numbers on a different page (such as 2), choose **Tools**, **Options**. On the **General** tab, in the **Start publication with page** box, type the page number where you want to begin numbering, and choose **OK**.

Hide Other Page Numbers

If you want to hide another page number in the publication (for example, if you have a text frame that needs to stretch down over the page number and you don't want the page number showing through the text), draw an empty text frame over the page number you want to hide.

How to Use the Design Gallery to Add Flair to Your Publication

Publisher has a Design Gallery of ready-made objects such as reply forms, pull quotes, and coupons that you can insert into your publication. The Design Gallery objects are already formatted with fonts, colors, and borders that save you the time of formatting (although if an object isn't quite right, you can change the formatting yourself after you insert it into your publication).

Begin

1 Click Where You Want the Object

In your publication, click where you want to insert the object. (You can move the object after it's inserted if you want.)

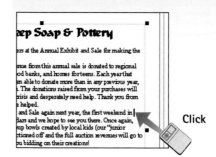

Click

2 Open the Design Gallery

Click the **Design Gallery Object** button. The Design Gallery dialog box opens.

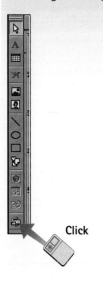

Click

3 Choose an Object by Category

Objects on the **Objects by Category** tab are sorted by category. If you're looking for a specific object, such as a picture frame with a caption, you can look through all the picture captions in one place. In this task, I'm using the **Objects by Category** tab to find a picture caption.

Click

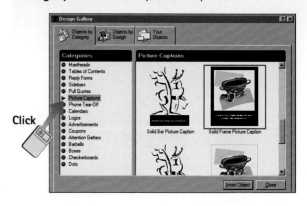

4 Choose an Object by Design Set

Objects on the **Objects by Design** tab are sorted by design set. They're the same objects as on the **Objects by Category** tab, but they're sorted into color-and-design sets so you can easily find different objects for a publication that share a coordinated design theme.

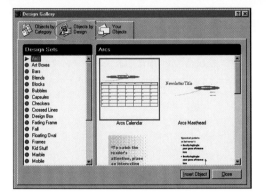

5 Find and Insert an Object

Click the object you want, and then click **Insert Object**. The object is inserted and the Design Gallery closes.

6 Change and Format an Object

To change the default text in the object (such as the picture caption here), click it and type new text. To change a picture, color, border, or other detail in the object, use normal formatting techniques: Right-click the object you want to change, and use commands on the shortcut menu. To learn about the Wizard button at the bottom of the object, see Task 17.

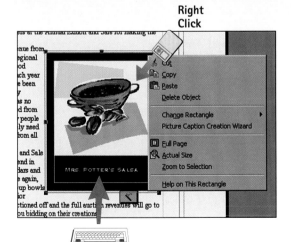

How-To Hints

Format the Objects

To learn about changing font or text frames, see Tasks 3, 4, and 5. To learn about changing and layering pictures, see Tasks 7 and 13. To learn about grouping objects, see Task 14. To learn about formatting borders and fill colors, see Tasks 10, 11, and 12.

Explore the Objects

Individual object types behave in unique and efficient ways, so it's worth your while to explore each one you use. For example, in a phone tear-off, you select the text in one tear-off and type your own information; after you click away from the object, all the tear-offs are updated with your entry. If you resize a phone tear-off sideways, more tear-offs are added.

End

How to Use the Page Wizard for Special Elements

When you insert a Design Gallery object into your publication, you may find that the selected object has a **Wizard** button at the bottom; all objects that offer more than one design have a wizard. The object's wizard enables you to change the object's design after it's inserted, so you can see how different designs look in your publication. It's a lot faster than deleting the object and inserting a different one, but the results are the same.

Begin

1 Insert a Design Gallery Object

Click the **Design Gallery Object** button. In the Design Gallery, click the object you want, and then click **Insert Object** (for this task, insert an object that has several designs, such as an **Attention Getter**). The object is inserted and the Design Gallery closes.

Click

Click

2 Click the Object's Wizard Button

Click the object to select it (if it's not already selected), and then click the **Wizard** button at the bottom of the object.

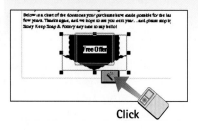

Click

3 The Wizard List Appears

An object's wizard is a list of all the different Design Gallery possibilities for that object type.

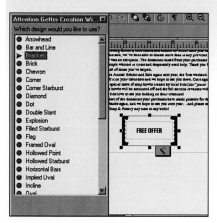

4 Try a Different Design

Click different items in the wizard list to test different design choices. If you need to move the wizard out of the way, drag it by its title bar. If you need to see the object from a different magnification, change the **Zoom** setting at the bottom of the publication window.

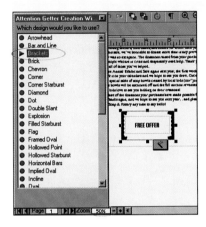

5 Move and Resize the Object

You can move the object, reshape it, or resize it while the wizard is open.

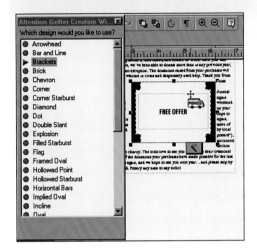

6 Close the Wizard

When you like what you see, click away from the object to close the wizard. If you want to change the object again later, click it and repeat the previous steps. To change the text in the object, you don't need the wizard; click the placeholder text to select it, and then type new text.

End

How-To Hints

Redesign the Object

If you want to change the design of the object, you can ungroup the individual objects that make up the main object by choosing **Arrange, Ungroup Objects**. You'll be warned, however, that this makes the wizard non-functional for that particular object; the object becomes a collection of text frames and graphics shapes that you can redesign as you please without the wizard.

How to Use Shapes

Shapes are the basic building blocks of any graphic design. All logos and graphics elements are made up of lines, rectangles, and ovals. Even custom shapes are combinations of these elements, but they're pre-drawn for you to save time.

Wherever you want to add a simple shape or a splash of color, you can draw and format one of Publisher's shapes. You can also place text on a colored shape by layering a transparent text frame on top of a drawn shape (refer to Task 13 to learn how).

Begin

1 Click a Shape

Click one of the Shape Tools. The pointer becomes a crosshair symbol. If you click the **Custom Shapes** tool (shown here), click a shape on the shortcut menu.

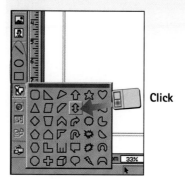

Click

2 Drag to Draw the Shape

On the page, drag to draw the shape you want.

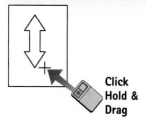

Click
Hold &
Drag

3 Change the Shape

When you release the mouse button, the shape is selected and has handles around its perimeter. Change the shape by dragging different handles. To move the shape, point to the border (but not to a handle); when the pointer becomes a moving van, drag the shape to a new location.

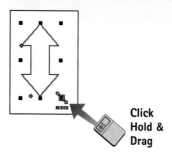

Click
Hold &
Drag

4 Draw Perfect Shapes

When you draw a shape, you can draw perfect circles, squares, 45-degree lines, and default custom shapes by holding down Shift while you draw. To center a shape perfectly, hold down Ctrl, and begin to draw from the centerpoint.

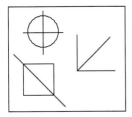

5 Change the Colors

Click the shape to select it, and click the **Fill Color** button on the Formatting toolbar. Choose from the default publication color scheme, or click **More Color Schemes**, **More Colors**, or **Fill Effects** to create more interesting colors. To change the border, click the **Line/Border Style** button, and choose a different thickness or **More Styles**. (Refer to Task 12 to learn more about colors.)

Click

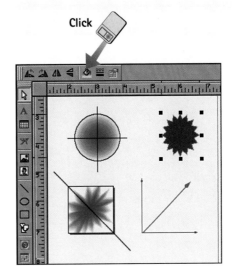

6 Create a Custom Shadow

To create a custom shadow for an object, create duplicate objects and layer them. Create one object, select it, and hold down Ctrl. Move the object slightly, and release Ctrl after you release the mouse button. A copy is created on top of the original. Change the color of the object behind to create a custom shadow effect.

How-To Hints

Delete a Shape

To delete a shape, click to select the shape, and then press Delete. To delete a group of shapes, drag to draw a selection rectangle that surrounds the entire group, and press Delete.

End

How to Get Clip Art Online

Your Publisher CD contains a lot of clip art, but if you can't find exactly the right one, you can find more on the Internet. Microsoft provides an easy-to-access site for more clip art, from which clips are added to your ClipArt Gallery. But if you don't want to go through the hassle of telling Microsoft all about yourself and remembering a password, you can also conduct your own Internet searches for non-Microsoft clip art (see Task 6 in Chapter 7 to learn how).

Begin

1 Open the ClipArt Gallery

Use any method you like to open the ClipArt Gallery; a quick way is to click the **Clip Gallery** tool and then draw a frame on a publication page. The Microsoft Clip Gallery 4.0 dialog box appears.

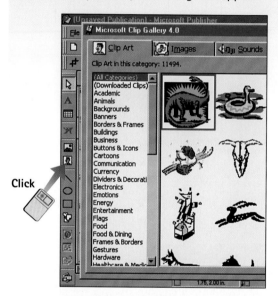

Click

2 Choose Clips from the Web

In the Microsoft Clip Gallery 4.0 dialog box, click **Clips from Web**. You'll see an informational message in which you must choose **OK** to proceed.

Click

3 Microsoft's Web Site Opens

Your browser is launched and jumps to the Microsoft Web site. Before you can go any farther, read the license agreement and click **Accept**.

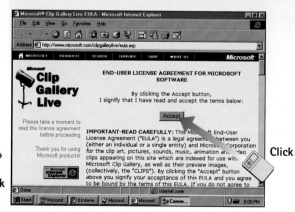

Click

4 Browse the Clip Gallery Page

Choose a category from the **Browse clips by category** list to look through general categories of clip art files.

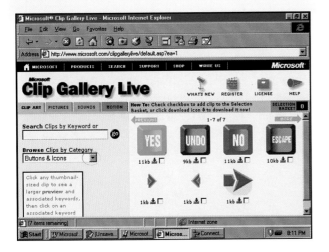

5 Browse by Keyword

Type a keyword in the **Search clips by keyword** box, and then click **Go** to find specific clip art files. Click a file you like to download it—you'll have to fill out a lot of online paperwork, though, so Microsoft can keep track of you before you can download. It might be easier to find clip art elsewhere.

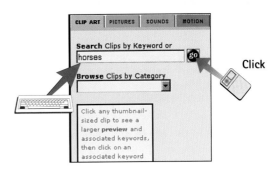

Click

6 Search Elsewhere

On the browser toolbar, click the **Search** button to open the Search bar and search the rest of the Internet. Different search engines are available in the Search bar; for example, in the Lycos search engine, type a search word such as "clip art" and click **Go Get It**. See Task 6 in Chapter 7 to learn more about searching the Web for graphics.

Click

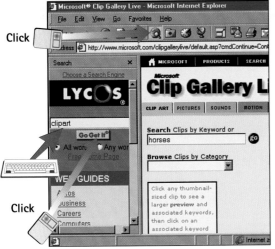

Click

How-To Hints

More Sources

You can buy clip art on CDs these days and store hundreds of very big files on a CD-ROM instead of on your hard drive. Check out catalogs targeted at computer graphics and desktop publishing; after you give your mailing address to one of these companies, you'll find several catalogs arriving in your mailbox—and you'll have lots of clip art collections to choose from.

End

How to Create a Custom Design Set

A design set is a set of coordinated publications—such as business cards, brochures, and letterheads—that have the same look, logos, and color scheme. The result is a synchronized look to an entire set of publications.

You can start with one publication in a design set and customize it so that no one else is likely to have the same design. All the other publications in that design set are synchronized with the changes you make in that one publication.

Begin

1 Open a Publication in a Design Set

To start with an existing Design Gallery publication, choose **File, New**. On the **Publications by Design** tab, select a publication similar to what you want. Click **Start Wizard**, and then click **Finish** to create a default publication. (When asked if you want to skip past the wizard's questions, click **Yes**.)

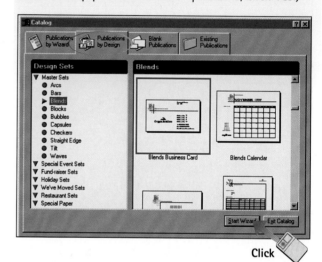

Click

2 Customize the Information

Enter your personal and company information in the appropriate text frames. Every time you change this information, all your new wizard-created publications will be synchronized to use the new information.

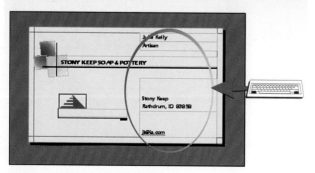

3 Change the Logo

Try changing the color and border on the logo to customize it (see Tasks 11 and 12 to learn how). All your wizard-created publications will be synchronized to use the changed logo. See Task 22 to learn more about logos.

Click

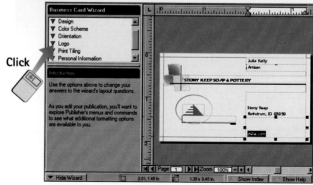

4 Save the Color Scheme

Choose **Format**, **Color Scheme**. In the Color Schemes dialog box, select the color scheme you want for all your publications, or create your own custom color scheme on the **Custom** tab. On the **Standard** tab, if you click the **Include scheme in Personal Information** check box, every new wizard-created publication will use this color scheme. Choose **OK** to close the dialog box.

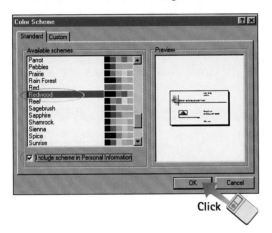

5 Save the Publication

Choose **File**, **Save**. In the Save dialog box, navigate to a folder where you want to save the publication, type a filename, and choose **Save**. After you save the publication, all new publications in the design set are synchronized to reflect your changes.

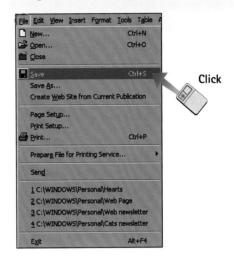

6 Check the Synchronization

Choose **File**, **New** and use the wizard to create a different publication; the changes you made earlier are part of the wizard's default repertoire.

End

How to Use Smart Objects

A Smart Object is any object in a publication that has a wizard of its own to help you change it. Smart Objects include objects such as logos, coupons, advertisements, and calendars.

You'll find Smart Objects in wizard-created publications when you choose **File**, **New** to start a publication, but you can also save time by inserting Smart Objects in your own publications. You'll find them among the Design Gallery Objects.

Begin

1 Insert a Design Gallery Object

Click the **Design Gallery Object** button, and double-click an object to insert it into your publication (see Task 16 to learn about using the Design Gallery).

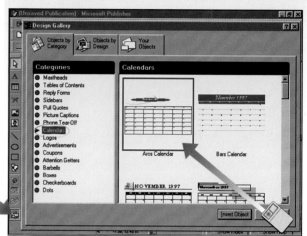

Click

Double Click

2 Create a Calendar

To make a full-page calendar, insert a Design Gallery Calendar. Resize the calendar to fit the page, and then click the Wizard button. To create the proper dates for the month you want, click **Dates**, and then click **Change Dates**. In the Change Calendar Dates dialog box, select the month and year you want and choose **OK**.

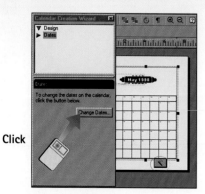

Click

3 Experiment with a Coupon

To include a coupon in a flyer or newsletter, insert a Design Gallery Coupon. Use the wizard to change borders, add more text or graphics frames, or switch to another Design Gallery coupon.

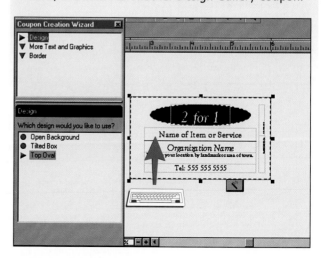

4 Try an Advertisement

To create an advertisement, insert a Design Gallery Advertisement. The wizard makes it easy to switch designs, even after you enter your advertisement text.

5 Check Out the Repeating Graphics

If you need a space filler on a page, the repeating graphics in the **Barbells**, **Boxes**, **Checkerboards**, and **Dots** categories make it easy. No wizard is involved, but if you resize the graphics, the number of repeating shapes changes to fill the space; if you change the color of one of the repeating graphics and then click away from the object, all the objects change color.

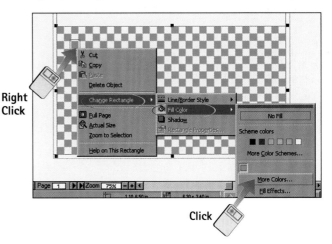

6 Ungroup a Smart Object

To ungroup the individual objects in a Smart Object, select the Smart Object, and choose **Arrange**, **Ungroup Objects**. You can move, resize, and format the objects individually and group them again, but you cannot revive the wizard. To use the wizard again, delete the group of objects and insert another Smart Object.

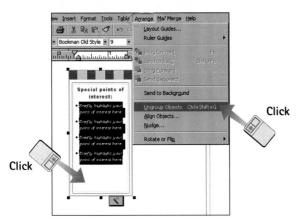

How-To Hints

Change the Page Orientation

If you need to change the page orientation to create a calendar that's wide rather than tall, choose **File**, **Page Setup**. Under **Choose an Orientation**, click **Landscape** or **Portrait**, and then choose **OK**.

End

How to Customize a Logo

Creating a custom logo to identify your business is easier when you don't have to start from scratch. With Publisher, you can start with Design Gallery logos for inspiration, and simply change one to customize it and make it your own.

Begin

1 Choose a Design Gallery Logo

Open a publication in which you want to use the logo. Click the **Design Gallery Object** button. In the Design Gallery, on the **Objects by Category** tab, click the **Logos** category. Double-click a logo that looks like a good starting point for your new custom logo. The logo is inserted on the new page.

Click

Double Click

2 Replace the Text

Click the text frame in the logo, and type your text in place of the placeholder text.

3 Replace the Picture

Double-click the logo's picture frame, and choose a new clip art picture to replace the placeholder picture.

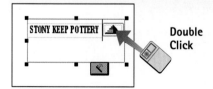

Double Click

4 Select a Different Design

To change the design, even after you've changed text and the picture, click the **Wizard** button. In the Wizard, click **Design**, and click different designs to see each effect.

Click

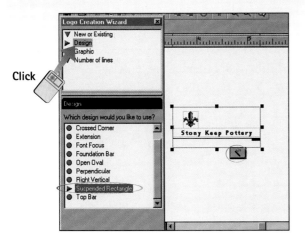

5 Make More Detailed Changes

To make more detailed changes, ungroup the logo and stop using the wizard. With the logo selected, choose **Arrange**, **Ungroup Objects**. With the logo objects ungrouped, you can add objects, change their shapes and sizes, and add your own drawn objects; but you won't be able to return to using the wizard for this particular logo.

6 Finish and Save Your Publication

Finish your publication, and choose **File**, **Save** to save it.

Click

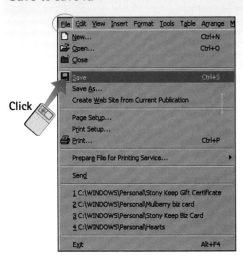

End

How-To Hints

Keep It Simple

A logo is a pretty important graphic identifier for your business, so it's worth putting a lot of serious thought into what you want before you start using one. Look at other folks' business cards and get a feel for what works; go to the library and spend time poring through graphic design books. Get a pencil and a lot of paper, and play with designs until you come up with one that's unique and comfortable for you. Then open Publisher and create your logo.

How to Create Pull Quotes and Masteads

Pull quotes are commonly used in newsletters and books to call attention to a particular sentence or phrase in the body text, usually a sentence that encapsulates an important idea concisely. Mastheads are the front-page titles of newsletters that usually identify the newsletter with a unique title, a graphic, and a date.

Both pull quotes and mastheads can take considerable time to create and format yourself, but Publisher provides several ready made pull-quote and masthead objects that you can insert into your own publications. You can use them as is or use their wizards to customize them.

Begin

1 Open the Design Gallery

Open your publication and click where you want the object. Then click the **Design Gallery Object** button.

Click

2 Choose a Category

Choose the **Pull Quotes** or the **Mastheads** category, depending on which object you want.

3 Select and Insert the Object

Find a pull quote or masthead that you like, and double-click it to insert it in the publication. You can reposition it precisely after you've inserted it.

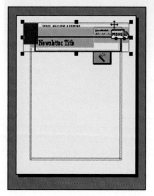

4 Fill In the Masthead

In a masthead, replace placeholder text by selecting it and typing your own text. To fill in the current date, click the date text frame, choose **Insert**, **Date and Time**, and double-click a date format. After the text is in place, you can click the **Wizard** button and try different designs. Change border, frame, and text colors using the buttons on the Formatting toolbar.

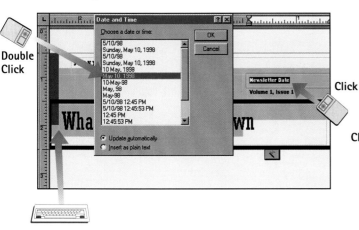

Double Click

Click

Click

5 Fill In a Pull Quote

A pull quote usually "pulls a quote" out of the surrounding text. The easiest way is to find a quote you want in the body text, select it, and choose **Edit**, **Copy**. Then click the pull-quote text to select it, and choose **Edit**, **Paste**. Click the **Wizard** button to try different pull quotes styles, and resize the pull quote if it will look better.

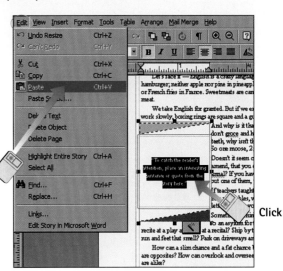

Click

Click

6 Save and Reuse Your Publication

To save your publication, choose **File**, **Save**. After you've saved it, you'll find it if you choose **File**, **Open**, and click the **Existing Publications** tab.

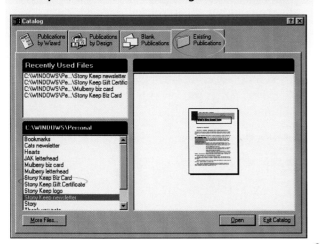

End

How-To Hints

Publisher's Saving Grace

A publication is built from lots of parts and pieces that are painstakingly assembled into the perfect positions; to help you keep all your work, Publisher prompts you to save often. The Save prompt appears by default every 10 minutes; if that's too often for you, or not often enough, you can change the number of minutes. Choose **Tools**, **Options**, and on the **Editing and User Assistance** tab, change the number in the **Minutes between reminders** box. To stop the prompts completely, clear the **Remind to save publication** check box.

How to Save a Publication as a Web Page

If you've spent time creating a brochure or a newsletter for print, there's no need to re-create it as a Web page from scratch; you can convert it from a printed publication to a Web page. Only Publisher-designed newsletters and brochures can be converted to Web pages using this technique.

Begin

1 Create a Newsletter or Brochure

Choose **File, New**. In the Catalog dialog box, on the **Publications by Wizard** tab, click a newsletter or brochure and then click **Start Wizard**.

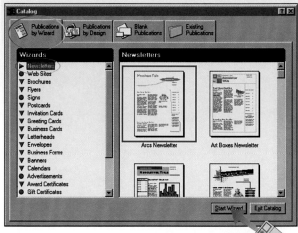

Click

2 Finish the Newsletter or Brochure

Use the wizard to complete your newsletter or brochure.

3 Open the Publication Wizard

If the wizard isn't displayed when you finish the publication (or if you're using a previously created newsletter or brochure), click the **Show Wizard** button in the lower-left corner of the Publisher window.

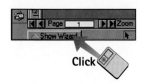

Click

4 Choose the Converter

Scroll to the bottom of the wizard list, and click **Convert to Web Site**. Below the wizard list, click the **Create** button.

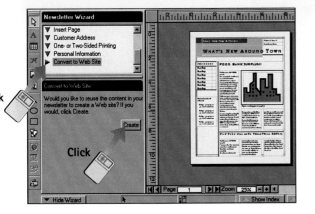

Click

Click

5 Start the Converter

In the Convert To Web Site dialog box that appears, leave the **Use the Web Site Wizard** option selected, and choose **OK**. When asked if you want to save changes, click **Yes** and save the file.

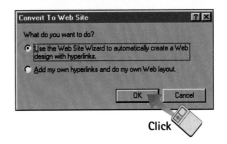

Click

6 The File Is Converted

Your file is converted to a Web page file. If you are set up to post on a Web site, this is the file you'll post (talk to your local Webmaster to learn more). You can edit this Web page file just as you would any Publisher page.

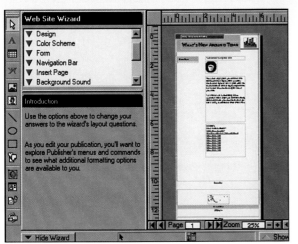

How-To Hints

Create a Web Site from Scratch

You don't have to convert a print publication; on the **Publications by Wizard** tab, click the **Web Sites** category and select a Web site template. Then use the wizard to create your Web page.

End

How to Convert a Publisher Web Page to a Print Publication

If you've created a Web page in Publisher, you can convert it to a printable publication in much the same way that you convert a Publisher newsletter or brochure to a Web page.

Begin

1 Open the Web Page

Choose **File**, **Open** and locate the Web page file on the **Existing Publications** tab in the Catalog. Click the filename and choose **Open**. If you need to navigate through other folders to find your file, click the **More Files** button and locate the file with the Open Publication dialog box; then click the filename and choose **Open**.

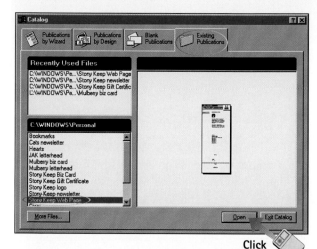

Click

2 Show the Wizard

If the wizard isn't open, click the **Show Wizard** button in the lower-left corner of the Publisher window.

Click

3 Choose the Converter

Scroll to the bottom of the wizard list and click **Convert to Print**.

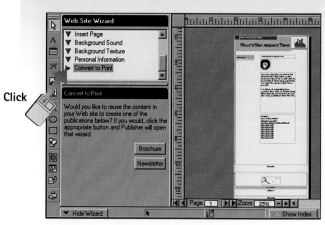

Click

4 Start the Converter

Below the wizard list, click either the **Brochure** or the **Newsletter** button (for this task, I'll convert the Web page to a brochure). When asked if you want to save changes, click **Yes**. Any changes to the file are saved, and the converter goes to work.

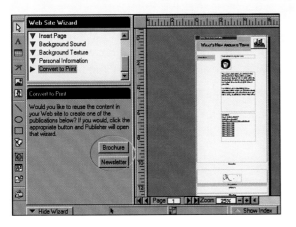

5 Look at the Result

The finished brochure is displayed. You can use the Brochure Wizard to make changes.

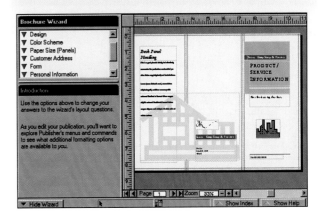

6 Make More Changes

You don't have to use the wizard to make changes; you can change individual text and picture frames with the Formatting tools (refer to Tasks 5, 7, 10, 12, and 13 to learn how).

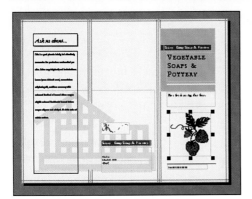

End

How to Use Side-by-Side Help and Tippages

Help in Publisher 98 comes in Tippages and side-by-side help windows.

Tippages appear when Publisher thinks you might want a tip, and disappear when you click somewhere. Help files you look up appear in side-by-side windows at the right side of your screen. You can show and hide them easily, but the files are unpredictable. Often the index is the most direct way to find the help you need.

Begin

1 Tippages Arrive Unannounced

A Tippage looks like this. It appears unannounced and unsolicited while you're working. After you read it, click anywhere and it disappears.

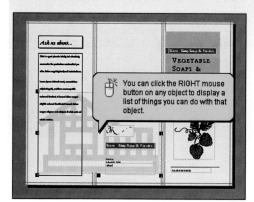

2 Turn Tippages On or Off

To turn Tippages on or off, choose **Tools, Options**. On the **Editing and User Assistance** tab, clear the **Show tippages** check box to turn them off (mark the check box to turn them on again). To reset the Tippages tips, click **Reset Tips**, and choose **OK**.

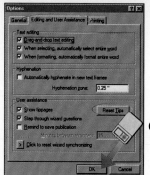

Click

3 Get Help on Your Current Project

Click the **Show Help** button in the lower-right corner of the Publisher window. In the help window that appears, click the **Contents** button to see a list of topics that apply to your current project. The **Show Help** button becomes a **Hide Help** button when help is open; click it to hide the help window.

Click

4 Narrow the Help Topic

Click a general topic to see more specific topics. If a **More Info** tab appears, click it to get more specific help. To step to previous help files, click the left-pointing arrow next to the **Contents** button.

5 Try a Demo

If you see a "View a demo" topic, click it for a multistep demonstration of a concept. Click the arrows in the demo window to step through the demonstration. Click **Done** to quit the demo.

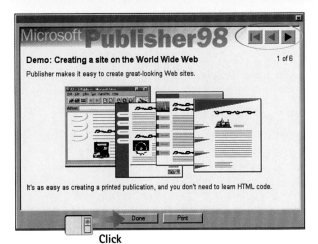

Click

6 Look Up a Topic in the Index

Click the **Show Index** button to show the index. When you **Type a keyword**, the index list scrolls to the alphabetical location of the word. Click an index topic; then click potentially helpful files that appear in the help window. The **Show Index** button becomes a **Hide Index** button when the index is open; click it to hide the index window.

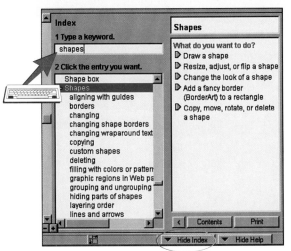

How-To Hints

More Help

Publisher is capable of very intensive desktop publishing activities—more than I can present in this particular book; as usual, the help files that come with the program are often sadly lacking in useful help. If you want to learn more about using Publisher, check out the book *How to Use Microsoft Publisher 98* (0-7897-1-6666).

End

How to Set Up a Publication for Outside Printing

If you want professional printing quality for your publication, you'll want to take your work to a professional printer.

First, locate a professional printer to discuss the project. Tell them what you want, and find out what they need from you. Print Publisher's Printing Service Checklist and use it to guide your conversation with your printer.

After you talk to your printer, have Publisher check your publication for potential layout errors. Print the color separations that you'll take to the printer.

Begin

1 Look Up Printing Help

Click the **Show Index** button in the lower-right corner of your screen. In the index **Type a keyword** box, type `printing service checklist`. The next window appears before you finish typing.

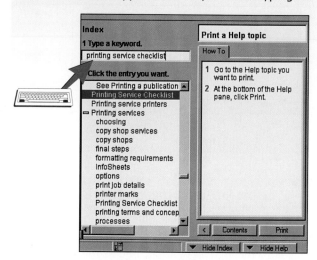

2 Print a Useful Checklist

In the help window that appears, read the information, and then click the button for **Click here to print a copy of the Printing Service Checklist**. (Be sure your printer is turned on.) Read the other printing help files while you have them open. Click **Done** when you finish reading.

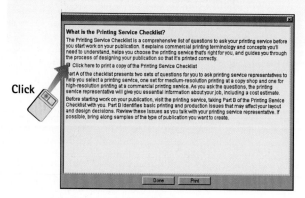

Click

3 Check for Design Errors

Choose **Tools, Design Checker**. Click **Options** to see what the design checker looks for, and then choose **OK** twice to start the Design Checker. If the Design Checker finds any problems, use the buttons in the Design Checker dialog box to **Ignore** the problem or to **Close** the Design Checker and correct the problem. Run the Design Checker again until it tells you it's complete.

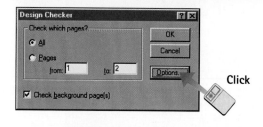

Click

4 Set Up a Color Publication

If you're printing with one or two colors (called spot colors) in addition to black and gray, your printer will want a separate page for each color (called color separations). Choose **File**, **Prepare File for Printing Service**, **Set Up Publication**.

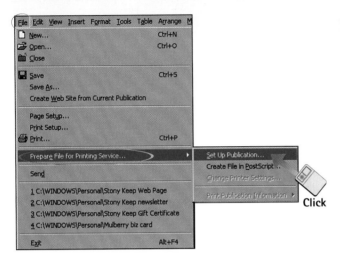

Click

5 Set Up Color Separation Proofs

In the Set Up Publication dialog box, click an option for your colors. For one or two colors, click the **Spot color(s)** option, and select the colors you want under **Select spot color(s)**. Then click **Next**. Accept the default choices in the next few steps, and click **Next** and **Done** to finish the setup.

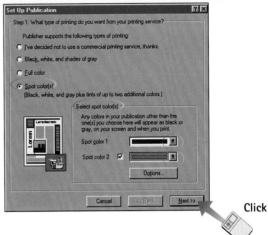

Click

6 Print Color Separation Proofs

Click each object you want colored, and then select a color from the **Fill Color** button on the Formatting toolbar. After applying your spot colors, choose **File**, **Print Proof**. In the Print Proof dialog box, click the **Print Color Separations** check box, and choose **OK**. Separate pages are printed for each color. Take them all to your printer.

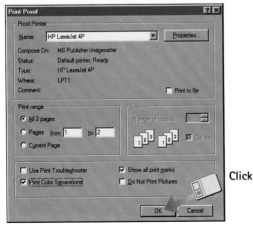

Click

How-To Hints

Print Overrun?

If your printer has the standard 2MB of memory, it won't be able to print color gradients, WordArt, or complex graphics. You can reduce your printer's resolution to a lower dpi (dots per inch), which won't look as good, or you can buy more memory for the printer.

Learn More About Printing

Printing is a deeply detailed business, with its own technology and terminology. To learn more about printing, spend time talking to your printer, and get a good book about the art and business of printing (your printer may be able to recommend one).

End

How to Write and Edit Long Text Files with the Word Story Editor

You can edit your text in a Publisher text frame the same way as you would in Word, but it can get time-consuming to chase text around through multiple text frames on different pages. The answer is to use the Word Story Editor, which opens a Word window in which you can edit your story easily. When you're done, you save the text in the Story Editor and close it.

Begin

1 Select the Text Frame

Click to select the text frame you want to edit.

Click

2 Choose the Story Editor

Choose **Edit, Edit Story in Microsoft Word.**

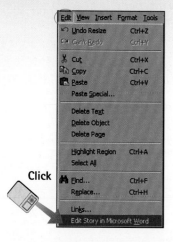

Click

3 The Word Window Opens

A Word window opens with your text in it. You can double-click the title bar to maximize the window for easier editing.

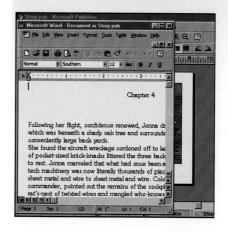

4 Edit the Text

Make your changes, run the spell-checker, change fonts—do whatever editing procedures you want just as if you're working in Word. (See Chapter 2, "How to Use Word 97," to learn how to use Word.)

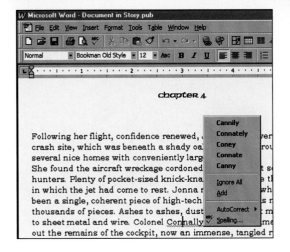

5 Update the Text Frame

Choose **File**, **Update** when you want to save your changes. In the Story Editor, the Update command replaces Word's Save command; when you choose **Update**, the Publisher text frame is updated with your changes.

Click

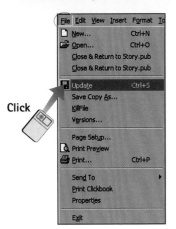

6 Close the Story Editor

Click the **X** button in the upper-right corner of the Word Story Editor window (the one on the title bar) to close it and return to Publisher.

Click

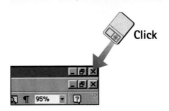

End

How-To Hints

Which Window Do I Close?

If the Word Story Editor window is maximized, click the upper **X** close box (the one on the title bar) to close the whole window; the Publisher window underneath appears after the Word window closes. If you get confused about which window you're closing, try resizing the Word window (click the middle button on the title bar) so you can see the Word and Publisher windows separately, as shown in step 3. Then click the **X** button on the Word title bar to close the Editor window (not just the story window).

How to Print Envelopes

Although they take more time, printed envelopes look much more professional than handwritten or labeled envelopes. You can set up a good-looking envelope using a wizard and then customize it to your preferences just as in any other publication.

Begin

1 Open the Catalog

Choose **File**, **New** to open the Catalog.

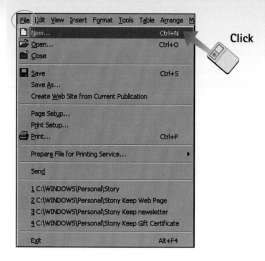

Click

2 Choose an Envelope Wizard

On the **Publications by Wizard** tab, click **Envelopes**. Wizards are available to set up purchased, preprinted envelopes that don't require a color printer, but we'll use **Plain Paper** to set up an envelope for a black-and-white printer. Double-click the envelope for which style you want to start the wizard.

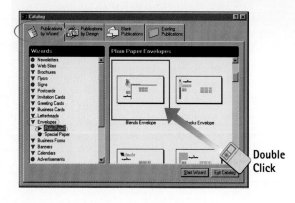

Double
Click

3 Follow the Wizard

Follow the wizard steps to create the envelope; in the size step, a #10 envelope is the standard business size.

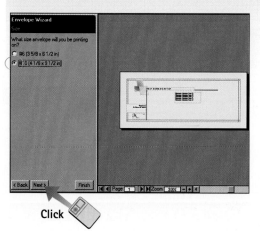

Click

4 Make More Changes

After the wizard finishes, you can move text frames around to customize the envelope, delete or change any pictures, and fill in the mailing address and return address. If you want to change the color scheme to shades of gray, choose **Format**, **Color Scheme**, and select **Black & Gray** on the **Standard** tab of the Color Scheme dialog box; then choose **OK**.

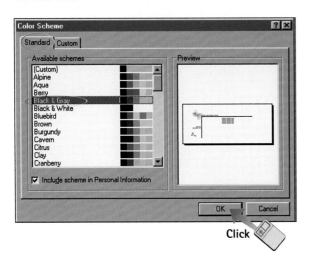

Click

5 Save and Close the Envelope

Choose **File**, **Save**. In the Save As dialog box, type a filename and click **Save**. To close the publication, choose **File**, **Close**.

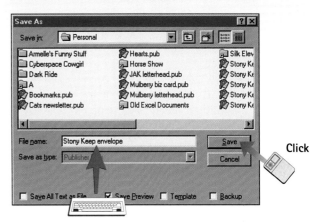

Click

6 Open and Reuse the Envelope

Whenever you need to print another envelope, just open your saved publication, change the mailing address, and print it. Choose **File**, **Open**, and locate your envelope on the **Existing Publications** tab.

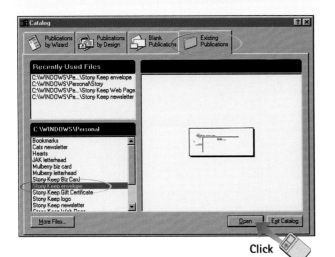

Click

How-To Hints

Envelope Texture

If you're printing envelopes on a laser printer, smooth paper works better than textured paper. Although both look great when they come out of the printer, textured paper doesn't hold the ink as well and looks ratty by the time it's been handled in the mail.

End

Project

In this project, I'll create a story-letter, which is set up just like a newsletter but contains the next chapter of an unpublished novel. The document will have a masthead, text in columns, graphics with text wrapped around them, a mock order form to order the story-letter, and a pull quote to intrigue a reader.

To create this story-letter, I'll use text that's already been written and saved in a Word file, and I'll import it to the publication text frame.

Because there's a lot of work in this project, save your work regularly as you go.

1 Start with a Blank Page

If you've just started Publisher, click **Exit Catalog** to close the Catalog. If you've been working in Publisher and the Catalog isn't open, close the publication on which you're working. You should have a single blank page in your Publisher window.

2 Insert More Pages

If this is a four-page publication, it can be printed on 11-by-17-inch paper (folded in the middle to make four pages), or double-sided on two sheets of 8.5-by-11-inch paper. Either way, it needs three more pages. Click the **Next Page** button three times (click **OK** each time). Then click the **First Page** button to return to the first page.

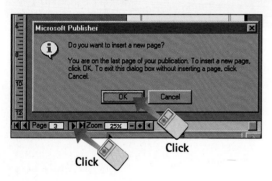

Click

Click

3 Create Page Numbers

To add page numbers, choose **View, Go to Background** to switch to the background. Draw a text frame at the bottom of the page, and then choose **Insert, Page Numbers** to create automatic numbers. (Refer to Task 15 to learn about page numbers.)

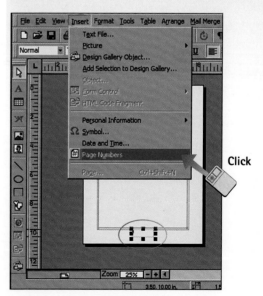

Click

4 Format the Page Numbers

With the text frame selected, click **Center** on the Formatting toolbar to align the page number in the center. Add the word **Page** and a space in front of the number. (Press F9 to zoom in and out from the text frame.) Then choose **View**, **Go to Foreground**.

5 Insert a Masthead

Be sure you're on the first page, and click the **Design Gallery Object** button. Under **Categories**, click **Mastheads**, and double-click a masthead you like. After the masthead is pasted on the page, move it into position at the top of the page, and resize it to fit within the page guides if you want. (See Task 23 to learn about mastheads.)

6 Customize the Masthead

Select the masthead, and press F9 to zoom in. Give the masthead an appropriate name, title, and volume and issue numbers. Click the **Newsletter Date** text and enter an appropriate date. Press F9 to zoom out again.

7 Insert an Order Form

Insert an order form on page 3 to encourage more orders for your publication; if you insert the order form first, you can draw the text frames to fit around it later. Choose **View**, **Two-Page Spread** to see the layout better; then switch to page 3 (click the **Next Page** button). Click the **Design Gallery Object** button, and then double-click a **Reply Form**.

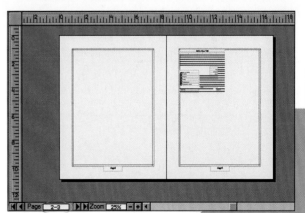

Continues

8 Customize the Order Form

Move the reply form to a good spot; then zoom in and customize it. Reword text, ungroup the object to add and delete individual text frames, and draw a rectangle frame around the form. (Refer to Task 14 to learn about ungrouping and Task 18 to learn about drawing rectangles.)

9 Draw a Box for an Address

A blank rectangle makes a space for a mailing address label after all the copies of the story-letter are printed. Switch to page 4; then draw a rectangle in the middle of the lower half of the page (picture the publication folded for mailing to help you position it).

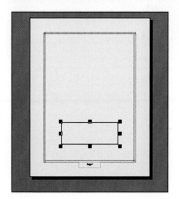

10 Insert a Return Address

Draw a text frame to add a return address to the lower half of the last page (picture the page folded for mailing to help you position it). Enter your return address in the text frame.

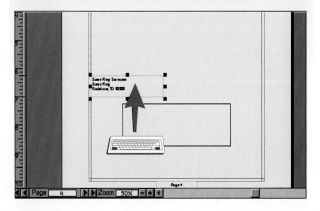

11 Draw Text Frames for the Story

Beginning on Page 1, draw text frames to hold the story. Because narrow frames are easier to read than wide frames, I'll create two long text frames on each page and draw them around the objects I've already created. (Refer to Tasks 3 and 4 to learn about text frames.)

12 Import the Text

Right-click the first text frame on page 1, and choose **Change Text**, **Text File**. In the Insert Text File dialog box, locate the file you want to import, and choose **OK**. When asked if you want Publisher to AutoFlow your text, click **No**. (Refer to Task 4 to learn about importing text.)

13 Show the Connect Frames Tools

Choose **Tools**, **Text Frame Connecting** to show the Connect Frames toolbar.

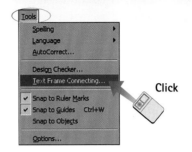

Click

14 Connect Text Frames

With the frame with text in it selected, click the **Connect Frame** button. The mouse pointer becomes a mug symbol. Click the next text frame to flow the story into it. To flow text to frames on other pages, click the **Connect Frame** button, and then switch pages and click the next text frame. (Refer to Task 9 to learn about flowing text.)

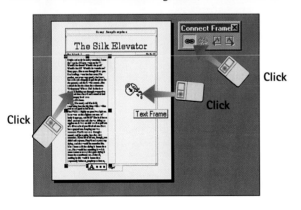

Click

Click

Click

Text Frame

15 Flow the Text into All the Frames

After you flow text into each frame, click the **Connect Frame** button again to flow remaining text into the next frame. Continue to connect all your frames—even the empty ones. When you insert pictures and wrap text around these empty frames, there's someplace for the text to flow.

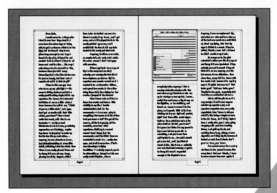

Continues

16 Insert Pictures

Draw a picture frame between the two text frames on each page, and insert clip art or one of your own graphics files to illuminate the story. (Refer to Task 7 to learn about picture frames.)

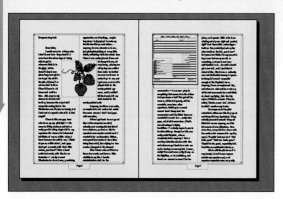

17 Wrap Text Around the Pictures

Right-click each picture, and choose **Change Frame, Object Frame Properties.** In the Object Frame Properties dialog box, click the **Picture only** option, and choose **OK**. (Or click the **Wrap Text to Picture** button on the Formatting toolbar. (Refer to Task 8 to learn about wrapping text.)

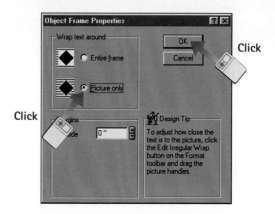

18 Insert a Pull Quote

Click in the text where a pull quote would look good. Click the **Design Gallery Object** button, and double-click a suitable **Pull Quote** object. (Refer to Task 23 to learn about pull quotes.)

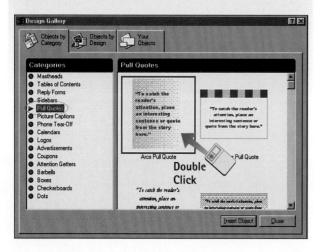

19 Position the Pull Quote

Drag the pull quote to position it at the side of a text frame or between the two text frames so that no lines of text are broken across the pull quote object. Add pull quote text from the body of your story.

20 Resize Pictures

Resizing the pictures can help flow text more evenly into the connected text frames. If there's empty space in the last text frames, make the pictures larger; if the text doesn't quite fit, make the pictures smaller. Wait to do any resizing until all the objects, such as pull quotes, have been inserted.

Click
Hold &
Drag

21 Insert a Closing Graphic

Inserting a picture at the end of a story gives the story—and the publication—a neat sense of packaging with all the ends tied up.

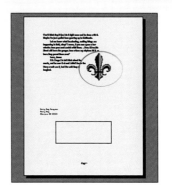

22 Save the Publication

Choose **File**, **Save** to save the publication. When it's time to produce the next issue, you can open this one, replace the text and insert new pictures, and be finished quickly.

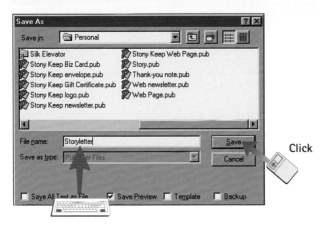

Click

23 Print the Publication

Choose **File**, **Print** to print each page of the publication. If you're going to have many copies of the publication commercially printed, take all the pages to your printer, select nice paper, and tell the printer what you want.

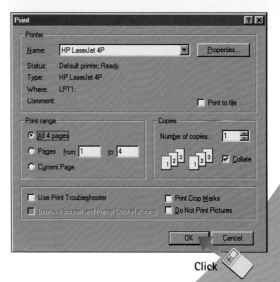

Click

End

Task

CHAPTER 6

How to Use the Small Business Financial Manager 98

*T*he Small Business Financial Manager 98 is an *add-in*, a small, non–self-contained program, that works within Excel. It's essentially a collection of prebuilt worksheets and wizards to help you organize your business financial data as quickly and painlessly as possible.

You can create all the different financial reports that you might need to keep track of your business performance (or get a bank loan), but beyond that, you can choose from a variety of different types of each report.

You can start the Small Business Financial Manager from an icon that's installed on your desktop or from the Accounting menu in Excel 97. ●

1

How to Import Existing Data

The Small Business Financial Manager uses data imported from your existing accounting software to generate a variety of financial reports and to analyze what-if scenarios. The more detailed the data in your accounting software, the more detailed your analyses, reports, and scenarios will be.

When you installed Small Business Financial Manager, you were given the opportunity to choose which software converters to install; the Financial Manager will import data from any of those file types.

Start Excel before you begin this task.

Begin

1 Start the Import Wizard

In Excel, choose **Accounting**, **Import Wizard**.

Click

2 Select New or Existing Data

In step 1 of the Import your Accounting Data wizard, select the **Import** option to import data for the first time. If you've imported this data before and you're importing updated data from the same accounting files, click the **Update** option. Then click **Next**.

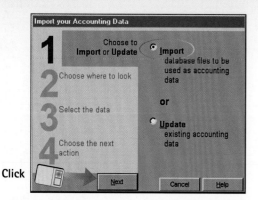

Click

3 Look for the Data

In the second step of the wizard, select an option that tells the wizard where to search for data (the wizard can search your whole hard drive or just a few folders). If you choose the **In specific folders** option, click each folder you want to search, and then click the **Add folder to list** button. When your search list is complete, click **Next**.

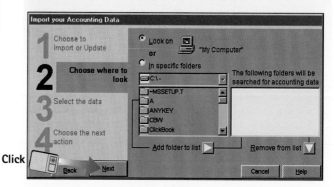

Click

4 Select a Data Type

In the third wizard step, click the data you want to import, and then click **Next**.

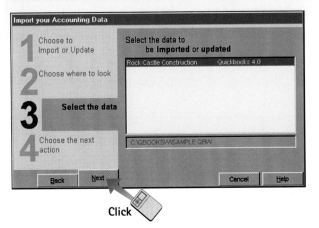

Click

5 Begin the Import

The next dialog box tells you the import might take a while depending on a number of factors. If you can spare the time, click **Yes**. (If not, click **No** and do the import later.)

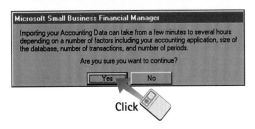

Click

6 Finish Up

In step 4, the wizard tells you the import is complete. Choose an option and click **Finish**. If you choose **Remap your Accounting Data**, see the How-To Hints that follow. (If you choose this option but don't need to remap your accounts, you can choose **OK** or **Cancel** in the Map Your Accounts dialog box.)

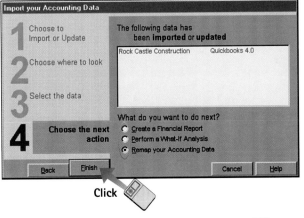

Click

End

How-To Hints

Remap the Categories

If Small Business Financial Manager couldn't match your accounting categories with its categories, it won't be able to find the data. To remap categories, you match your categories with the Financial Manager's. Choose **Accounting**, **Remap Data**, and then click a company and choose **OK**. Move accounts to different categories by cutting them (use the **Cut** button in the dialog box) and pasting them in new categories (use the **Paste** button in the dialog box).

2

TASK

How to Create a What-If Scenario

What-if is a numbers game that can teach you a lot about the state of your business and help you to make better business decisions. You play the what-if game by looking at financial reports and then changing the numbers to see what the results will be. For example, what if the cost of a raw material goes up by 2%? Or what if employees all get 5% raises?

Small Business Financial Manager has several what-if scenarios already set up. You plug in the numbers that match your questions and then review the answers.

Start Excel before you begin this task.

Begin

1 Start the What-If Wizard

In Excel, choose **Accounting**, **Select Analysis Tool**. In the Select a Financial Manager Analysis Tool dialog box, click **What-If Analysis** and then click **Next**.

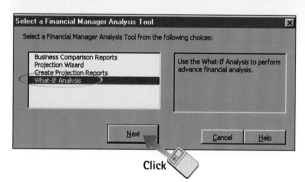

2 Select the Company to Analyze

In the Perform a What-If Analysis dialog box, click the name of the company you want to analyze, and then click **Next**.

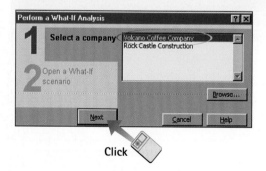

3 Select a Scenario

If you are creating a new scenario, click the **New** option, type a scenario name, and enter a Begin Date and an End Date. If you want to play with scenarios you created previously, click the **Existing** option, and select the scenario name. Then click **Finish**.

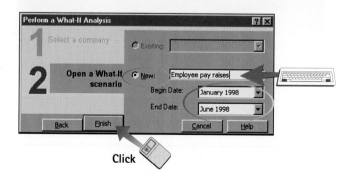

4 Save the Scenario

In the Save Scenario Workbook As dialog box, save the workbook normally; then wait as the workbook is built.

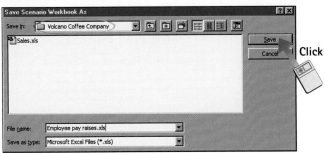

Click

5 Change a General Category

A What-If Overview worksheet appears. In the **Analysis Category** section of the worksheet, click the general category in which you want to change numbers.

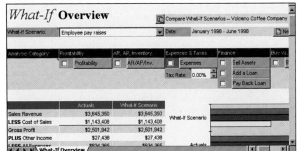

6 Change a Specific Category

In the general category worksheet, select specific categories of data to change. Click the arrows to change the values. Keep an eye on the totals as you change numbers so you'll have a change-by-change look at the results. Click the **What-if Overview** button to return to the overview.

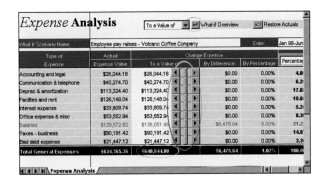

How-To Hints

Save and Create More Scenarios

Save each scenario by clicking the **Save** button near the upper-right corner of the What-If Overview worksheet. Then click the **New** button (next to the Save button) to create another scenario by changing values again. The saved scenarios are saved with the worksheet; use normal Excel techniques to save the workbook. To start a new set of scenarios, click a new worksheet or open a new workbook.

Summarize Several Scenarios

To compare the results of different scenarios side-by-side, create a summary. In the worksheet, click the **Compare What-If Scenarios** button at the top of the What-If Overview worksheet.

End

How to Create a Business Comparison Report

A business comparison report compares your business with others in your industry so you can measure your performance against your competitors.

Start Excel before you begin this task.

Begin

1 Choose an Analysis Tool

In Excel, choose **Accounting**, **Select Analysis Tool**.

Click

2 Select Business Comparison Reports

In the Select a Financial Manager Analysis Tool dialog box, click **Business Comparison Reports**, and then click **Next**.

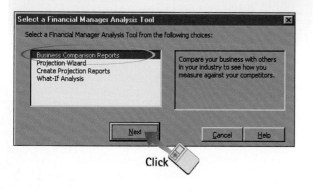

Click

3 Choose a Range

In step 1 of the Business Comparison Wizard, select a company name and a date range to analyze, and then click **Next**.

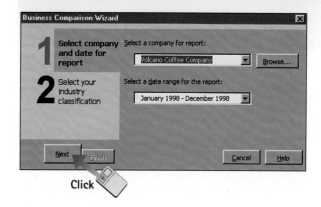

Click

4 Select the Industry

In step 2 of the wizard, select your industry classification (all standard government industry classifications are included). Click the small plus symbols to expand classifications into their subclassifications, and keep selecting until you reach your narrowest subclassification. Then click **Finish**.

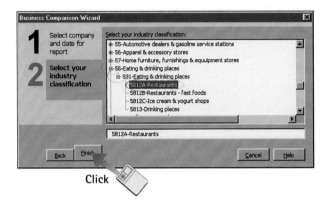

Click

5 Look at Key Ratio Comparisons

The Key Ratios worksheet compares the key ratios for your business to those for the industry standards.

Business Comparison Report

Change Wizard Choices		Income Statement	Balance Sheet	Help
Company Name	Volcano Coffee Company			
Industry Classification	5812A - Restaurants			
Report Date Range	January 1998 - December 1998			

Key Ratios	Your Company	RMA Industry Averages	Your Ranking	Show/Hide Info
Current Ratio	6.34	0.50	Top 25%	Show Info
Debt to Worth Ratio	0.02	2.50	Top 25%	Show Info
Pretax Profit to Total Assets Ratio (%)	38.6%	19.9%	Top 50%	Show Info
Sales to Total Assets	0.74	1.90	Bottom 25%	Show Info

Industry comparative data provided by RMA as a subset of its Annual Statement Studies. For more information and comment on statistical representativeness visit http://www.rmahq.org/Annual_Studies/studies_fr.html

Key Ratios / Income Statement Comparison / Balanci

6 Look at Other Comparisons

Click the other worksheets to see income statement comparisons and balance sheet comparisons between your business and the industry standards. Use standard Excel techniques to save and close the workbook (see Task 3 in Chapter 1, "Getting Started with Office Small Business Edition," to learn how to save files).

Balance Sheet Comparison

	Show Detail	Key Ratio
Date: December 1998		

Description	Volcano Coffee Company Dollar Value	Percentage	RMA Indus Averag
ASSETS			
Total Current Assets	10,106,030	94.8%	10
Total Other Assets	552,606	5.2%	8
TOTAL ASSETS	10,658,636	100.0%	100
LIABILITIES & OWNERS' EQUITY			
Total Current Liabilities	1,593,698	15.0%	2
Total Other Liabilities	103,916	1.0%	3
TOTAL LIABILITIES	1,697,614	15.9%	6
Total Owners' Equity	8,961,023	84.1%	3
TOTAL LIABILITIES & OWNERS' EQUITY	10,658,636	100.0%	100

Key Ratios / Income Statement Comparison / **Balance Sheet Compariso**

End

4

How to Create Income Statements

Your accounting software can probably produce an income statement for you (most do), but you may not have much choice about the way the income statement is presented. In the Small Business Financial Manager, however, you can choose from several built-in designs. After you import a copy of the data in your accounting software (see Task 1 to learn how), you can follow the steps in this task to create an income statement.

Start Excel before you begin this task.

Begin

1 Start the Report Wizard

In Excel, choose **Accounting, Report Wizard**. (In the Microsoft Small Business Financial Manager startup screen, you can click **Report** instead.)

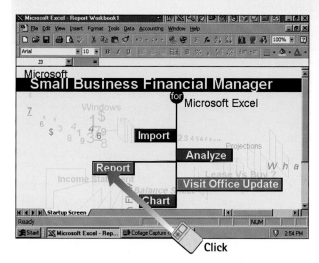

Click

2 Choose Income Statement

Wait until the wizard starts. In step 1 in the Create a Financial Report dialog box, click in the **Financial Reports** list on **Income Statement**. Select a **Company Name**, and click **Next**.

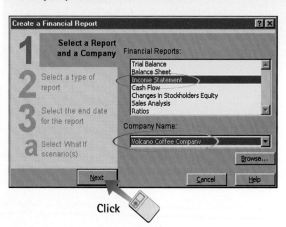

Click

3 Choose Income Type

In step 2 in the Create a Financial Report dialog box, click in the **Report types** list on the type of income statement you want, and then click **Next**.

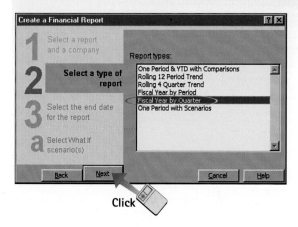

Click

4 Choose an End Date

In step 3 in the Create a Financial Report dialog box, click an **End date for the report**. If you chose a report that includes the current period in addition to the year-to-date figures, the end date specifies the month that you'll see as the current period. Then click **Finish**.

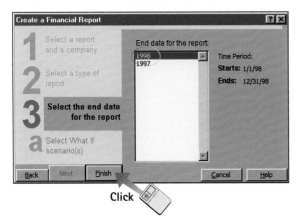

Click

5 Look at the Report

The report is an Excel worksheet; you can save it with normal Save procedures. Click the small minus buttons (the Hide buttons) on the left side of the worksheet to hide details for sections of the report. (Click the **1** and **2** buttons above the Hide buttons to hide all the details for a specific level.)

	Account	Description	Quarter 1, FY1998	Quarter 2, FY1998	Quarter 3, FY1998
33	Revenue				
34	5000	In Store sales	537,075	593,481	640,076
35	5100	Telephone sales	348,735	385,361	415,616
36	5200	Catalog sales	322,236	356,079	384,035
37	5800	Consulting sales	523,692	578,691	624,126
38	**Total**	**Revenue**	**1,731,739**	**1,913,611**	**2,063,853**
40	Cost of Sales				
41	6000	Direct material	156,173	172,575	186,124
42	6100	Direct labor	199,579	220,539	237,854
43	6200	Other direct cost	117,644	129,999	140,206
44	6900	Sales and marketing	69,785	77,115	83,169
45	**Total**	**Cost of Sales**	**543,181**	**600,227**	**647,353**

6 Show and Hide Details

After you hide details for a section, click the small plus buttons (the Show buttons) on the left side of the worksheet to show details for sections of the report. (Click the **1** and **2** buttons above the Show buttons to show all the details for a specific level.)

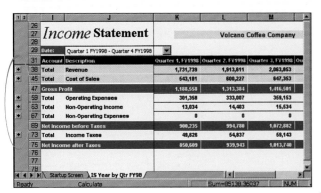

End

How-To Hints

Report Names

Your accounting software may call this type of report a "profit and loss" report; whether it's called an income statement or a profit and loss report, it's the same thing.

TASK **5**

How to Create Balance Sheets

A balance sheet is the essence of your company's financial health. It "balances" your assets, liabilities, and the value of your equity.

Your accounting software produces a balance sheet, but you may not have much choice about how the data is presented. Most balance sheets give you a choice between year-to-date or year-to-date plus current period, but with the Small Business Financial Manager balance sheets, you can choose from a variety of accounting periods.

Start Excel before you begin this task.

Begin

1 Start the Report Wizard

In Excel, choose **Accounting**, **Report Wizard**. (In the Microsoft Small Business Financial Manager startup screen, you can click **Report** instead.)

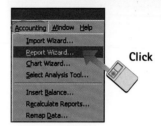

Click

2 Choose Balance Sheet

In step 1 of the Create a Financial Report dialog box, click in the **Financial Reports** list on **Balance Sheet**. Select a **Company Name**, and click **Next**.

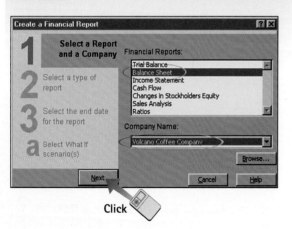

Click

3 Choose a Type of Balance Sheet

In step 2 of the Create a Financial Report dialog box, click in the **Report types** list on the type of balance sheet you want, and then click **Next**.

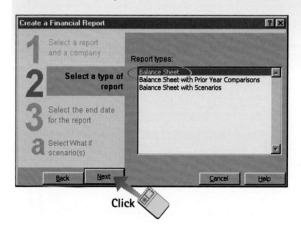

Click

4 Choose an End Date

In step 3 of the Create a Financial Report dialog box, click an **End date for the report**, and then click **Finish**.

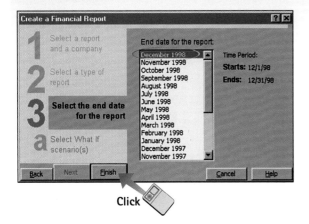

Click

5 Look at the Report

The balance sheet is an Excel worksheet; formulas appear in the Formula bar, and you can save the workbook with normal save procedures.

1 2		F	G	H	I
	25	*Balance* Sheet			Volcano Coffe
	26				
	27	Date:	December 1998		
	28				
	29	Account	Description	December 1998	
	30	ASSETS			
·	31	Current Assets			
·	32	1000	Cash and equivalents	2,757,544	
·	33	1100	A/R - trade	6,751,816	
·	34	1110	A/R - other	157,583	
·	35	1199	Allowance for bad debts	(93,046)	
·	36	1200	Inventory	486,109	
·	37	1900	Other current assets	46,023	
-	38	Total	Current Assets	10,106,030	
·	39	Other Assets			
·	40	2000	Fixed assets	1,005,918	
·	41	2100	Accumulated depreciation	(491,646)	
·	42	2900	Other assets	38,334	

Startup Screen / BS 12-98 /

6 Show and Hide Details

Click the small plus and minus buttons (the Show and Hide buttons) on the left side of the worksheet to show and hide details for sections of the report.

1 2		F	G	H	I
	25	*Balance* Sheet			Volcano Coffe
	26				
	27	Date:	December 1998		
	28				
	29	Account	Description	December 1998	
	30	ASSETS			
+	38	Total	Current Assets	10,106,030	
+	43	Total	Other Assets	552,606	
	44	TOTAL ASSETS		10,658,636	
	45	LIABILITIES & OWNERS' EQUITY			
+	50	Total	Current Liabilities	1,593,698	
+	54	Total	Other Liabilities	103,916	
	55	TOTAL LIABILITIES		1,697,614	
+	61	Total	Owners' Equity	8,961,023	
	62	TOTAL LIABILITIES & OWNERS' EQUITY		10,658,636	
	63				
	64				
	65				

Startup Screen / BS 12-98 /

End

TASK 6

How to Create a Trial Balance

The best use of a trial balance is to obtain a snap-shot of your company's financial health at any given point in time and to track the status of specific items. You may want to see how much you're spending or what your earnings are from specific items or services. Sometimes you need to check whether the trial balance is "in balance."

Start Excel before you begin this task.

Begin

1 Start the Report Wizard

In Excel, choose **Accounting**, **Report Wizard**. (In the Microsoft Small Business Financial Manager startup screen, you can click **Report** instead.)

Click

2 Choose Trial Balance

In step 1 of the Create a Financial Report dialog box, click in the **Financial Reports** list on **Trial Balance**. Select a **Company Name**, and click **Next**.

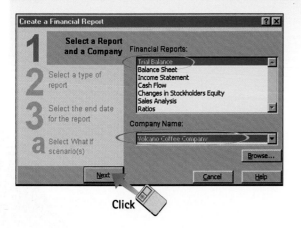

Click

3 Choose a Type of Trial Balance

In step 2 of the Create a Financial Report dialog box, click in the **Report types** list on the type of trial balance you want, and then click **Next**.

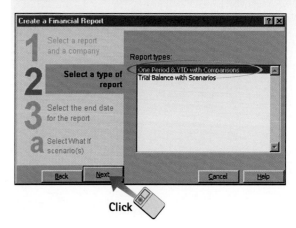

Click

4 Choose an End Date

In step 3 of the Create a Financial Report dialog box, click an **End date for the report**, and then click **Finish**.

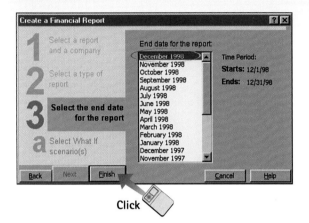

Click

5 Look at the Report

The trial balance, a complete audit report of the general ledger totals and changes, is an Excel worksheet. You can save it with normal save procedures.

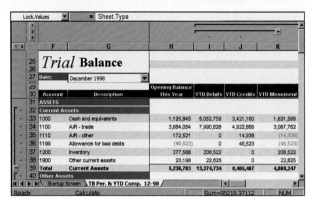

6 Show and Hide Details

Click the small plus and minus buttons (the Show and Hide buttons) on the left side of the worksheet and across the top to show and hide details in rows and columns.

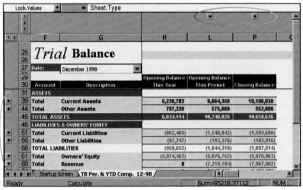

End

7

TASK

How to Create a Cash Flow Report

One of the more difficult reports to obtain from accounting software is a good cash flow report. Accountants charge a good deal of money to prepare these, and the reports take a long time to prepare.

The Small Business Financial Manager has several built-in worksheets that produce cash flow reports with excellent detail.

Start Excel before you begin this task.

Begin

1 Start the Report Wizard

In Excel, choose **Accounting**, **Report Wizard**. (In the Microsoft Small Business Financial Manager startup screen, you can click **Report** instead.)

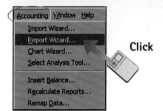

Click

2 Choose Cash Flow

In step 1 of the Create a Financial Report dialog box, click in the **Financial Reports** on **Cash Flow**. Select a **Company Name**, and click **Next**.

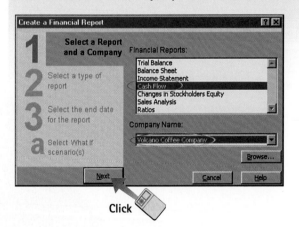

Click

3 Choose a Type of Cash Flow

In step 2 of the Create a Financial Report dialog box, click in the **Report types** list on the type of cash flow you want, and then click **Next**.

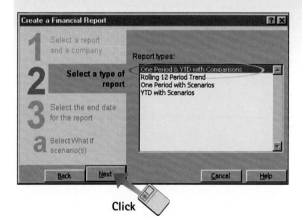

Click

4 Choose an End Date

In step 3 of the Create a Financial Report dialog box, click an **End date for the report**, and then click **Finish**.

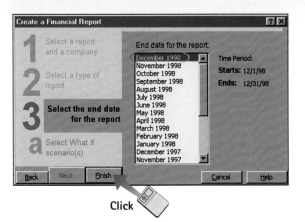

Click

5 Look at the Report

A detailed statement of money in and out is displayed in an Excel worksheet. You can save it with normal save procedures.

6 Show and Hide Details

Click the small plus and minus buttons (the Show and Hide buttons) on the left side of the worksheet to show and hide details for sections of the report.

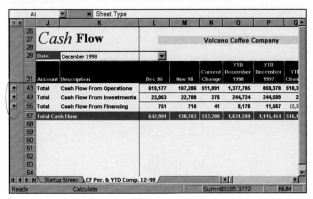

End

Task

CHAPTER 7

How to Use Internet Explorer 4

As a small-business person, you may or may not want to advertise your business to the world on the Internet, but you'll want to be comfortable with the Internet so you can conduct research, locate new supply sources, and download software files or more clip art for your publications. The tasks in this part show you how to get connected and introduce you to the basics of using the *World Wide Web* (the portion of the Internet where you can find Web sites with information or advertising).

Keep these words of wisdom in mind as you find your way around the Web: You may be frequently prompted for username and password information, depending on how your ISP is set up. This book can't predict when extra dialog boxes will prompt you for connection data, so you'll have to deal with these even when they're not mentioned in this book. Web sites also change names, locations, and appearances often. Any Web site shown or mentioned in this book may change before you find it, but try anyway. ●

How to Set Up Internet Explorer 4 with the Internet Connection Wizard

Before you can use the Internet, you need to connect through an *Internet service provider (ISP)*. An ISP is your gateway to the interconnected computers that form the Internet.

You can connect to Microsoft Network easily through the Internet Connection Wizard. If there's no local access number for Microsoft Network, you can set up an account with a local ISP (look in *The Yellow Pages* or ask a connected friend). Remember, you pay the ISP for connection time, and if there's no local access number, you also pay the phone company for long-distance calls.

Begin

1 Choose the Connection Wizard

Click the **Start** button, and choose **Programs, Internet Explorer, Connection Wizard**.

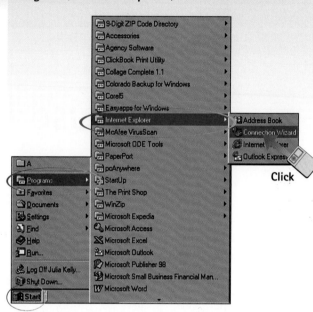

Click

2 Start the Wizard

In the Internet Connection Wizard dialog box, click **Next**.

Click

3 Choose a Connection Type

To set up a new account with one of the national ISPs, leave the top option selected and click **Next**.

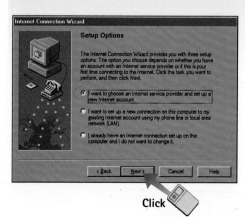

Click

4 Start the Automatic Setup

Click **Next** to instruct the wizard to begin running the necessary programs.

Click

5 Check for a Connection

In the next step, enter the first three digits of your area code and telephone number, and click **Next**. Internet Explorer 4 goes online to the Microsoft Referral Service to see if there's a local access number for you.

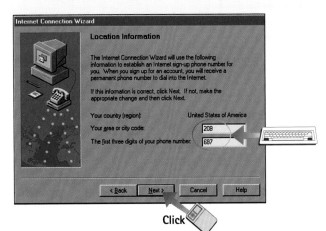

Click

6 Is There Local Access?

If there's a local access number listed, choose a number and continue to follow the wizard (it will eventually want credit card information for billing). If there's no local access number (as shown here), choose **Cancel** and go find yourself a local ISP.

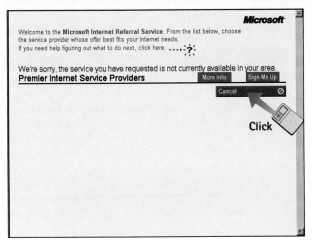

Click

End

How-To Hints

Are You Connected?

Before you set up your Internet account, be sure your modem is installed and connected to a phone line—setting up an account always requires going online.

Try a Disk Instead

Many ISPs provide connection software on a disk as well as online, and waiting for a disk in the mail is often much easier and less stressful than long waits in front of the computer. Call your local ISP, set up an account, and ask them to send you a connection software disk and instructions. (If you get a referral to a local ISP, ask if they reward members who refer their friends and associates, and be sure they know who sent you to them.)

Consider a Second Phone Line

Make sure you are connected to a modem and phone line before you begin. While you are connected, don't try to use that phone line, and be aware that no one else can call you on that line.

How to Use the Active Desktop

When you install Internet Explorer 4 and click **Yes** to install the active desktop, your onscreen desktop appearance changes dramatically. The active desktop gives you opportunities to jump onto the Internet from almost anywhere on your computer screen, thereby integrating your computer with the Internet. Your desktop looks and works like a Web page, and you get extra stuff called active content that provides up-to-the-minute current Web pages from news, weather, and other content providers (you learn how to use the active content, called channels, in Task 3).

Begin

1 Use Web Graphic for Background

Go online and find a graphic you really like (perhaps at a museum's Web site). Right-click the graphic, and then choose **Set as Wallpaper**; the graphic appears on your desktop as a new background. To turn the background on or off without deleting the graphic file, right-click the desktop, choose **Properties**, and change settings on the **Background** tab.

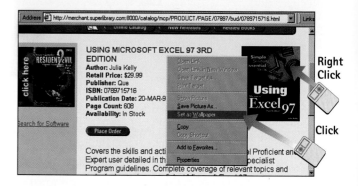

2 Single-click or Double-click Mode

The active desktop settings include single-click hyperlinks in place of the classic Windows 95 double-click icons. To switch to double-click icons, choose **Start**, **Settings**, **Folder Options**. On the **General** tab, click the **Classic style** option, and choose **OK**. (Choose the **Web style** option to switch to single-click mode.)

3 Use the Favorites Bar

In any folder window, choose **View**, **Explorer Bar**, **Favorites** to show the Favorites bar in the window. Click an item to start your browser and jump to that Web page. To save a new favorite, open that Web page and choose **Favorites**, **Add to Favorites**. Type a **Name** you want listed in the Favorites list, accept the default settings, and choose **OK**.

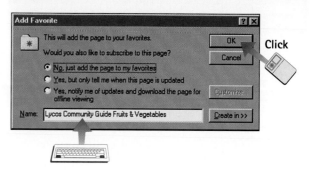

4 Use the History Bar

In any folder window, choose **View**, **Explorer Bar**, **History**. The History bar appears on the left side of the window and lists the Web pages you've visited recently. To revisit a Web page, click the day you were last there, and then click the page you want.

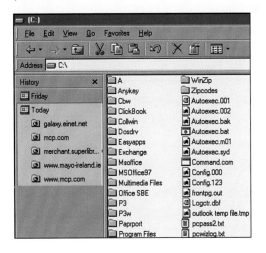

5 Use the Search Bar

In any folder window, choose **View**, **Explorer Bar**, **Search**. You'll be connected online. With the Search bar, you can conduct repeated Internet searches without losing the search engine page. Select an engine in the **Select provider** list box, and use the search page that appears in the Search bar. Web pages appear on the right, and the search engine remains available on the left.

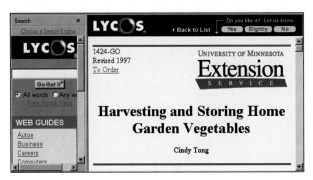

6 Add Shortcuts to the Start Menu

To add your own shortcuts to the Start menu, drag a folder or file icon from a folder window and drop it on the **Start** button; a shortcut is added to the Start menu.

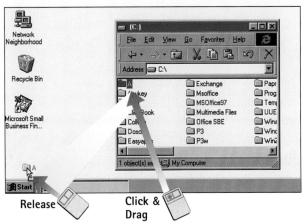

Release   Click & Drag

End

How-To Hints

Is the Active Desktop Too Busy?

You can turn the active desktop on and off so that you don't have to look at it at all times. Right-click a blank spot on the desktop, and choose **Active Desktop**, **View As Web Page** to turn it on or off.

Get Off the Phone!

To get off the Internet and release the phone line, choose **File**, **Work Offline**. The Web pages you've already looked at are still available in your History bar.

How to Use Channels

Channels are Web sites that come to your computer like television channels. You can't navigate to a channel as you can a Web page, but after you subscribe to a channel, you can view it by clicking a **Channel** button on the Channel bar.

Channels are updated on your schedule; you can update them manually, or you can leave your computer on and schedule an automatic update overnight.

You can also open channels from the Channel Guide, a component that's part of your active desktop, or from a folder window (choose **View, Explorer Bar, Channels**, and then click a button in the Channel bar).

Begin

1 Click Channel in Channel Guide

If your active desktop is off, turn it on by right-clicking the desktop and clicking **Active Desktop, View As Web Page**. When the active desktop is on, the Channel Guide appears. Click the channel you want. Internet Explorer 4 dials up the channel (you may see a message asking if you'd like an overview of Active Channels—it's your choice).

2 Subscribe to the Channel

The first time you open a channel, you have the opportunity to subscribe. On the channel's preview page, click the button, graphic, or link that indicates subscription.

Click

3 Choose an Update Method

In the Modify Channel Usage dialog box, choose an option for whether and when you want your browser to check the channel for updated information and/or download the changed pages. Then choose **Customize**. (Choose **OK** if you selected the **No** option.)

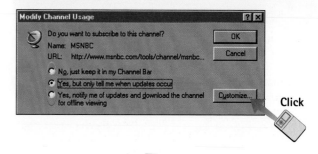

Click

4 Follow the Subscription Wizard

Follow the Subscription Wizard to finish subscribing; the option you choose in step 3 determines which questions the Subscription Wizard asks. In the last step, choose **Finish**.

Click

5 Update Channels Manually

If you set manual updates in your subscription, or if you want an off-schedule update, you can update manually. In any folder or browser window, choose **Favorites, Update All Subscriptions**. Your browser goes online, checks for changes, and then notifies you or downloads the pages.

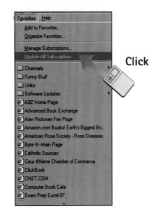

Click

How-To Hints

Keep the Channel Bar in View

In Full Screen view, the Channel bar is hidden. To view the bar, click the pushpin icon. Click the pushpin again to hide the Channel bar.

Use Toolbars

In Full Screen view, the toolbars and menu bar are hidden. To see them, point to the top of the screen. To show or hide a specific toolbar, right-click the menu bar and click the name of the toolbar. To switch between hiding and showing the toolbars and the menu bar, right-click the top bar and click **AutoHide**.

Delete a Channel

Delete channels that clutter up your Channel Guide. Right-click the channel you want to delete, and click **Delete**. In the Confirm Folder Delete dialog box, click **Yes**. If you subscribed to the channel, you must delete it from your Subscriptions list, too. In your browser window, choose **Favorites, Manage Subscriptions**. Right-click the subscription to delete, choose **Delete**, and close the dialog box.

6 Change Subscription Settings

Right-click the channel you want to change, and then choose **Properties**.

Right Click

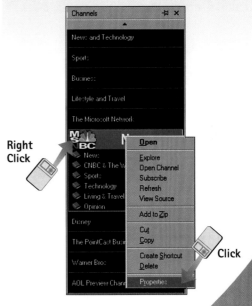

Click

End

How to Use the New Taskbar

The new taskbar that's installed with the active desktop has four new toolbars; they're handy to varying degrees and are easy to show or hide. You can change the height of the taskbar so that you can display all your toolbars.

You can also display and minimize program windows by clicking their taskbar buttons instead of searching for the tiny minimize button, and you can tile multiple program windows (have Windows resize them so you view all open windows onscreen) so that you can drag and drop data between two programs.

Although the new taskbar is installed with the active desktop, it's completely functional whether the active desktop is turned on or off.

Begin

1 Use the Quick Launch Toolbar

The Quick Launch toolbar has buttons to launch your Internet Explorer browser, minimize windows to show your desktop instantly, launch your browser in Channel view (a full-screen view with the Channel Bar displayed), and start Outlook Express (a mini version of Outlook that you don't need if you have Outlook installed). To show or hide the Quick Launch toolbar, right-click the taskbar and choose **Toolbars, Quick Launch**.

2 Use the Links Toolbar

The Links toolbar contains buttons that are hyperlinks to different Microsoft Web sites, but you can delete those buttons and add links to your favorite Web sites instead. To show or hide the Links toolbar, right-click the taskbar and choose **Toolbars, Links**.

3 Change the Links Toolbar

To delete a Links button, right-click it and choose **Delete**. To add a new Links button, drag either a hyperlink from a Web page or the Web icon from the browser's Address box onto the Links toolbar, and drop it. A button is created that jumps to the hyperlink or the URL in the Address box.

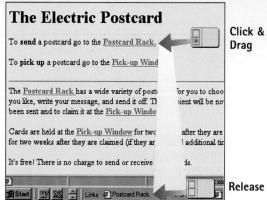

The Electric Postcard

To **send** a postcard go to the Postcard Rack.

To **pick up** a postcard go to the Pick-up Window.

The Postcard Rack has a wide variety of post... for you to choose you like, write your message, and send it off. Th... ...ient will be no... been sent and to claim it at the Pick-up Windo...

Cards are held at the Pick-up Window for two... after they are for two weeks after they are claimed (if they ar... additional tir...

It's free! There is no charge to send or receive ...ds.

Click & Drag

Release

4 Use the Address Toolbar

To show or hide the Address toolbar, right-click the taskbar and choose **Toolbars**, **Address**. You can type a URL or a hard-drive path into the Address box, and then press Enter. The Web page or folder you entered opens. You can also select from a list of recently visited pages and folders by clicking the down arrow on the right.

5 Use the Desktop Toolbar

To show or hide the Desktop toolbar, right-click the taskbar and choose **Toolbars**, **Desktop**. The Desktop toolbar has buttons for every shortcut icon on your desktop, so you can trigger those shortcuts without clearing your desktop to access them.

6 Change the Taskbar Size

If you have a lot of toolbars displayed or a lot of buttons on one toolbar, you can't read the button names. To change the taskbar height, point to the top border and drag the two-headed arrow up to make it taller and down to make it shorter.

End

How-To Hints

Toggle Your Programs

Every open program has a button on the taskbar; to toggle between open and minimized, click this button.

Clear Your Desktop Fast

To minimize all your open program windows at once, either display the Quick Launch toolbar and click the **Show Desktop** button, or right-click the taskbar and click **Minimize All Windows**.

Tile Windows Easily

Right-click the taskbar and click a window-tiling command: **Cascade Windows**, **Tile Windows Horizontally**, or **Tile Windows Vertically**. All open windows are tiled perfectly.

How to Search the World Wide Web

It's ironic that one of the Internet's principal attractions is one of its major sources of frustration. The tremendous volume of information available on the Web means there's hardly a subject not covered; it also means that to find a single piece of data you must sort through a mountain of similar data. This is where a good search engine and the ability to use it are invaluable.

The following examples were created using the Excite search engine. Most search engines work in a similar fashion, but because each search engine has its own design, the specifics may vary somewhat.

Begin

1 Begin at the Help Menu

To search the Web from within any Office 97 program, choose **Help, Microsoft on the Web, Search the Web.**

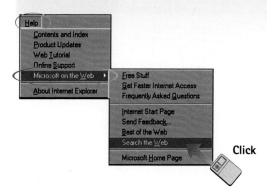

Click

2 Select a Search Engine

Internet Explorer 4 starts and opens to the Microsoft Find It Fast Web page. This page has links to several major Internet search engines, as well as categories of Web sites. Click a search engine name to open its home page (this task uses Excite).

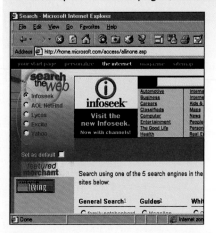

3 Enter Search Words

Enter a word or phrase in the text box, and click **Search** to start the engine hunting (the button is different in other search engines, but you get the idea).

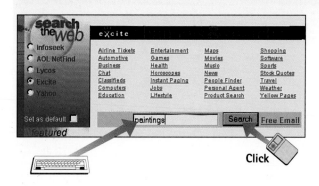

Click

4 Click a Link in the Results List

The result of the search is a list of links to Web pages that contain your word or phrase; the list may be very long or may have no links at all. Repeat the search with other words or phrases to narrow or expand the search. In the results list, click a likely hyperlink to jump to that Web page.

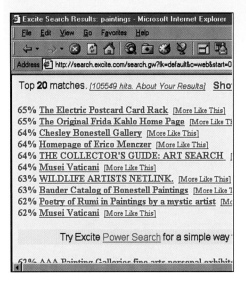

5 Get Search Help

If you have a problem finding what you want, you can call on the search engine for help. Most engines provide a search help link on their home page that can help you with your choice of search words or phrases.

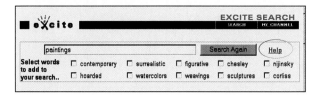

6 Try Other Search Options

In addition to search tips, most search engines provide search options to improve your chances of success. Click a search option (or similar) link to see the available options. Many search engines also enable you to search newsgroups as well as commercial Web sites (you'll have to scroll up and down the page to locate them, as in this Excite search options page).

End

How-To Hints

Got Cookies?

Lots of Web sites send "cookies" that are stored on your computer without your knowledge. Although not harmful, they do contain information that allows a Web site to identify you and see where you've been. Unfortunately, avoiding cookies is practically impossible because you must either accept them blindly or reject them one at a time as they are sent. To reject them, choose **Start**, **Setting**, **Control Panel**. Double-click **Internet**. In the Internet Properties dialog box, click the **Advanced** tab, and scroll down to **Cookies**. Click the **Prompt before accepting cookies** option, and choose **OK**. You can also outsmart the marketing geniuses behind the "cookie conspiracy." Open the Cookies folder—c:\windows\cookies—and delete all the files except index.dat.

How to Find Files on the Web

Information is not the only thing you'll find in abundance on the Internet. The Net is also knee-deep in software, sound, video, graphics, and text files. Because files are more easily categorized and organized than Web pages, finding them is generally much simpler than locating relevant information sources.

After you find a site that has files you want, see Task 7 to learn how to download them.

Begin

1 Find Computer & Internet Files

In Word, Excel, Publisher, or Outlook, choose **Help, Microsoft on the Web, Best of the Web**. Your browser starts and jumps you to Microsoft's collection of the "best" sites on the Web. In the **best of the web** column, click the **Computers & Internet** link.

2 Find Shareware Files

Among Microsoft's choices are several excellent *shareware* sites. Follow the links from **Computer software** to **Shareware and freeware**, and then visit a site by clicking its link.

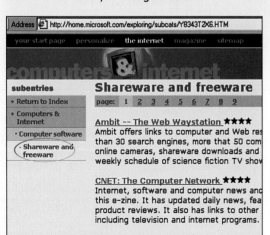

3 Find Graphics Files

To find graphics files, click in the browser window **Address** box. The current URL is highlighted, so your typing replaces it. Type the URL `www.clipartconnection.com` (the browser adds the `http://` part), and press Enter. This URL takes you to The ClipArt Connection, which has lots of graphics files and links to more clip art sites.

4 Find Sound Files

If you want to find sound files, start your search at Sound Ring, an organization of Web sites that have sound clips. In the browser **Address** box, type **www.sound-ring.com** and press Enter.

5 Find Updates and Patches

One of the most important but often overlooked benefits of finding files on the Internet is the ability to download software updates, patches (bug fixes), and drivers. One site that contains a nice selection of patches and drivers is Windows95.com. In the **Address** box, type **www.windows95.com**, and press Enter. When the Web page opens, select an appropriate category to find the files that capture your interest.

6 Use Other Search Engines

In addition to the specific Web pages cited previously, you can always use any search engine to hunt for other file collections. Play with the engine's search options to see what else you can find (shown are HotBot's search options). To find other search engines, click the **Search** button on the browser toolbar (see Task 2 to learn about the Search bar).

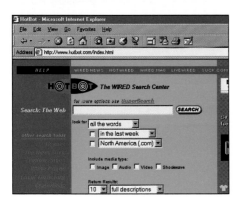

How-To Hints

Find a Specific Company

Many companies use their name followed by .com as their Web site address (*URL*). To speed up your search for a specific company, try typing **www.companyname.com** in the **Address** box.

End

How to Download Files from the Internet

After you find a file you want (perhaps a shareware program or a clip art file), you can transfer a copy of the file from the Internet site to your computer. This is called *downloading*.

Downloading is relatively simple, but it requires some forethought. You need enough room on your hard drive to hold the file. Also remember that downloading large files can keep your computer occupied for a considerable time (large files of 5MB or more can take hours). Even with a fast modem, download time depends on the modem's connection speed and how many others are downloading from that Web site simultaneously.

Begin

1 Find a File

Find the Web site that has the file you want (see Task 6 to learn how to find downloadable files).

Click

2 Start the Download

Click the file's link to start the download process. If the file must be purchased, follow the directions given by the Web site.

Click

3 Save the File on Your Hard Drive

In the File Download dialog box, click the **Save this program to disk** option, and choose **OK**.

Click

4 Choose a Hard Drive Location

When you are ready to download, the Save As dialog box appears. Navigate to the folder where you want the file saved (just as you would any document), and then click **Save**.

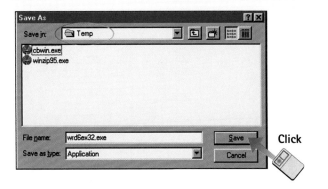

Click

5 Wait... and Wait Some More

After the download begins, a dialog box appears that gives you as many details as Windows 95 can find about the file size, time remaining, and so forth. If you decide you can't spend hours waiting for the download, click **Cancel** to stop the download, and try it again later.

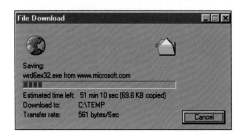

End

How-To Hints

Virus Alert

Be aware that any file you obtain from the Internet (or any source, really) can contain a computer virus. To keep your computer as protected as possible against viruses, consider purchasing an anti-virus program. Programs such as McAfee VirusScan and Norton Anti-Virus can check for viruses while you are downloading the file to ensure that a tainted file doesn't get into your hard drive.

Plan Your Download Times

If you have to download large files, try to do it during a time when most other users won't be using the Internet. If you're on the East Coast, download early in the morning before the rest of the country has had a chance to wake up; if you're on the West Coast, download late at night when everyone else is asleep.

How to Get Online Support

One of the many advantages of being connected to the Internet is the availability of online help. From the vast number of technical support calls that Microsoft receives, the company's support department has developed a large database of knowledge, tips, common questions (with answers), and the latest update information and files.

To use this wealth of information, which is literally at your fingertips, take a minute to check out the online support available from within any Microsoft Office 97 program.

Begin

1 Choose Online Support

In Word, Excel, Publisher, or Outlook, choose **Help, Microsoft on the Web, Online Support.**

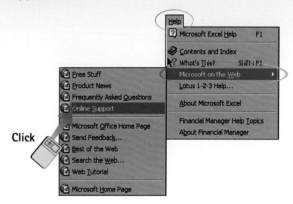

Click

2 Open the Online Support Page

Your browser starts and jumps to the Microsoft Support page for the program in which you chose the Online Support command. (For example, if you chose the command from the Excel menu, your browser jumps to the Excel support page.) You might be asked to register before you can open the page.

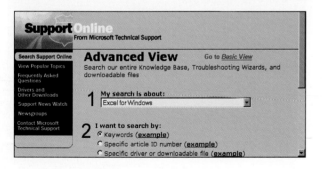

3 Search for Your Topic

If you need help on a specific topic, use the support page's Search feature. Type a word or phrase for which you want to search, and click **Find.**

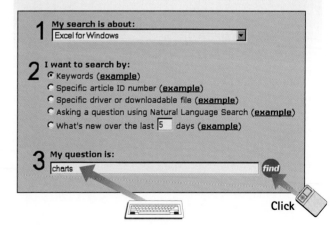

Click

4 Select Your Topic

The Microsoft Support search engine searches the Microsoft Support files in the same way an Internet search engine searches the Web. The result is a list of Microsoft articles that contain the search word(s); click the link that most closely matches your topic.

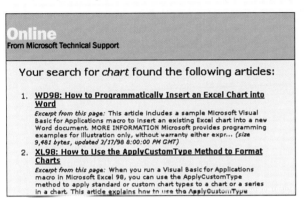

5 Try the FAQs

Another source of answers is the Frequently Asked Questions (FAQ) area. On the left side of the Web page is a Search Support Online menu; click the **Frequently Asked Questions** link, if there is one.

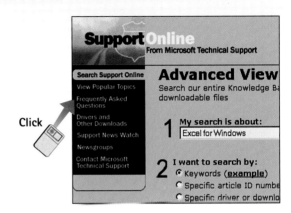

6 Read Questions and Answers

Select the program about which you want information, and click the **Go** button; then click your program version. Click a question that looks appropriate. (You may find it's easier to get help from a good book than from Microsoft Support.)

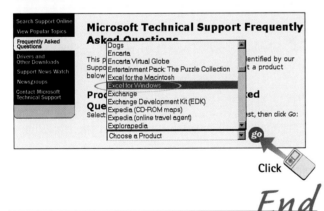

End

9

How to Hyperlink the Web into Your Office Document

You can include pages of Internet information within a letter, memo, or other document, but that's inefficient and impractical. When the information in a Web page is precisely what you need to include in a document, you can simply point your correspondent to the Web page by including a *hyperlink*, a "live" Internet address, in the document. When your correspondent clicks the hyperlink, his browser launches and jumps directly to that Web page.

Hyperlinks can be underlined text links, but they can also be graphics, which take up more page space but are more entertaining.

Begin

1 Start a Text Hyperlink

Click in the document where you want to place the hyperlink, and choose **Insert**, **Hyperlink** (or click the **Insert Hyperlink** button on the Standard toolbar).

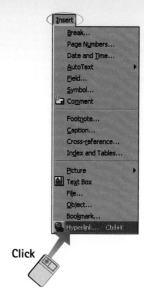

Click

2 Type the URL

In the Insert Hyperlink dialog box, click in the **Link to file or URL** box, and type the URL, beginning with **http://**, and then choose **OK**.

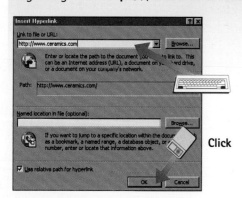

Click

3 Finish the Text Hyperlink

After the hyperlink is created, right-click the new hyperlink and choose **Hyperlink**, **Select Hyperlink**. Type a name to replace the URL, and then click away from the hyperlink. To test the hyperlink, click it.

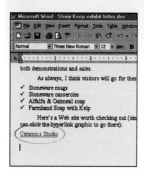

4 Start a Picture Hyperlink

Click in the document where you want to place the hyperlink, and choose **Insert, Picture, Clip Art**. Insert a clip art graphic (see Task 26 in Chapter 2, "How to Use Word 97," to learn how to insert a clip art graphic in a Word document).

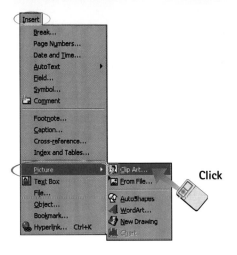

Click

5 Type the URL

With the graphic selected (it should have handles around its edges), choose **Insert, Hyperlink**. In the Insert Hyperlink dialog box, click in the **Link to file or URL** box and type the URL, beginning with **http://**, and choose **OK**.

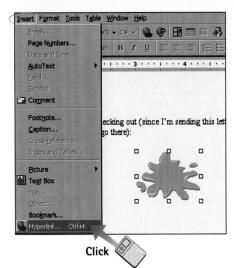

Click

6 Test the Picture Hyperlink

To test the hyperlink, click it. When you point to the image, a ScreenTip appears displaying the hyperlink URL, which tells you where clicking the link will take you.

End

How-To Hints

Works for Files, Too

You can use this procedure to create hyperlinks to files on your hard drive or network, too. Type the path to the file (instead of the URL) in the Insert Hyperlink dialog box, or use the **Browse** button to locate and link to the file.

If the URL Is Long and Complicated

It's often easier to get a long, complex URL entered correctly if you jump to that page in your browser first. Select and copy the URL from the browser's Address box, and then paste the copied URL into the Insert Hyperlink dialog box or directly onto your document or email page. If you paste it directly into your document, the URL becomes a hyperlink after you press Enter or the Spacebar.

Task

8

How to Put the Office 97 Small Business Edition Applications Together

*T*he advantage of using the Office 97 Small Business Edition suite of software is that the applications interact and work well together. Not only can you copy data in a file in one program and paste it into a different file in another program, but you can also *embed* and *link* data *objects* between files in different programs.

Embedding an object inserts a chunk of formatted data into a file; the embedded object is connected to the program in which it was created. Linking an object inserts a picture of formatted data into a file; the linked object, or picture, is connected to the source file from which it was copied.

Another way in which the programs work together is through *hyperlinks*, which enable you to jump to a different file or to a Web site without first opening a program or searching for the file or Web site. When you use hyperlinks in a document, you can bring multiple files in multiple programs as close as a mouse click, or you can grant instant Web site access to an email correspondent who uses Outlook. ●

How to Edit Linked and Embedded Data

When you know the difference in objects' edit behavior, you can make a decision about which type of object to use to insert data in another file.

Use an embedded object to insert formatted data and change the data or formatting using the original program's tools. The embedded object isn't connected to the source file from which you copied it; any changes affect only the embedded object.

Use a linked object to place copies of the same data in different files. Linked objects show what's in the source file. When you edit a linked object, you change the source file; all linked copies are automatically updated with the changes.

Begin

1 Edit an Embedded Object

Double-click the embedded object (in this example, an Excel chart embedded in a Word letter).

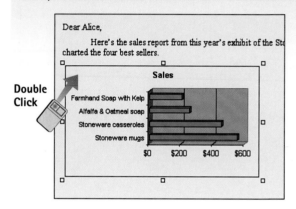

2 Use the Source Tools

The source program tools appear. Be sure the object window shows just what you want in the embedded object when you're finished editing.

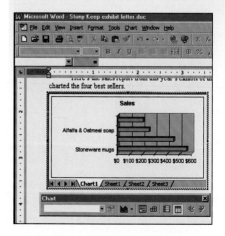

3 Return to the Main Document

When you finish editing, click outside the embedded object, in the main document. The source program tools disappear, and whatever was displayed in the object window is displayed in the embedded object.

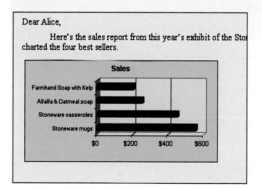

4 Edit a Linked Object

Double-click the linked object (in this example, a Word paragraph linked in an Excel worksheet).

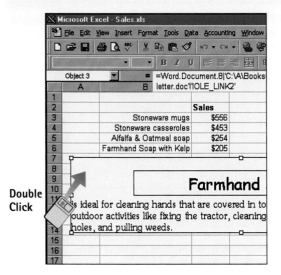

Double Click

5 Edit the Source File

The source program and source file open. (If a document with a linked object is removed from the computer where the source file and program are, you can't edit the linked object.)

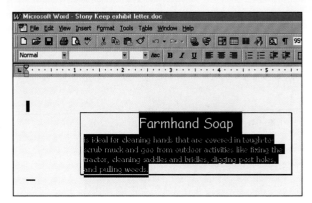

6 Return to the Main Document

When you finish editing, save your changes and close the source program and file. All linked copies of the source data automatically reflect the changes.

End

How-To Hints

Embedded Objects Are Big But Portable

Because an embedded object is separate from its source file, it contains all the data and formatting codes it needs. Because the object is separate from its source, you don't need the source file to edit the object (although you do need the source program).

Linked Objects: Small But Less Portable

A linked object is not a container of data and formatting codes; it contains directions to the source file. Because the object shows what's in the source file, you cannot edit this object if it can't find its source file.

Opening a File with a Linked Object

When you open a file that contains a linked object, you'll be asked whether you want to update the link. If the source file is available on your computer, click **Yes;** the current source data is displayed in the linked object. If you don't want the object updated with current changes, click **No** so that the old linked data is displayed.

How to Use Excel Data in a Word Document

Task 1 discusses why you might want to use one type of object instead of the other. If you don't need to include formatting from the source file but only want to transfer data from one file into another, you can copy and paste the data rather than using objects. Copied-and-pasted data becomes a part of the file in which it's pasted and retains no connection to its source.

This task shows you how to copy and paste data from Excel to Word without using objects, and then how to create linked and embedded Excel objects in a Word document.

Begin

1 Copy Excel Data

Select the cells you want to copy, and use any technique you like to copy them (choose **Edit**, **Copy**; click the **Copy** button on the Standard toolbar; or press Ctrl+C).

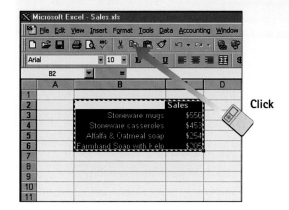
Click

2 Paste Data in a Word Document

Switch to the Word document, and click where you want to paste the Excel data. Choose **Edit**, **Paste** (or click the **Paste** button on the toolbar, or press Ctrl+V). The Excel data is pasted into the Word document as a Word table, and it becomes Word data (not an object). Edit it like any Word table (see Task 13 in Chapter 2, "How to Use Word 97").

Click

3 Copy an Excel Chart

Click the Excel chart to select it, and use any technique you like to copy it (choose **Edit**, **Copy**; click the **Copy** button on the Standard toolbar; or press Ctrl+C).

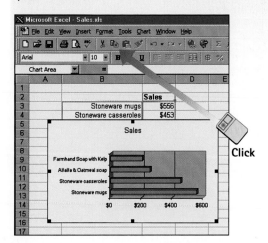
Click

4 Paste-Embed the Chart into Word

Switch to the Word document, and click where you want to paste the Excel chart. Choose **Edit, Paste Special**. In the Paste Special dialog box, click the **Paste** option, select **Microsoft Excel Chart Object**, and choose **OK**. The chart is pasted as an embedded object.

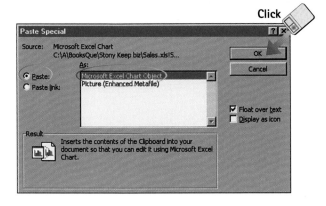

5 Paste-Link the Chart into Word

Switch to the Word document, and click where you want to paste the Excel chart. Choose **Edit, Paste Special**. In the Paste Special dialog box, click the **Paste link** option, select **Microsoft Excel Chart Object**, and choose **OK**. The chart is pasted as a linked object.

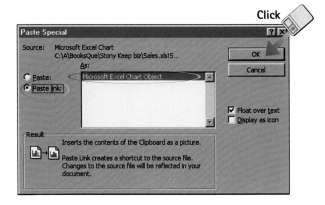

6 They Look the Same

Although they behave differently, chart objects look the same whether linked or embedded; whether you did step 4 or step 5, the result looks similar to this.

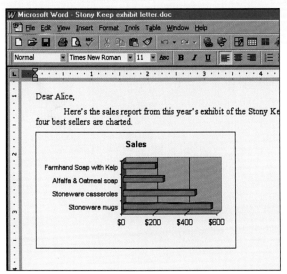

How-To Hints

Link or Embed Worksheet Cells

To link or embed a worksheet table, select and copy the cells and then follow step 4 or 5 to link or embed a picture of the formatted cells into your Word document.

Drag-and-Drop Data

When you drag-and-drop Excel data into a Word document, the data is pasted as an embedded object.

End

How to Use Word Data in an Excel Worksheet

This task shows you how to copy and paste paragraphs from Word to Excel without using objects, and then how to create linked and embedded Word objects in an Excel worksheet.

Begin

1 Copy Word Data

Select the paragraphs you want to copy, and use any technique you like to copy them (choose **Edit, Copy**; click the **Copy** button on the Standard toolbar; or press Ctrl+C).

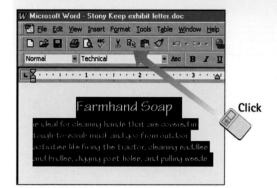
Click

2 Paste Data in an Excel Worksheet

Switch to the Excel worksheet, and click where you want to paste the Word text. Choose **Edit, Paste** (or click the **Paste** button on the toolbar, or press Ctrl+V). The Word text is pasted into the Excel worksheet (each paragraph in a separate cell) and becomes Excel data (not an object). Edit the data like any worksheet cells (see Task 3 in Chapter 3, "How to Use Excel 97").

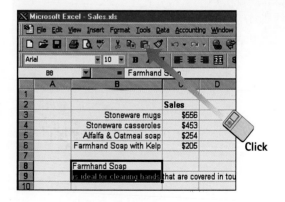
Click

3 Copy Formatted Word Text

Select the Word text, and use any technique you like to copy it (choose **Edit, Copy**; click the **Copy** button on the Standard toolbar; or press Ctrl+C).

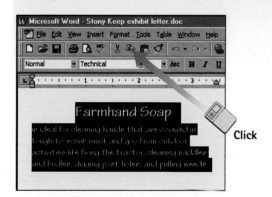
Click

4 Paste-Embed the Text into Excel

Switch to the Excel worksheet and click where you want to paste the Word object. Choose **Edit**, **Paste Special**. In the Paste Special dialog box, click the **Paste** option, select **Microsoft Word Document Object**, and choose **OK**. The selected text is pasted as an embedded object.

Click

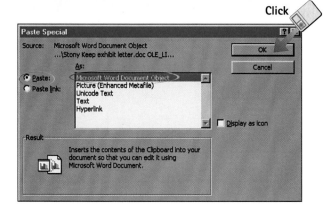

5 Paste-Link the Text into Excel

Switch to the Excel worksheet and click where you want to paste the Word object. Choose **Edit**, **Paste Special**. In the Paste Special dialog box, click the **Paste link** option, select **Microsoft Word Document Object**, and choose **OK**. The selected text is pasted as a linked object.

Click

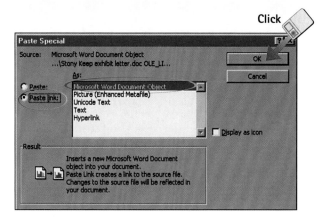

6 Format the Object

Linked and embedded objects look similar. To change an object's formatting, right-click the object and click **Format Object**. On the **Colors and Lines** tab, set the colors you want, and choose **OK**.

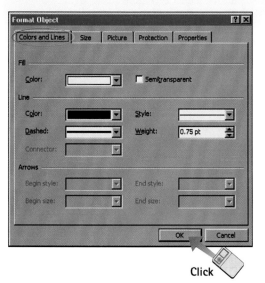

Click

How-To Hints

Drag-and-Drop Data
When you drag-and-drop Word text into an Excel worksheet, the text is pasted as cell entries, not as an object.

End

How to Use Word Text in a Publisher Document

You can write all the text directly in your Publisher 98 document while you create it, but if the text you want to use is already in electronic form, why retype it? You can import it into your Publisher document without even opening Word. Text in a Publisher text frame can be edited and formatted using Word tools, which can make changes in a long segment of text much easier.

Text that's imported from another document is copied and converted; the source file isn't changed in the process. If you want to use only a small portion of the text in a Word file, you may find it easier to open Word, copy the text you want, and paste it into a Publisher text frame.

Begin

1 Create a Text Box

In a Publisher document, text must be entered in a *text frame*. Click the Text Frame Tool, and drag to draw a rectangle on the document page.

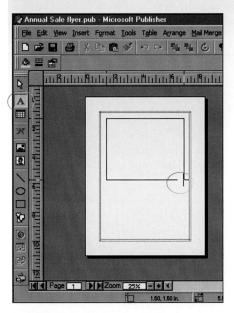

2 Choose Insert, Text File

Click the text frame to select it, and choose **Insert**, **Text File**; or right-click the text frame, point to **Change Text**, and click **Text File**.

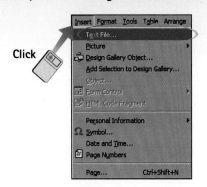

Click

3 Insert the File

In the Insert Text File dialog box, navigate to the file that contains the text you want to import, and double-click the filename.

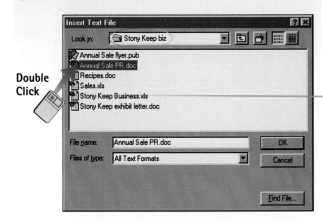

Double Click

4 The File Is Converted and Inserted

The entire contents of the file are converted and inserted into the Publisher document. If you're asked whether the text should autoflow (because the text is larger than your text frame), you can click **Yes** to let Publisher create new pages and text frames for the text, or you can click **No** to create and connect new text frames yourself (see Task 4 in Chapter 5, "How to Use Publisher 98," to learn how).

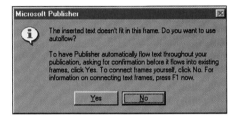

5 Copy Part of a Larger File

To use a small part of a large Word file, it's easier to copy the text you want from the Word document. To copy selected text, use any technique you prefer for copying (choose **Edit**, **Copy**; click the **Copy** button; or press Ctrl+C).

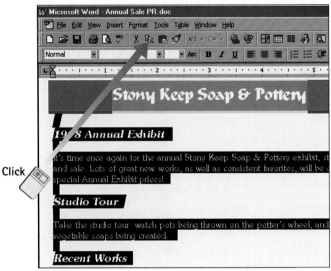

Click

6 Paste the Text in Publisher

Click in the Publisher text frame where you want to paste the text, and use any technique you prefer for pasting (choose **Edit**, **Paste**; click the Paste button; or press Ctrl+V).

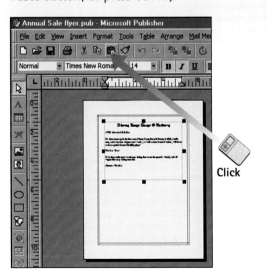

Click

End

How to Add Hyperlinks to a Document to Open Other Documents

Hyperlinks came into being with the World Wide Web as the means by which you can jump directly from one Web page to another. Office 97 brought hyperlinks into your computer documents. You can add hyperlinks to Word documents, Excel worksheets, and Outlook email messages.

Begin

1 Decide on Hyperlink Location

Click in the worksheet cell or document text to place the insertion point where you want the hyperlink to appear. In this example, I'm creating an index of chapter files for this book.

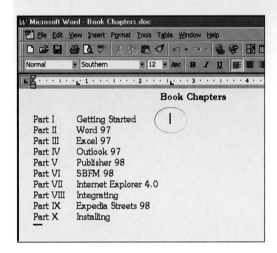

2 Choose Insert, Hyperlink

To insert a hyperlink, you can choose **Insert, Hyperlink**; click the **Insert Hyperlink** button on the Standard toolbar; or press Ctrl+K.

3 Find the Hyperlink File

In the Insert Hyperlink dialog box, click in the **Link to file or URL** box, and then click the **Browse** button.

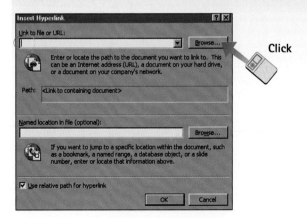

4 Link to the File

In the Link to File dialog box, navigate to the file you want the hyperlink to open, click the filename to select it, and choose **OK**. In the Insert Hyperlink dialog box, choose **OK** to finish the hyperlink.

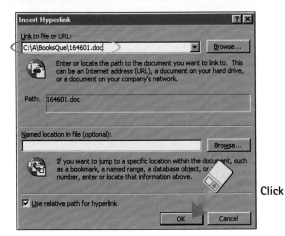

Click

5 Rename the Hyperlink

The hyperlink name will consist of the hard drive path or complete URL. To create a shorter, more memorable name, right-click the new hyperlink and choose **Hyperlink**, **Select Hyperlink**. The hyperlink is selected, so you can change its spelling without triggering it to open a file.

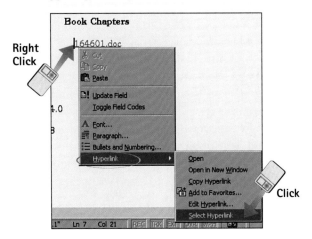

Right Click

Click

6 Type a New Name

Type a new name for the hyperlink, and then click away from it. When you point to the hyperlink, a ScreenTip shows the path, but the name in your document is more reader-friendly. Click the hyperlink to test it; the file it points to opens.

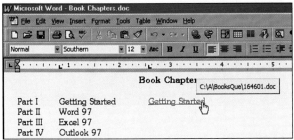

End

How-To Hints

Jump to a Specific Part of a File

You can have a hyperlink jump to a specific section of a file if you've named the portion to which you want to jump (for example, a named range in a worksheet or a bookmark in a Word document). When you create the hyperlink in step 3, click in the **Named location in file** box, click **Browse**, and click the named range or bookmark; then choose **OK**.

Remove a Hyperlink

You can't click a hyperlink in a Word document or worksheet cell to select it because you'll trigger the hyperlink. To delete a hyperlink from a worksheet cell, select the cell with keystrokes (arrow keys, Shift, or Tab) and press Delete. To delete a hyperlink from a Word document, right-click the hyperlink, and choose **Hyperlink**, **Select Hyperlink**, and then press Delete.

Project

This project combines tasks in Word, Excel, and Publisher to create a letter to mail to customers. The initial text is written in Word because Word is so easy for most people to use, and a chart is created from data in Excel. A new Publisher document opens, and the Word text and Excel chart are combined in the Publisher document, along with a title, pull quote, and page border to create an eye-catching finished letter. If you need help remembering how to do any step, refer to the Part and Task in this book that cover the particular procedures.

1 Write Text in Word

Write the main document text in Word, and save and close the Word document (see Task 2 in Chapter 2 and Task 3 in Chapter 1 to learn how).

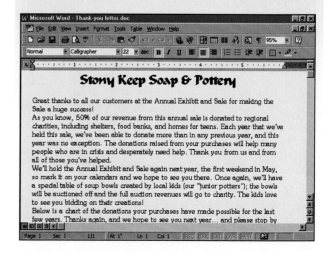

2 Create a Chart in Excel

Use Excel's ChartWizard to chart data in an Excel worksheet. (See Task 22 in Chapter 3 to create an Excel chart.)

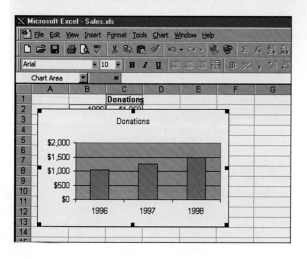

3 Format Chart Elements

To use special color blends, right-click a chart element to select it, and click **Format element**.

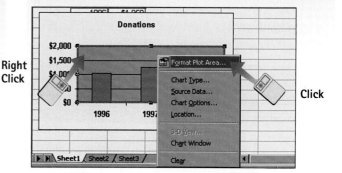

Right Click

Click

4 Try Unusual Color Effects

In the Format *Element* dialog box, on the **Patterns** tab, click the **Fill Effects** button and experiment with color combinations. Save but don't close the workbook.

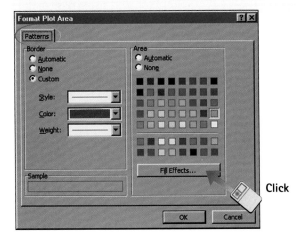

Click

5 Start Publisher

Start Publisher, and close the Catalog that appears when Publisher starts (click the **Exit Catalog** button in the lower-right corner of the Catalog dialog box). This project uses an empty Publisher page.

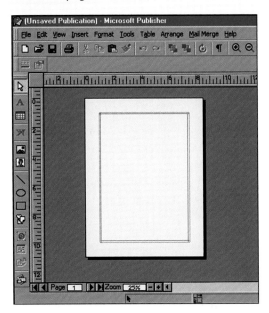

6 Create a Text Frame

Click the Text Frame Tool, and drag to draw a Text Frame on the page. (To learn how to create text frames, see Task 3 in Chapter 5.)

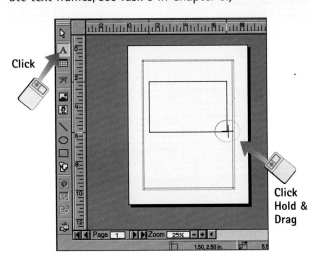

Click

Click
Hold &
Drag

7 Import Text from Word

Click the Text Frame to select it, and choose **Insert**, **Text File**. (To learn how to import text in a text frame, see Task 4 in Chapter 5.)

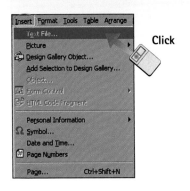

Click

Continues

8 Find the Word File

In the Insert File dialog box, navigate to the file where you saved the text in step 1. Click the filename to select it, and then click **Insert** to insert it in the text frame.

9 Create a Picture Frame

Click the **Picture Frame** tool, and drag to draw a picture frame on the page. The picture frame is where a copy of the Excel chart gets pasted.

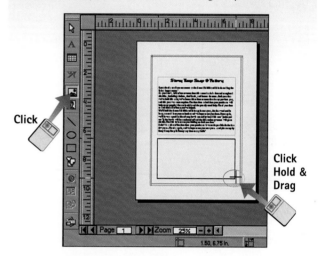

Click

Click Hold & Drag

10 Copy the Excel Chart

In Excel, click the chart to select it, and then click the **Copy** button on the Standard toolbar to copy the chart.

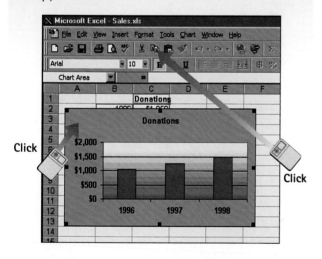

Click

Click

11 Paste the Chart

Return to Publisher and click the picture frame to select it. Then choose **Edit**, **Paste Special**.

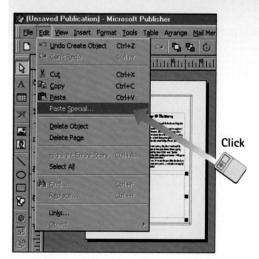

Click

12 Embed the Chart

In the Paste Special dialog box, be sure the **Paste** option and **Microsoft Excel Chart Object** are selected. Choose **OK** to paste an embedded copy of the chart.

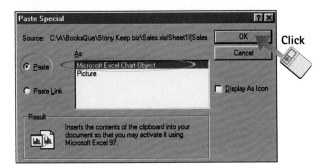

13 Look at the Page

Shown is the page completed to this point. The next few steps walk you through editing the text and adding a title, border, and pull quote.

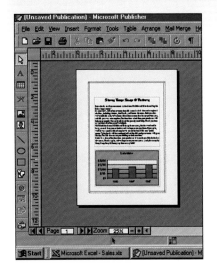

14 Edit Text with Word Tools

You can edit text directly in the Publisher page, of course, but sometimes it's easier to handle large-scale editing jobs with Word tools. I'll demonstrate by using Word tools here—right-click in the text frame, point to **Change Text**, and click **Edit Story in Microsoft Word**.

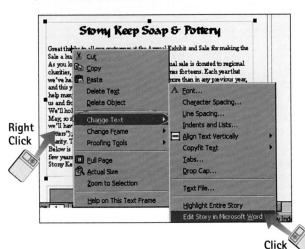

15 Make Your Changes

The text appears in a Word window, along with Word's tools. When you've made your changes, click the **Save** button on the Standard toolbar to save them, and then close the Word window. You'll return to the Publisher window, and the text is changed.

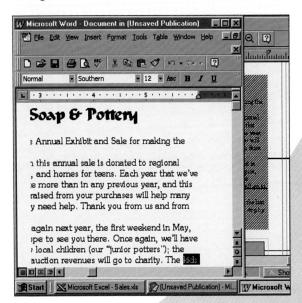

Continues

16 Add a Title

To add a title, draw another text frame at the top of the page and enter your text. (For this example, I cut the title text from the first text frame and pasted it into the new title text frame.) (If you need to move the text frame to make room for the title text frame, see Task 3 in Chapter 5.)

17 Add a Page Border

To create a page border, click the **Rectangle** tool and draw a rectangle around the page; then choose **Format, Line/Border Style, More Styles**.

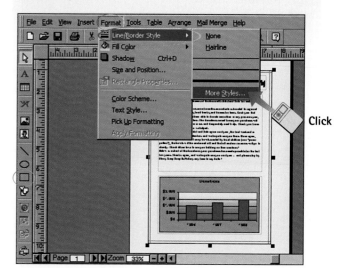

Click

18 Format the Page Border

On the **BorderArt** tab in the Border Style dialog box, select one of the **Available Borders** and choose **OK**.

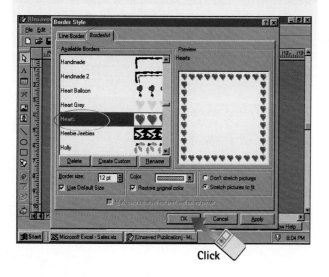

Click

19 Open the Design Gallery

You can add a pull quote to illuminate a concise idea in the text. The Design Gallery has a lot of ready-made pull-quote objects that you can use. Click in the text where you want a pull quote, and then click the **Design Gallery Object** button.

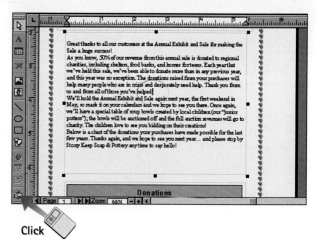

Click

20 Add a Pull Quote

In the Categories list of the Design Gallery dialog box, click **Pull Quotes**; select a design and click **Insert Object**.

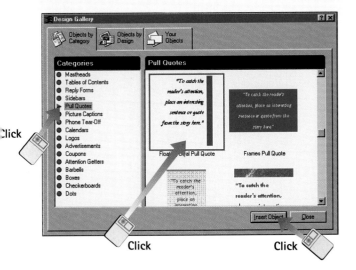

Click

Click

Click

21 Enter the Pull Quote Text

Pull quotes are text quotes that are copied, or pulled, from the body text. Find a pithy sentence, select it, and choose **Edit**, **Copy**. Select the pull quote text and choose **Edit**, **Paste**.

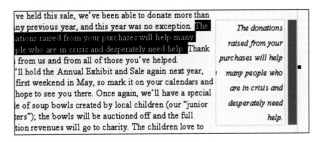

22 Print the Document

Save the document, and then choose **File**, **Print**. Set printing options in the Print dialog box and choose **OK**. If you want to print special documents on special paper, be sure the special paper is loaded in your printer.

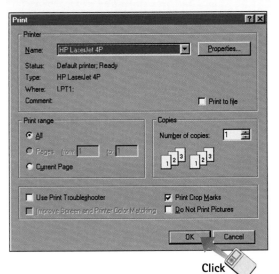

Click

23 Look at the Finished Document

Time to take a step back and look at this document now that it's finished.

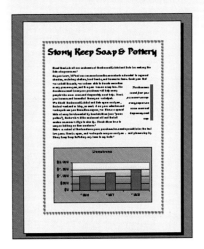

End

Task

How to Use Expedia Streets 98

*E*xpedia Streets 98 is a very useful mapping program that covers the entire United States, including Alaska and Hawaii. You can find street addresses anywhere in the country, print the street map, locate facilities, and mark and label your own spots on the map. For a trip across the country, you can highlight a route for navigation, print maps, and make hotel reservations.

The Expedia Streets windows and menus look and behave just a bit differently than other Small Business Edition programs, but you'll get used to them quickly.

You should be aware that the Expedia Streets maps are copyrighted, so don't print any maps for sale or publication, and don't include a map on a Web page. You can copy a map to a document as long as you keep the copyright information with the map and as long as the map is not sold. For more information, choose **Help**, **Contents**; on the **Index** tab, go to **Copyrighted material**. ●

How to Open and Exit Expedia Streets 98

Expedia Streets runs from its CD because there's such a vast amount of map data involved. You can keep the Expedia Streets CD in your CD drive all the time and start it as any other program, or you can place the CD in the drive only when you want to run Expedia Streets.

You can minimize the program to get it out of your way temporarily rather than closing it; when you do exit the program, you can leave the CD in your drive or remove it (but you should exit the program before you remove it).

Begin

1 Put the CD in the Drive

Place the Expedia Streets 98 CD in your CD drive, and wait several seconds for the start screen to appear. You don't need to click anything to start the program.

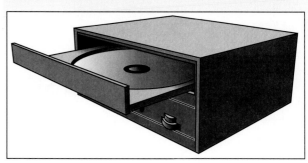

2 Start from the Start Button

If the CD is already in your CD drive because you used Expedia Streets earlier and then exited the program, choose **Start**, **Programs**, **Microsoft Expedia**, **Streets 98** to start the program again.

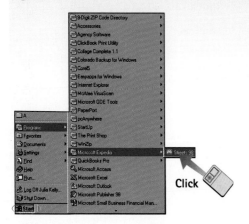

Click

3 Close the Start Screen Dialog Box

The Start Screen dialog box is an easy way to get started exploring Expedia Streets. If you don't want to see it when you start, click the **Don't show this screen again** check box—all the options in the Start Screen dialog box are also commands on the top toolbar. Click **Close** to close the dialog box.

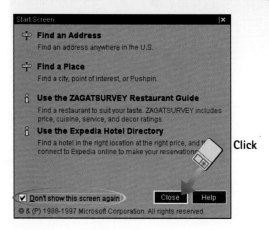

Click

4 Minimize the Map

To move the map temporarily out of your way, minimize it by clicking its button in the taskbar. Click the taskbar button again to return the map to view.

Click

5 Exit the Map Quickly

To exit Expedia Streets quickly, click the small **X** button in the upper-right corner of the screen.

Click

6 Exit the Map with the Menu

To exit Expedia Streets with two clicks, choose **File, Exit**.

Click

End

How to Use the Map Tools

The Expedia Streets window has two toolbars in addition to the menu bar. Although you see the toolbar buttons mentioned in other tasks, I cover them all here so you have a single reference for the map tools.

Begin

1 The Upper Toolbar

The upper toolbar text labels make the buttons easy to identify. **Back** and **Forward** jump back and forth between views you've already seen; **Find** enables you to search for addresses, places, and points of interest (see Task 4); **Guides** gets you information about restaurants and hotels (see Tasks 8 and 9); and **Expedia Online** launches your browser to the Expedia Streets Web page.

2 Zoom Buttons

On the left end of the lower toolbar are the **Zoom In**, **Zoom Out**, and **Zoom Slider** buttons. They're all ways to change your viewing altitude (see Task 3). You can also zoom in and out by right-clicking anywhere on the map and choosing a **Zoom** command.

3 Selector and Hand

Next to the zoom tools are the **Zoom Area** button and the **Move Map** button. Use the **Zoom Area** button to zoom in on a specific area of the map, and use the **Move Map** button to move the map around so you can see what's off the screen (see Task 3).

4 Route and Spot Highlighters

The Route Highlighter draws highlighted lines on the map to help you follow a route when you're traveling. It also measures the distance (see Task 5). The **Highlight a Place** button places a high-lighted spot on cities, places, or pushpins so you don't lose track of them after you find them (this button also turns off the highlighted spots).

5 Points of Interest and Pushpins

Points of Interest are items such as restaurants, hotels, schools, museums, theaters, golf courses, nightclubs, and shopping centers (see Task 4). Pushpins are markers for your own locations and labels (see Task 7).

6 Map Scale

At the lower-right corner of the map window is a map scale that gives you an idea of the scale of your current view. Every time you zoom, the scale changes.

End

How to View the Map

Expedia Streets starts with a map of the entire contiguous United States, but you can zoom in to as close as a few square blocks or zoom out to an altitude of 8,700 miles above the earth.

In this task you learn how to change your altitude, zoom in closer on an area, move the map to see nearby areas, and then zoom back to a view of the whole map. Because all the data is accessed from the CD, you'll need to wait a moment for the map view to change (depending on the speed of your CD drive).

Begin

1 Change Your Altitude

On the lower toolbar, click the **Zoom Slider** arrow, and then click an up or down slider button to change viewing altitude (your altitude is shown at the bottom of the Zoom Slider box). To determine which slider button to click, point at one of them to see a ScreenTip. You can also drag the altitude arrow. Click anywhere to close the Zoom Slider box.

Click

2 Zoom on the Center of the Map

Click the **Zoom In** and **Zoom Out** buttons to zoom closer and farther from the point in the center of your screen. You can also right-click anywhere in the map and choose **Zoom In** or **Zoom Out**.

3 Zoom In on a Specific Area

Click the **Zoom Area** button. When the mouse pointer has a rectangle symbol (which is the default pointer), drag to draw a rectangle around the area you want to zoom in on. Click inside the rectangle (the pointer changes to a plus symbol inside the rectangle). If you change your mind, click anywhere outside the rectangle to remove it.

Click

4 Move Map with the Hand

Click the **Move Map** button. With the hand-symbol mouse pointer, drag a spot on the map to a new position. The map moves around in your Expedia Streets window.

Click
Hold &
Drag

5 Move Map with Perimeter Arrows

Point to the perimeter of the map in the direction that you want to move (for example, if you want to move your view up, point to the top border of the map). When the pointer becomes a big, white arrow, click to move by jumps.

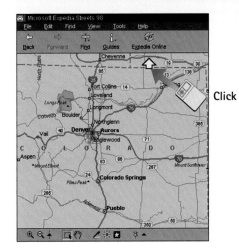

Click

6 Return to Expanded View

When you want to start over again with a bird's-eye view of the whole country, right-click anywhere in the map, and point to **Zoom**. Click **To 48 States** for the contiguous United States, or click **To Entire U.S.** to include Alaska and Hawaii.

Right
Click

Click

End

How-To Hints

View the Terrain

If you're not zoomed in too closely, you can switch your map view to include terrain levels. Choose **View**, **Display Terrain** to switch between terrain view and flat-map view.

How to Find and Mark Locations on the Map

Unlike a standard road map, you don't have to search for locations yourself in Expedia Streets; you can instruct the program to look them up for you. You can look up specific addresses or find places such as cities or national parks. You can also find points of interest and restaurants and hotels, either near a specific map location or anywhere in the country.

Begin

1 Find an Address

Choose **Find, An Address**. In the Find Address dialog box, type as much of the address as you know. (If the program can't find the address, try typing it differently, or leave out the street number.) Then click **Find**. If you get a list of Found Addresses, click the correct one and choose **OK**, or choose **Cancel** and try again.

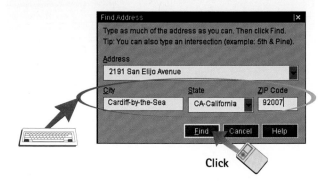

Click

2 Show the Address on the Map

A pushpin appears with the address on the map. You can zoom in or out to figure out your route to get there, and the pushpin will remain in place. To relabel the pushpin, drag to select the text and type a new label. You can show several addresses in the same vicinity by repeating step 1. (See Task 7 to learn more about pushpins.)

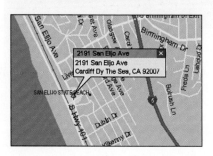

3 Find a Place

Choose **Find, A Place**. Type the name of the city or **Place** (choose a **State** to narrow the search), and click **Find**. In the list of Found Places, click the place you want. For more information about the place, click **Information**. Choose **OK** to close the dialog box.

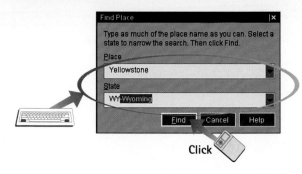

Click

4 Find Faraway Points of Interest

To find a point of interest anywhere in the country, choose **Find, A Point of Interest**. In the Find Points of Interest dialog box, type the **Point of Interest Name**, and narrow your search with a **Category**, **City**, or **State**. Click **Find**. Next, you may need to select from a list of **Found Places**; click a place, and choose **OK**.

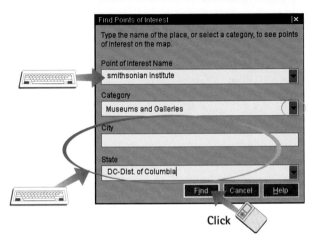

5 Find Nearby Points of Interest

On the lower toolbar, click the **Points Of Interest** button, and click the map. In the Find Nearby Points of Interest dialog box, click a category, and then click a place in that category (the location appears on the map). For information such as phone numbers and addresses, click **Information**. To expand the search, drag the slider at the top of the dialog box.

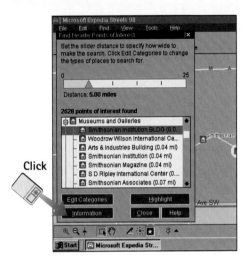

6 Remove Points of Interest

Right-click near the point of interest you want to remove, and choose **Show Points of Interest**. Scroll through the list in the Show Points of Interest dialog box, and clear the check boxes next to the points of interest you want to remove from view. Then choose **OK**. (If the label remains on the map, choose **Edit, Clear Labels**).

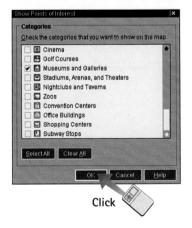

How-To Hints

Too Many Icons?

If you find your map inexplicably covered with icons and pushpins, you can delete all of them and start with a fresh map. Choose **View, Show Pushpin Sets**; click **Clear All**, and then choose **OK**.

More Point-of-Interest Information

To open a Guides window with information about a specific point of interest, double-click the point-of-interest icon. If you right-click the point-of-interest icon, a shortcut menu lists commands for zooming in on the area and for showing more nearby points of interest.

End

How to Highlight a Travel Route and Mileage

Although a map program is great fun when you're armchair-traveling from your computer, it becomes truly useful when you're actually traveling. Whether you're heading out on sales calls and appointments with clients or planning a vacation, you can highlight your route on a map and take a printed copy with you.

You can test different routes and check the mileage before you settle on one. Unfortunately, there's no automatic recording of the mileage you measure; however, you can place a pushpin and label at the end of a route, and then type the mileage you measured into the label (see Task 7).

Begin

1 Click the Route Highlighter

On the lower toolbar, click the **Route Highlighter** button. The Route Highlighter dialog box appears, and the pointer becomes a pen-and-crosshair symbol.

Click

2 Mark Your Route

Click to mark the start of your route, and then click at various points along the route. At the end of the route, double-click to turn off the highlighter pen. You cannot draw a route by dragging; routes are drawn in straight-line segments. The more segments you create to follow the twists and turns of your route closely, the more accurate the mileage measurement is.

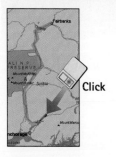

Click

3 Look at Route Mileage

Each time you click a route segment, the new segment mileage is added to the distance in the Route Highlighter dialog box. Look at the distance before you double-click to end the route because the Route Highlighter dialog box closes when you end the route. If you missed the distance, you can remeasure the route by following steps 5 and 6.

4 Erase Highlighted Routes

To erase the last route you highlighted, choose **Edit**, **Clear Highlights**, **Last Route**. To erase all the highlighted routes on the map, choose **Edit**, **Clear Highlights**, **All Routes**.

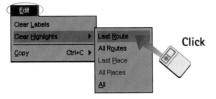

Click

5 Test with Temporary Measurement

To take a temporary measurement without leaving any highlights on the map, choose **Tools**, **Measuring Tool**.

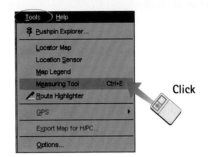

Click

6 Measure Different Routes

Click to mark segments of the route you want to measure, and look at the Distance in the Measuring Tool dialog box. To end a measurement, right-click the map.

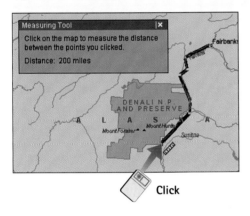

Click

End

How to Save and Print a Route

If you're creating a map to help you find your way to an office building downtown in one of those cities whose streets are laid out like a pile of spaghetti, you'll want to print the map so you can use it to navigate. And if your office is the place that's tough to find, you'll want to save the map so you can open it and print it whenever you need to send it to a client.

Begin

1 Save the Map

To save the map in which you're currently working, with all your highlighted routes, labels, addresses, points of interest, and pushpins, choose **File, Save Map**. (See Task 7 to learn more about pushpins.)

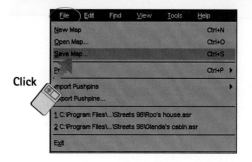

Click

2 Name the Map File

In the **Save As** dialog box, navigate to the folder where you want to save your maps, then type a **File name** and choose **Save**.

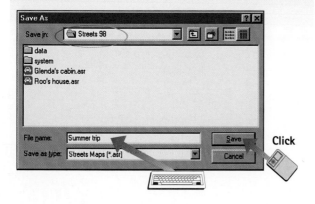

Click

3 Open a Saved Map

To open a saved map, choose **File, Open Map**. Navigate to the folder where you saved the map, and double-click the map name. You can also open a recently saved map by double-clicking its name at the bottom of the **File** menu.

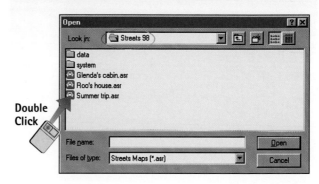

Double Click

4 Print a Map

To print a map, choose **File**, **Print**, **Map**.

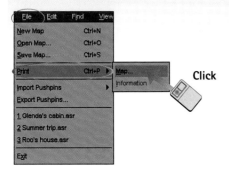

Click

5 Title the Map

In the Print Map dialog box, type a title for the map (either one line or two), and choose **Print**. Depending on the amount of detail in the map, it may take a few minutes for your computer to get the data together and send it to the printer.

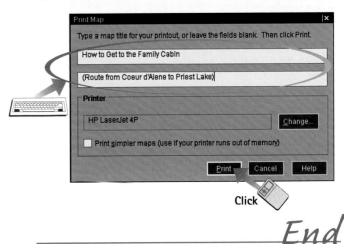

Click

End

How-To Hints

If the Map Won't Print

If your printer doesn't have enough memory to print the map, you can print a simpler map that doesn't require as much printer memory. In the Print dialog box, click the **Print simpler maps (use if your printer runs out of memory)** check box before you choose **Print**.

7

How to Mark Your Map with Pushpins

Pushpins are used for adding your own bits of information to the map, such as "No street sign; turn left at the big green rock." Each pushpin has a label that you can turn on or off, and you can mark different places with different pushpins by changing the pushpin symbol.

Begin

1 Create a Pushpin

On the lower toolbar, click the **Pushpin** button. If you want to use a different symbol, click the arrow button next to the Pushpin button, and click a symbol.

Click

2 Click the Map

On the map, click where you want to place the symbol. The symbol and a blank label appear.

Click

3 Type a Title and Add a Note

The name of the label (the gray bar) is highlighted; type a name for the pushpin. Then press **Tab** or click the white area, and type any notes you want to attach to the pushpin. Click anywhere on the map to finish the label. To change the text, select it and type new text.

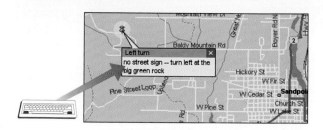

4 Hide and Show the Label

To hide the label, click the **X** button in its upper-right corner. To show the label again, right-click the pushpin and choose **Open**. To show just the label name, right-click the pushpin and choose **Show Name**.

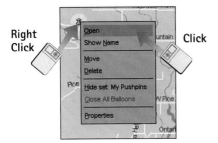

5 Move the Label

If you zoom in on an area with a push-pin, you may find the pushpin isn't exactly where you want it. To move it, right-click the pushpin and choose **Move**, and then click where you want the symbol.

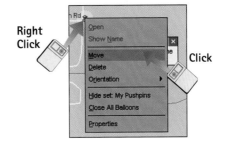

6 Delete a Pushpin

To delete a pushpin, right-click the symbol and choose **Delete**. When asked to confirm the deletion, click **Yes**.

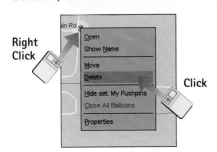

End

How-To Hints

Change an Existing Pushpin Symbol

Right-click the pushpin and choose **Properties**. In the Pushpin Properties dialog box, under **Symbol**, click the down arrow; then click a different symbol and choose **OK**.

Include a Hyperlink in a Label

To create a hyperlink to a Web site or a site on your company's intranet, right-click the pushpin symbol. Choose **Properties**. In the Pushpin Properties dialog box, click the **Type** tab, and then click **Web Link**. In the **URL** box, type the hyperlink, starting with **http://**, and choose **OK**. To use the hyperlink, click it.

How to Use the Hotel Guide and Travel Services

When you plan a trip, you can check out the hotels in the area and make reservations before you go. Expedia Streets has a large database of hotel information (more than 14,000 hotels) and offers an easy way to look up just the kind of accommodations you want.

When you decide where you want to stay, you can make reservations over the Internet through the Microsoft Expedia Travel Agent, which is a complete online travel service. You can also use the Microsoft Expedia Travel Agent to check airfares, reserve rental cars, and purchase plane tickets.

Begin

1 Open the Hotel Directory

On the top toolbar, click **Guides**, **Expedia Hotel Directory**.

Click

2 Look Up the Hotel Type You Want

In the Expedia Hotel Guide dialog box, type a **City** and choose a **State**. Narrow your selections by choosing a specific **Chain/Type** of hotel and a **Price** range. If you require special amenities, click those check boxes, and then click **Find**.

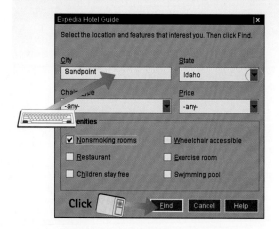

3 Locate a Hotel on the Map

A list of hotels that meet your requirements appears in the Found Expedia Hotel Guide dialog box; click a hotel name and wait a moment. The map zooms in on the location of the hotel, and a label and icon appear for the hotel.

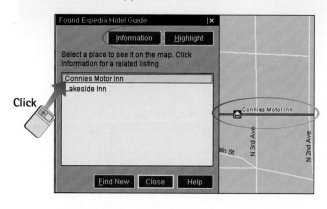

4 Look Up Hotel Information

To read more information about the hotel that's selected in the Found Expedia Hotel Guide list, click **Information**. A **Guides** window opens with hotel information. To read information about another hotel, click another name in the Found Expedia Hotel Guide list; the information in the **Guides** window changes.

5 Print Hotel Information

To print the Guides information, click the arrow in the upper-left corner of the Guides window, and choose **Print**. To close the Guides window, click the **X** in the upper-right corner.

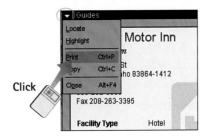

Click

6 Go Online to Make Reservations

To make hotel reservations online through the Microsoft Expedia Travel Agent, open the Guides window for the hotel and click the **Online Reservations** button (not all hotels have this feature available).

Click

How-To Hints

Erase All Those Labels

To erase labels and icons for hotels, restaurants, and other points of interest, choose **View**, **Show Points of Interest**. In the Show Points of Interest dialog box, clear specific check boxes to erase those labels, or choose **Clear All** to erase them all, and then choose **OK**.

End

How to Look Up Restaurant Reviews

If you're new in town, you can get restaurant reviews from Expedia Streets before you go out to eat. Expedia Streets lists 17,000 restaurants throughout the United States, so you'll be able to find restaurant information almost anywhere.

Expedia Streets lists pricing information for restaurants if it's available—those prices are based on the main meal or the latest meal served by the restaurant, and are based on the median entrée price for one person (taxes, tips, and drinks are not included in the price listings). If there's price or rating information shown in blue, click the blue type to read more.

Begin

1 Open the Restaurant Guide

On the upper toolbar, click **Guides**, **ZAGATSURVEY Restaurants**.

2 Select a Region and a Cuisine

In the ZAGATSURVEY Restaurant Guide dialog box, select a geographical region from the **Region** list box. If you want a particular type of cuisine, select it from the **Cuisine** list (leave **Cuisine** blank to look for all types).

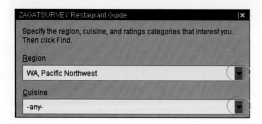

3 Choose Preferences

Under **Ratings Categories**, you can narrow your search by selecting a price range from the **Price** list box, a food quality range from the **Food** list box, and **Excellent Service** or **Noteworthy Decor** from the **Special** list box (or you can leave them reading -any-). Then click **Find**.

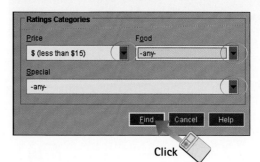

4 Click a Restaurant

In the Found ZAGATSURVEY Restaurant Guide window, click the name of a restaurant you want to know more about. The map zooms in to the restaurant's location, and a label and icon appear on the map.

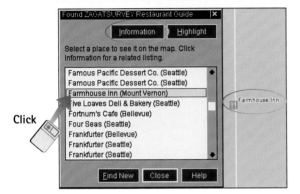

Click

5 Get More Information

In the Found ZAGATSURVEY Restaurant Guide window, click the **Information** button to open a **Guides** window about the selected restaurant. For information about another restaurant in the Found ZAGATSURVEY Restaurant Guide list, click the restaurant name.

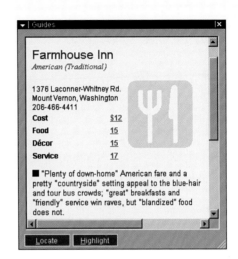

6 Drill Deeper

For more information, especially about ZAGATSURVEY, click the hyperlinks (the blue text) in the **Guides** window. To close the **Guides** window or the Found ZAGATSURVEY Restaurant Guide window, click the **X** in the upper-right corner.

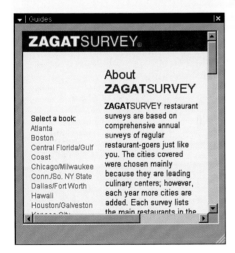

End

How to Paste a Custom Map into a Document

You can send maps to others either as map files or as part of a Word document. If you send a map file to someone, he'll need to have Expedia Streets installed before he can open the map. If he doesn't have Expedia Streets, you can still send him a map as a picture pasted in a document. If you send a map in a document, either as a document file or as a printed document, all he must do is open the document.

Begin

1 Set Up the Map

Zoom in until all the detail you want is shown—but nothing extra because everything displayed on your screen will be included in the picture.

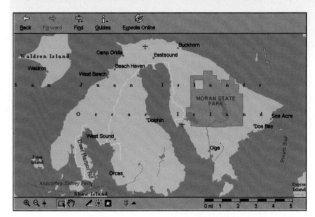

2 Copy the Map

With the map displayed, choose **Edit, Copy, Map**.

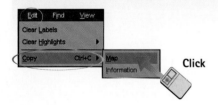

Click

3 Switch to the Document

Switch to your document by clicking the document's button on the taskbar.

Click

4 Prepare to Paste the Map

In the document program, click where you want to paste the map.

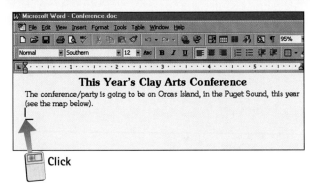

Click

5 Paste the Map

Choose **Edit, Paste**.

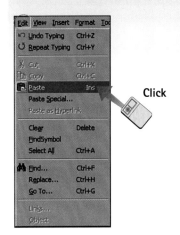

Click

6 Resize the Picture

The map is pasted as a picture in your document. To resize it, click the picture to select it, and then drag a corner handle. (If you drag a top, bottom, or side handle, you'll alter the proportions of the map.)

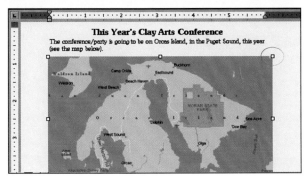

End

Task

CHAPTER 10

How to Install the Microsoft Office 97 Small Business Edition Programs

*I*nstallation of the Microsoft Office 97 SBE programs is fairly simple. Each program in Office 97 SBE is installed separately, which means you must perform a few more steps. However, this process makes it easy for you to install only the programs you want, when you want to install them.

To install Microsoft Office 97 SBE, insert the CD disk #1 into your CD-ROM drive. Wait a few seconds, and the Microsoft Office 97–Small Business Edition install dialog box automatically appears on your screen.

To install any of the Microsoft Office SBE programs, start at the Install dialog box. The tasks in this chapter walk you through the installation of the different programs; each is installed a little bit differently.

If you're curious about a program listed on the Install dialog box, point to the program's icon. The program name is highlighted in black, and a quick explanation of the program appears on the right side of the dialog box.

TASK *1*

How to Install Word 97, Excel 97, and Small Business Financial Manager 98

Word 97, Excel 97, and Small Business Financial Manager 98 are the core programs for Microsoft Office 97 SBE. Each is installed using the same basic procedures and dialog boxes. Although you'll see illustrations of the installation procedure for Word, the steps in this task apply to the installation of Excel and Small Business Financial Manager as well (see step 7 for specific information about the Small Business Financial Manager).

Begin

1 Choose a Program

On the Microsoft Office 97 SBE install dialog box, click the Microsoft Word, Microsoft Excel, or the Small Business Financial Manager icon, and then wait for the setup program to start.

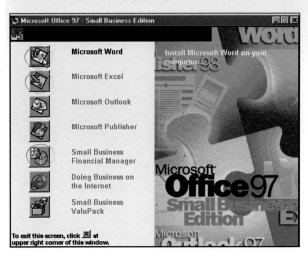

2 Close Other Programs

A Setup dialog box appears and tells you to close any open applications—at this point, if you have any other programs running, you should close them before continuing the installation; then click **Continue**.

3 Type Your Name and Company

In the Name and Organization Information dialog box, information from your Windows 95 setup is automatically entered. You can change this if you wish. Choose **OK**; in the Confirm Name and Organization Information dialog box, the information is repeated. Choose **OK** to see the dialog box where you'll enter your CD Key#.

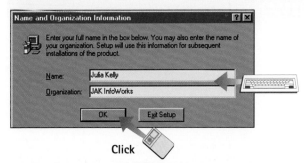

4 Type Your CD Key Number

On the back of the plastic case containing your Office 97 SBE CD, you'll find an 11-digit CD key number. Enter it in the CD Key space (don't type the hyphen; just type the 11 digits). Double-check to be sure you entered the correct number, and then choose **OK**. Choose **OK** again in the dialog box that tells you to write down your product identification number.

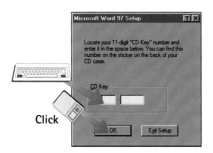

Click

5 Accept the Program's Folder

If you're installing the Small Business Financial Manager, you'll see a message about the SBFM template. If you're installing Word or Excel, Setup automatically installs the Office 97 SBE programs in the \Program Files\Microsoft Office folder. Choose **OK** to continue.

Click

6 Choose a Setup

Program setup starts; in the Setup dialog box, click **Typical**. If you see a dialog box with more check box options, click **Continue** to accept the defaults, or mark check boxes to add more files to your setup. Your program is installed; after installation, you're asked to **Register** or **Register On-line**. Click **Register**.

Click

7 Install the Financial Manager

If you're installing the Small Business Financial Manager, installation is the same as for Word and Excel, except that there's only a Custom installation in step 6; you choose which converters to install. The converters copy data from your existing accounting system into the SBFM so you can analyze it. After installation, you're asked to **Register** or **Register On-line**; click **Register**.

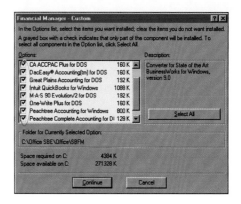

End

How-To Hints

Excel First

You must install Excel before you can install the Small Business Financial Manager.

How to Install Publisher 98

Installing Publisher differs from installing Word or Excel in that this program requires that you start with CD disk #1 and then switch to CD disk #2.

Begin

1 Choose Publisher

In the Microsoft Office 97 SBE Install dialog box, click the Microsoft Publisher icon, and wait for the setup program to start.

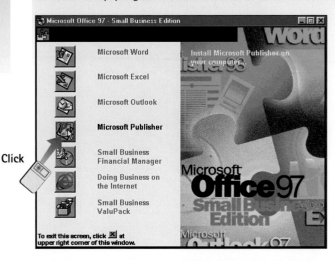

Click

2 Insert Disk #2

A message box tells you to insert CD disk #2. Switch disks and then choose **OK**. (If any other programs are open, close them before you continue.)

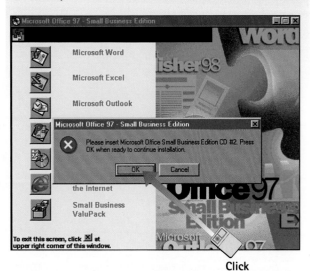

Click

3 Check Your Name and Company

In the Name and Organization Information dialog box, the name and organization information from your Windows 95 setup are automatically entered. You can change this if you wish or accept it as it is. Choose **OK**; in the Confirm Name and Organization Information dialog box, the information is repeated. Choose **OK** to open the next dialog box, where you enter your CD Key.

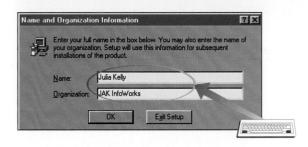

4 Type Your CD Key Number

On the back of the plastic case containing your Office 97 SBE CD, you'll find an 11-digit CD key number. Enter it in the CD Key space (don't type the hyphen; just type the 11 digits). Double-check to be sure you entered the correct number, and then choose **OK**. Choose **OK** again in the dialog box that tells you to write down your product identification number.

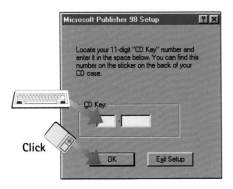

5 Accept Program Location

Setup automatically installs the Office 97 SBE programs in the \Program Files\Microsoft Office folder unless you instruct it otherwise. If you prefer another location for the installation, click **Change Folder** and indicate the new folder; otherwise choose **OK** to continue. During installation, you're asked to accept the License Agreement; click **I agree** to continue.

6 Choose a Setup

The setup program starts arranging files. In the Setup dialog box, click **Typical** (this book covers tasks that are available with a "typical" installation). If you see a dialog box with more check box options, you can click **Continue** to accept the defaults, or mark check boxes to add more files to your setup—doing so won't affect the tasks in this book. During installation, you're asked to register and restart—you don't have to register (you'll just get on Microsoft's mailing list), but you do have to **Restart** your computer before you'll be ready to work.

End

How to Install Internet Explorer 4

When you install Internet Explorer 4, you have three choices: a Minimal installation (the Internet Explorer 4 browser); a Standard installation (the Internet Explorer 4 browser, Outlook Express, and the Web Publishing Wizard); or a Full installation (all of the above and NetMeeting, FrontPage Express, and NetShow).

The tasks in this book use the Standard installation and the Active Desktop. The Active Desktop alters your desktop's appearance. In this task, I'll tell you how to turn off the Active Desktop until you learn more about it in Chapter 7.

Before you begin installation, close all open programs, including your Internet browser.

Begin

1 Select the Internet Icon

On the installation dialog box, click the **Doing Business on the Internet** icon.

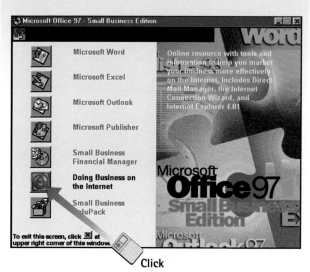

Click

2 Select the Internet Hyperlink

An HTML page on the CD opens in a browser window, with hyperlinks to other HTML pages on the CD. Click the **Microsoft Internet Explorer 4** hyperlink. If you're asked whether you want to make Internet Explorer 4 your default browser, click **Yes**.

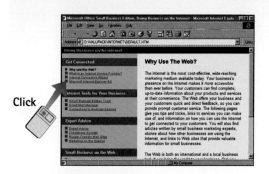

Click

3 Select the Hyperlink Again

Another HTML page from your CD opens; click the **Microsoft Internet Explorer 4** hyperlink on the right side of the page to begin installing Internet Explorer 4.

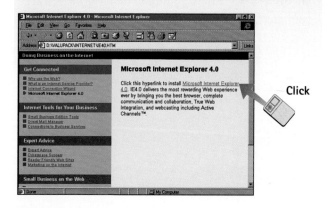

Click

4 Begin the Installation

In the dialog box that warns you about viruses, click **Open it**, and then choose **OK** (one would hope that Microsoft is not distributing viruses in its software). Keep clicking **Yes** and **OK** in any dialog boxes until the installation begins. Eventually the Setup dialog box appears. All you can do in this dialog box is click **Next**, and the Setup Wizard starts. In the piracy-threat message, click **I accept** and **Continue**. Follow the steps in the wizard until you see the Installation Option step. In the option list box, be sure **Standard Installation** is selected, and then click **Next**.

Click

6 Finish the Installation

Accept the default path, and click **Next**. File transfer takes a long time; answer any dialog box questions that appear. When installation is complete, several new icons appear on your desktop, and its appearance changes dramatically. When setup is complete, you can take a tour of Internet Explorer 4 or click **Exit**.

5 Choose the Active Desktop

The next step asks whether you want to install the Active Desktop. Click **Yes**; you can always turn off or uninstall Active Desktop later if you don't like it, and you learn how to use and modify it in Chapter 7. Then click **Next**.

Click

How-To Hints

The Active Desktop Is Bizarre

To return your desktop to the normal Windows 95 desktop without extra clutter from the Active Desktop, right-click the desktop and click **View as Web Page**. You can turn the Active Desktop components and appearance on and off any time you like after it has been installed.

Windows Are Too Big!

Web-style windows can be annoyingly large; to turn off the Web-page view of your windows, click **Start**, point to **Settings**, and click **Folder Options**. On the **General** tab, click **Classic style** (for normal Windows 95 settings), or click **Custom** and then click the **Settings** button to set only the options you want for your windows. An important option on the Custom Settings dialog box is the **Only for folders where I select "as Web page" (View menu)** option.

End

How to Install Expedia Streets 98

Expedia Streets 98 is a geographical mapping program that gives you a map of any city in the United States. The program can find street addresses for you, give you restaurant and hotel reviews, and calculate the mileage for a trip you plot on a map.

To install this program, you need to use the Expedia Streets 98 CD that came in your software package; to run the program, place the CD in your CD-ROM drive.

Begin

1 Insert the CD

Put the CD in your CD-ROM drive, and click **Continue** on the Microsoft Expedia Streets 98 Setup welcome screen.

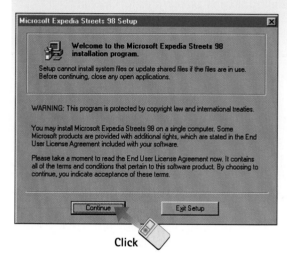

Click

2 Check Your Information

Type your name in the Name Information dialog box, and choose **OK**. Then choose **OK** to confirm the information, and choose **OK** again to acknowledge your product ID number.

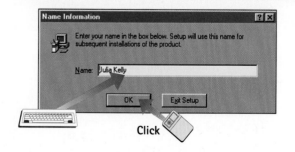

Click

3 Run the Setup

After you click **I Agree** to the software-piracy threat, the Microsoft Expedia Streets 98 Setup dialog box appears. Click the **Install Streets 98** icon. Click **Continue** and **OK** in the next couple of dialog boxes to start the installation, and choose **OK** when it's complete. When you're asked to **Register** or **Register On-line**, click **Register** to continue.

Click

4 Open the Program

After installation, you can start the program by placing the CD in your CD-ROM drive, which starts the program automatically. If it doesn't start automatically, or if you've exited the program and left the CD in its drive, click **Start**, **Programs**, **Microsoft Expedia**, **Streets 98**. The start screen looks similar to the one shown.

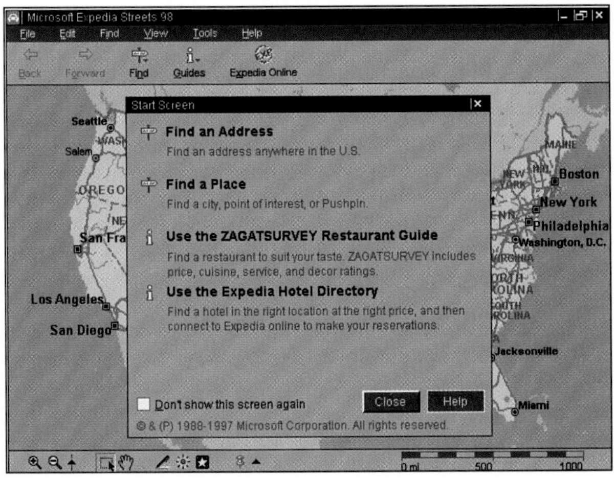

End

How-To Hints

Exit Expedia Streets 98

Click **File**, **Exit** to close the program.

Learn Expedia Streets 98

See Chapter 9, "How to Use Expedia Streets 98," to learn how to use this program.

Glossary

A

absolute reference A cell reference that specifies the exact address of a cell. An absolute reference takes the form $A$1, $B$3, and so on.

active cell The selected cell (it's surrounded by a dark border). You can enter or edit data in the active cell.

active document The document that is currently selected in your software window.

active window In a multiple-window environment, the window that you are currently using, or that is currently selected. Only one window can be active at a time, and keystrokes and commands affect the active window.

active worksheet The Excel worksheet or chart sheet on which you are currently working. When a sheet is active, the name on the sheet tab is bold.

add-in A small program that can be installed to add commands and functions to a main program such as Excel.

alignment The way text lines up against the margins of a page, within the width of a column, against tab stops, or in a worksheet cell.

applet An Outlook mini-program, such as Tasks or Calendar.

archiving The process of moving Outlook items out of Outlook and into storage files, where they are saved for future reference.

argument Information you supply to a function for calculation. An argument can be a value, a reference, a name, a formula, or another function.

attachment A complete file or item that is sent with an email message or stored with an Outlook item, such as a task or journal entry.

AutoCalculate An Excel feature that automatically calculates any selected cells.

AutoCorrect An Excel feature that corrects text or changes a string of characters to a word or phrase automatically.

AutoFill An Excel feature that enables you to create a series of incremental or fixed values on a worksheet by dragging the fill handle with the mouse.

AutoText A formatted block of boilerplate text that you can insert wherever you need it.

axes Borders on the chart plot area that provide a frame of reference for measurement or comparison. On column charts, data values are plotted along the Y axis and categories are plotted along the X axis.

B

background, Publisher A page layer that holds elements you want to repeat on every page of your publication.

Bcc Blind copy; A copy of an email message that you send without the primary recipient's knowledge.

browser A program for surfing the Internet (such as Netscape or Internet Explorer).

C

Cc Copy; when you send an email message, you can send Cc (copies) to other recipients.

cell The intersection of a column and a row.

cell address The location of a cell on a sheet; this consists of a row address and a column address, such as F12, which indicates the intersection of column F and row 12. Also referred to as *cell reference*.

cell reference The set of row and column coordinates that identifies a cell location on a worksheet. Also referred to as the *cell address*.

chart A graphical representation of worksheet data. Charts are linked to the data from which they were created and are automatically updated when the source data changes.

chart area The entire region surrounding the chart, just outside the plot area. When the chart area is selected, uniform font characteristics can be applied to all text in the chart.

chart sheet A sheet in a workbook that's designed to contain only a chart.

chart type The way chart data is displayed; column, bar, and pie are common chart types.

ChartWizard A wizard that guides you through the steps required to create a new chart or to modify settings for an existing chart.

close box A small box with an X in it that's located in the upper-right corner of every Windows 95 window; click it to close the program, file, or item in the window.

column A vertical range of cells. Each column is identified by a unique letter or letter combination (such as A, Z, CF).

column heading The label at the top of a column in a table view (also called the *field name*).

comment Extra information provided for an Excel cell or Word text. The comment remains hidden until you point to the Comment indicator symbol.

constant A cell value that does not start with an equal sign. For example, the date, the value 345, and text are all constants.

criteria Information in a specific field that identifies items you want to find, such as a last name of Smith or the category Business; criteria are used to filter a view to find only those items containing the criteria.

cursor The flashing vertical line that shows where text is entered (for example, in a cell during in-cell editing). Also referred to as the *insertion point*.

D

data marker A bar, area, dot, slice, or other symbol in a chart that represents a single data point or value originating from a worksheet cell. Related data markers in a chart comprise a data series.

data point An individual value plotted in a chart that originates from a single cell in a worksheet. Data points are represented by bars, columns, lines, pie or doughnut slices, dots, and various other shapes, called *data markers*.

data series A group of related data points in a chart that originate from a single worksheet row or column. Each data series in a chart is distinguished by a unique color or pattern.

data source The underlying worksheet data that's displayed in a chart or PivotTable.

delimiter A character (such as a tab, space, or comma) that separates fields of data in a text file.

document Any independent unit of information (such as a text file, worksheet, or graphics object) that is created with a program. A document can be saved with a unique filename by which it can be retrieved.

Document Map A vertical display of the headings in a Word document. For easy document navigation, click an entry to move quickly to that part of the document.

document window A rectangular portion of the screen in which you view and edit a document. A document window is typically located inside a program window.

download To transfer a file from the Internet to your computer through telephone lines and a modem.

E

email Electronic mail; a system that uses the Internet to send messages electronically over telephone wires instead of on paper.

embed To insert an object from a source program into a destination document. When you double-click the object in the destination document, the source program opens and you can edit the object. See also *link*.

embedded chart A chart that's located on a worksheet instead of on a separate chart sheet.

export The process of converting and saving a file to be used in another program. See also *import*.

F

field In a list or database, a column of data that contains a particular type of information, such as Last Name or Phone Number or Quantity.

field name The name of the field, also commonly called a *column heading*.

fill handle The small black square in the lower-right corner of the selected cell or range. When you position the mouse pointer over the fill handle, the pointer changes to a black cross and the contents can be AutoFilled.

filter A set of criteria you can apply to show specific items and hide all others.

flag A visual symbol indicating that some sort of follow-up to an email message is requested; flags appear in the Flag Status column in Table views.

floating palette A *palette* that can be dragged away from its toolbar.

floating toolbar A toolbar that is not docked at the edges of the application window. A floating toolbar stays on top of other windows within the application window.

font A typeface, such as Arial or Tahoma.

font formatting Characteristics you can apply to text to change the way it looks; these include bold, italic, color, and font size.

footer Text that appears at the bottom of every printed page. See also *header*.

formula A sequence of values, cell references, names, functions, or operators that produces a new value from existing values. A formula always begins with an equal sign (=).

Formula bar A bar near the top of the Excel window that you use to enter or edit values and formulas in cells or charts. This bar displays the formula or constant value from the active cell or object.

function A built-in formula that uses a series of values (*arguments*) to perform an operation and then returns the result of the operation. You can use the Function Wizard to select a function and enter it into a cell.

G

graphics object A line or shape (button, text box, ellipse, rectangle, arc, picture) you draw using the tools on the toolbar, or a picture you paste into Excel.

gridlines Lines to visually separate columns and rows.

gridlines (chart) Lines you can add to your chart that extend from the tickmarks on an axis across the plot area. Gridlines come in various forms:

horizontal, vertical, major, minor, and various combinations. They make it easier to view and evaluate data in a chart.

handles Small black squares located around the perimeter of selected graphic objects, chart items, or chart text. By dragging the handles, you can move, copy, or size the selected object, chart item, or chart text.

header Text that appears at the top of every printed page. See also *footer*.

hyperlink Colored, underlined text that you can click to open another file or go to a Web address.

import The process of converting and opening a file that was stored or created in another program. See also *export*.

insertion point A flashing vertical line that shows the text entry point. Also referred to as the *cursor*.

Internet The worldwide network of networks, in which everyone is connected to everyone else.

Internet service provider (ISP) A private enterprise that provides a server through which you can connect to the Internet (also called *Local service provider* and *mail service*).

intranet A miniature Internet that operates within a company or organization.

key The criteria by which a list is sorted.

label Text you provide to identify data, such as column headings.

Landscape The horizontal orientation of a page; opposite of *Portrait*, or vertical, orientation.

layout guides In Publisher, guidelines on the background page that represent boundaries for all pages in your publication.

link To copy an object, such as a graphic or text, from one file or program to another so that a dependent relationship exists between the object and its source file. The dependent object is updated whenever the data changes in the source object.

list A range of cells containing data that is related to a particular subject or purpose. In Excel, the terms "list" and "database" are used interchangeably.

Local service provider See *Internet service provider*.

mail merge The process of creating several identical documents (such as form letters or mailing labels) that each pull a different set of information (such as addresses) out of a database.

mail service See *Internet service provider*.

mathematical operators Characters that tell Excel which calculations to perform, such as * (multiply), + (add), - (subtract), and / (divide).

merge fields The placeholder text in a mail merge document where database information is inserted in each finished, or merged, copy of the document.

message An email message, or any text typed into the large message box in an item dialog box.

mixed reference A combination of a *relative reference* and an *absolute reference*. A mixed reference takes the form $A1 or A$1, where A is the column cell address and 1 is the row cell address. The $ indicates the fixed, or absolute, part of the reference.

N–O

name A unique identifier you create to refer to one or more cells. When you use names in a formula, the formula is easier to read and maintain than a formula containing cell references.

object A table, chart, graphic, equation, or other form of information you create and edit. An object can be inserted, pasted, or copied into any file.

Office Assistant Animated Office help system that provides interactive help, tips, and other online assistance.

Outlook Bar The vertical bar on the left side of the Outlook window; the Outlook Bar contains icons for Outlook applets and folders.

Outlook Bar group A group of icons displayed in the Outlook Bar, such as the Mail group, the Outlook group, and the Other group; display a group by clicking the button for that group.

overflow symbol In Publisher, a symbol at the bottom of a text frame that indicates too much text to fit in the frame.

P–Q

palette A dialog box containing choices for color and other special effects that you use when designing a form, report, or other object. A palette appears when you click a toolbar button, such as Border or Fill Color. See also *floating palette*.

Personal Address Book An address book that is separate from Contacts, although it stores similar information (name, address, phone numbers, email address, and so on). In a Personal Address Book you can create Personal Distribution Lists (which cannot be created in Contacts).

Personal Distribution List A group of names and email addresses; when you send mail to a Personal Distribution List, the email goes to everyone on the list.

placeholder text Text in a field or a Publisher text frame that's meant to be replaced. You click it and type your own text.

plot area The area of a chart in which data is plotted. In 2D charts, it is bounded by the axes and encompasses the data markers and gridlines. In 3D charts, the plot area includes the chart's walls, axes, and tick-mark labels.

Portrait The vertical orientation of a page; opposite of *Landscape*, or horizontal, orientation.

precision The number of digits Excel uses when calculating values. By default, Excel calculates with a maximum of 15 digits of a value (full precision).

Preview A view that displays your document as it will appear when you print it. Items, such as text and graphics, appear in their actual positions.

print area An area of a worksheet that is specified to be printed.

R

range Two or more cells on a sheet. Ranges can be contiguous or discontiguous.

record A single row in a database or list. The first row of a database usually contains field names, and each additional row in the database is a record.

reference The location of a cell or range of cells on a worksheet, indicated by column letter and row number.

reference type The type of reference: *absolute, relative,* or *mixed.*

relative reference Specifies the location of a referenced cell in relation to the cell containing the reference. A relative reference takes the form A4, C12, and so on.

row A horizontal set of cells. Each row is identified by a unique number.

S

scenario A named set of input values that you can substitute in a worksheet model to perform what-if analysis.

ScreenTips Helpful notes that appear on your screen to explain a function or feature.

shareware Software programs created by individuals or smaller software firms that are usually available for a reasonable cost after you try them out.

sheet tab The name tab at the bottom of a worksheet that identifies the worksheet.

sort A method of organizing items so that you can find the items you want easily.

sort key The field name or criteria by which you want to sort data.

source The document or program in which the data was originally created.

split bar The horizontal or vertical line dividing a split worksheet or document. You can change the position of the split bar by dragging it, or you can remove the split bar by double-clicking it.

T

tab, sheet The name at the bottom of a worksheet that identifies and selects the worksheet.

table Data about a specific topic that is stored in *records* (rows) and *fields* (columns).

Taskbar The horizontal bar across the bottom of the Windows 95 desktop; it includes the Start button and buttons for any programs, documents, or items that are open.

template Available in Word, Excel, and Publisher, templates provide predesigned patterns on which Office documents can be based.

text frame In Publisher, a frame that holds text on a page.

U–Z

URL (Uniform Resource Locator) A Web site address.

watermark A pale element placed in the background of a document page. Used for graphics or special text such as "Confidential."

Web See *World Wide Web.*

Windows Clipboard A temporary holding area in computer memory that stores the last set of information that was cut or copied (such as text or graphics). You transfer data from the Clipboard by using the Paste command.

wizards A set of dialog boxes that ask you questions to walk you through processes such as creating a file or an object based on your answers.

workbook An Excel document that contains one or more worksheets or chart sheets.

worksheet A set of rows, columns, and cells in which you store and manipulate data. Several worksheets can appear in one workbook, and you can switch among them easily by clicking their tabs with the mouse.

World Wide Web (WWW) The part of the Internet where Web sites are posted and available to Web browsers.

X axis On most charts, categories are plotted along the X axis. On a typical column chart, the X axis is the horizontal axis.

Y axis On most charts, data values are plotted along the Y axis. On a typical column chart, the Y axis is the vertical axis. When a secondary axis is added, it is a secondary Y axis.

Index

Borders and Shading dialog box, 42

Browse button (Word 97), 17

building
contact information
(Outlook 98), 146-147
footers in documents, 46
formulas in worksheets
(Excel 97), 86-87
headers in documents, 46
lines (Word 97), 18

bulleted lists
converting to numbered
lists, 39
creating, 38
symbols, selecting, 39
turning off, 39

Bullets and Numbering command (Format menu), Word 97, 39

business comparison reports (Small Business Financial Manager)
creating, 246-247
industry selection, 247
key ratios worksheet, 247

C

Calendar (Design Gallery), 216

calendar events, scheduling (Outlook 98), 140-141

cash flow reports (Small Business Financial Manager)
creating, 254
date range, 255
show/hide details, 255
types, 254
viewing, 255

Catalog dialog box (Publisher 98), 178

cells (Excel 97)
addresses
absolute, 108-109
mixed, 108-109
relative, 108-109
copying, 79
data
deletion, 80-81
edits, 80-81
entry, 78-79
formulas
entering, 86-87
ranges, 87

navigating, 79
numbers, formatting, 104-105
worksheets
deleting, 96-97
naming, 110-111

Channel Guide (IE4), subscribing, 262

channels (IE4)
Channel Bar, 263
deleting, 263
subscribing, 262
modifications, 263
update information, 262
manually, 263
views
full-screen, 263
normal view, 263

characters
copying, 30-31
worksheets, searching and
replacing, 112-113

Chart menu commands
Add Data (Excel 97), 124-125
Chart Type (Excel 97), 121

Chart Type command (Chart menu), Excel 97, 121

charts
colors, 121
data, modifying, 124-125
font selection, 121
modifying, 123
shapes, drawing, 126-127
titles
adding, 122-123
color, 122-123
moving, 122-123
text, 122-123
types, selecting (Excel 97),
120-121
worksheet data, creating,
118-119

ChartWizard (Excel 97), 118-119

clip art (Publisher 98)
commercial sources, 213
cropping, 189
inserting, 188
layering, 200-201
moving, 189
online sources, Microsoft Clip
Gallery Web site, 212-213
resizing, 189
sources, 188
text wrapping, 190-191

Clip Gallery
categories, editing, 67
contents, 66
images, adding, 67
link to online sources, 212-213

Clipboard
copying, 100-101
moving, 100-101

Close command (File menu), 5, 9

closing
Document Map, 49
documents, 9
programs, 4-5

color separations (Publisher 98), 229

colors
charts, 122-123
scheme selection (Publisher 98),
179
shapes (Publisher 98), 211
text, applying, 29

columns
multiple, 103
width adjustments, 40
worksheets
deleting (Excel 97), 94-95
inserting (Excel 97), 92-93
width (Excel 97), 102-103

commands
Accounting menu
*Import Wizard (Excel),
242-243*
Select Analysis Tool, 244-245
Chart menu
Add Data (Excel 97), 124-125
Chart Type (Excel 97), 121
Data menu, Filter (Excel 97),
116-117
Edit menu
Copy (Excel 97), 280-281
Copy (Word 97), 282-283
Paste (Excel 97), 280
Paste (Publisher 98), 285
Paste (Word 97), 282-283
Paste Special (Excel 97), 281
Paste Special (Word 97), 283
*Repeat Font Formatting
(Word 97), 31*
Favorites menu
Add to Favorites (IE4), 260
*Manage Subscriptions (IE4),
263*
File menu
Close, 5
Exit, 5

D

scenarios, financial
  category modifications (Small Business Financial Manager), 245
  creating additional (Small Business Financial Manager), 245
  selecting (Small Business Financial Manager), 244-245
  summary comparison (Small Business Financial Manager), 245

scheduling
  appointments (Outlook 98), 136-137
  calendar events (Outlook 98), 140-141

ScreenTips (Excel 97), 76

search engines (Web)
  hyperlinks, selecting, 267
  results, 267
  search words, 266

searching
  Contacts database (Outlook 98), 135
  data in worksheets, 112-113

Select Analysis tool (Excel), launching, 244-245

selecting
  borders (Publisher 98), 194-195
  chart types (Excel 97), 120-121
  color scheme (Publisher 98), 179
  data source (Mail Merge), 60
  document types (Mail Merge), 58
  font sizes, 33
  line spacing, 35
  paragraph spacing, 35
  search engines (Microsoft Find It Fast Web site), 266
  shapes (Publisher 98), 210-211
  text (Word 97), 20
  wizards, template uses, 56

sending email (Outlook 98), 162-163

setting
  default margins, 45
  recurring appointments (Outlook 98), 138-139

Shape tool (Publisher 98), 177

shapes
  AutoShapes tool (Excel 97), 126-127
  charts, drawing, 126-127
  colors (Publisher 98), 211
  customizing (Publisher 98), 210-211
  deleting (Publisher 98), 211

shareware files, locating on Web, 268

Show Pushpin Sets command (View menu), Expedia Streets 98, 303

Show/Hide button (Word 97), 19

Small Business Financial Manager
  accounting categories, remapping, 243
  balance sheets
    creating, 250
    data range, 251
    show/hide details, 251
    viewing, 251
  business comparison reports, creating, 246-247
  cash flow reports, creating, 254
  data, importing, 242-243
  income statements
    creating, 248
    selection, 248
  installing, 318-319
  trial balances, creating, 252
  what-if scenarios, 244-245

Smart Objects
  Design Gallery (Publisher 98), 216
  ungrouping, 217

software update files, locating on Web, 269

sorting data in worksheets, 114-115

sound files, locating on Web, 269

spell checking documents (Word 97), 22-23

Standard toolbar (Excel 97), 74

Standard toolbar (Word 97), 16

Start Screen dialog box (Expedia Streets 98), 296

sticky notes (Outlook 98)
  color, 155
  resizing, 154

Story Editor (Word 97), 230-231

subfolders, creating (Outlook 98), 157

subscribing channels (IE4), 262

Subscription Wizard (IE4), 263

SUM function (Excel 97), 82-83

T

Table and Borders button, 41

Table Frame tool (Publisher 98), 177

Table menu commands, Insert Table (Word 97), 40

Table of Contents, help features, 7

tables
  borders
    applying, 41
    inside, 41
    outside, 41
  columns, width adjustments, 40
  creating, 40
  elements, 40
  gridlines
    hiding, 41
    viewing, 41
  rows
    deleting, 41
    inserting, 41
  text, entering, 40

tabs (Word 97)
  custom
    creating, 36
    formatting, 37
    moving, 37
    removing, 37
  spaces, deleting, 37
  types
    center, 36
    decimal, 36
    left, 36
    right, 36

task lists (Outlook 98)
  creating, 144-145
  priorities, setting, 145

telephone contacts (Outlook 98), 150

templates (Word 97)
  custom
    deleting, 53-55
    saving, 53

scrollbars (Word 97), 17
toolbars (Word 97), 17

viruses
  Internet downloads, acquiring, 271
  MacAfee VirusScan software, 271
  Norton Anti-Virus software, 271

W – Z

watermarks, creating, 69

Web (World Wide Web)
  files
    computer, 268
    drivers, 269
    graphics, 268
    locating, 268-269
    shareware, 268
    software updates, 269
    sound, 269
  pages
    converting from Publisher 98 publication, 222-223
    converting to Publisher 98 publication, 224-225
  search engines
    results, 267
    selecting, 266
    words, 266
  searching with Office 97, 266

Web sites
  cookies
    defined, 267
    deleting, 267
    rejecting, 267
  FAQ pages, 273
  Favorites Folder (IE4), 11
  Microsoft Clip Gallery, 212-213
  Microsoft Find It Fast, 266
  URL addresses, 269

Web-style windows
  activating/deactivating, 323
  files, opening, 10
  navigating, 10

What's This? command (Help menu), 7

What-if Wizard (Small Business Financial Manager), 244-245

windows
  appearance, modifying, 11
  classic Windows 95, 11
  desktop, tiling, 265

Web-style, 11
  activating/deactivating, 323
  appearance, 10

Windows 95, 4

wizards
  features, 53, 56
  question process, 57
  selecting, 56
  zoom controls, 57

Word 97
  documents
    hyperlink insertion, 286-287
    typing areas, 15
    view options, 17
  installing, 318-319
  keyboard commands, 17
  menu commands, selecting, 16
  paragraphs, pasting into Excel 97 worksheets, 282-283
  pasting Excel data into documents, 280-281
  Story Editor, 230-231
  text, pasting in Publisher 98 documents, 284-285
  title bar elements, 14
  toolbars
    Formatting, 16
    Standard, 16

WordArt (Publisher 98), 177

Work Offline command (File menu), IE4, 261

worksheets (Excel 97)
  active cells, 90-91
  AutoCalculate function, 84-85
  AutoFill function, 88-89
  cells
    data deletion, 80-81
    data edits, 80-81
    data entry, 78-79
    deleting, 96-97
    naming, 110-111
    navigating, 79
    references, 108-109
  charts, creating, 118-119
  columns
    deleting, 94-95
    inserting, 92-93
    width, 102-103
  copying, 129
  data
    dragging and dropping, 98-99
    filtering, 116-117

searching and replacing, 112-113
sorting, 114-115
  deleting, 128-129
  formulas, entering, 86-87
  functions, selecting, 106-107
  moving, 129
  multiple, navigating, 128-129
  numbers, formatting, 104-105
  ranges, naming, 110-111
  renaming, 128-129
  rows
    deleting, 94-95
    inserting, 92-93
  shapes, drawing, 126-127
  sheet tabs, 77
  size, 77
  SUM function, 82-83

wrapping text around clip art (Publisher 98), 190-191

ZAGATSURVEY Restaurant Guide (Expedia Streets 98), 312-313

zoom controls
  document wizards, 57
  Expedia Streets 98, 298, 300
  Publisher 98, 176